Satellites and Shadows

Satellites and Shadows

The Militarization of Space

By

Dr. Emile Dorqan

Vij Books

New Delhi (India)

Published by

Vij Books
(Publishers, Distributors & Importers)
4836/24, 3rd Floor, Ansari Road
Delhi – 110 002
Phone: 91-11-43596460
Mobile: 98110 94883
e-mail: contact@vijpublishing.com
www.vijbooks.in

ISBN: 978-93-47436-37-6 (HB)

ISBN978-93-47436-99-4 (PB)

ISBN: 978-93-47436-54-3 (eBook)

This book was developed using advanced writing tools to support the drafting and ideation process. All content has been thoughtfully curated, refined, and reviewed to ensure quality and relevance.

Contents

Introduction

A missile test can erase a satellite in the span of a heartbeat. A flash, a plume, a silent impact hundreds of kilometres above the Earth—and an object that once carried weather forecasts, banking signals, or military communications becomes a cloud of glittering shrapnel. Yet the aftermath remains. Thousands of fragments, each travelling faster than a rifle bullet, circle the planet for decades. The strike is instantaneous; the consequences are patient. That is the new logic of power beyond the atmosphere: sudden acts, long shadows. Nations have always grappled with force and restraint, but never before have the remnants of a single decision circled the Earth with the precision of a clock's hand.

It is tempting to imagine space as a silent theatre: a realm of heroic astronauts, peaceful science, and distant stars. That myth endured for half a century because it was comforting. The public gaze was trained on lunar footprints, not orbital infrastructure; on iconic moments, not hidden dependencies. Yet quietly, satellites threaded themselves into daily life. They synchronised financial networks, guided ships through darkness, observed crops and coastlines, mapped storms, and enabled soldiers to coordinate across deserts and oceans. The sky filled with machines whose names few people knew, and on which everyone depended. Space ceased to be scenery. It became infrastructure.

That transformation seeded a new contest. Unlike the rivalries of the Cold War, which treated space as a stage for prestige, today's competition turns on utility, leverage, and vulnerability. The rough calculation is simple: societies run on data, data flows through orbit, and orbit can be shaped, stolen, blinded, or broken. The superpowers of the twentieth century built navies; the powers of the twenty-first build constellations. It is a shift that crept into being softly, without parades or speeches, announced instead by ground stations, cloud platforms, and launch pads that become busier every month. Military commands now treat orbits as operational terrain. Diplomats invoke space in the same breath as treaties on land and sea. Private firms deploy satellites faster than governments can regulate them.

And all the while, the possibility of conflict above our heads grows less theoretical.

This book is built for readers who want to understand that world without needing a physics degree or a security clearance. It maps the militarisation of space with clarity rather than jargon, rigour without fatalism. You will learn how to "read" an orbit strategically: why altitude signals intention, why a satellite's path can be as political as a treaty clause, and why the simplest numbers—speed, inclination, latency—constrain nations more than ideology ever could. You will see how anti-satellite weapons truly work, not as awe-inspiring weapons of science fiction, but as brittle tools of power whose effects can backfire spectacularly. And you will see why private constellations have become actors in geopolitics, shaping crises not by issuing statements, but by deciding where a signal flows, what a camera sees, and who receives a message at the moment it matters most.

The story begins not in a spaceport, but in an ordinary city. A commuter taps a card on a bus reader. A farmer checks the soil forecast on a phone. A bank executes thousands of trades every second with timestamps measured to nanoseconds. Somewhere in the background, a satellite provides the time, another provides imagery, a third provides communications. Remove them, and the modern world stutters. Some services would recover. Others would not. A single malfunction in timing signals can disrupt power grids and ATMs. A jammed communications satellite can strand troops and civilians alike. When nations plan for war, they first plan for what happens when their satellites go dark.

That dependence is the fulcrum on which contemporary strategy rests. Space used to be the "high ground" in metaphor only—an evocative phrase borrowed from military history. Today, it is literal. Whoever shapes the orbital environment shapes everything beneath it. But this new high ground behaves unlike any battlefield humanity has known. Borders are invisible. Distance gives no protection. Speed is constant and merciless. A fragment of metal the size of a coin can slice through steel. A malfunctioning satellite, tumbling uncontrolled, becomes a hazard to every object that shares its altitude. Even peaceful launches carry risk, because every object placed in orbit becomes another piece of celestial traffic in lanes that are already crowded.

That is why debris matters. The public tends to imagine space as endless and empty. Strategists know the truth: lower Earth orbit is an overpopulated highway. When a missile test smashes a satellite, it sprays a debris field across those lanes. Some fragments fall quickly and burn up. Many do not. They remain, menacing but invisible, each with the power to shred a spacecraft and spawn new fragments that expand the cloud. Scientists call this cascade the Kessler syndrome, but one need not know the term to grasp the essence. In space, destruction multiplies. A single event can litter orbit with thousands of threats that outlast the politics which caused them. Thus, every strike risks self-harm. Every show of force risks poisoning the very environment that grants it.

This paradox—power that is immediate, consequences that endure—is the organising theme of the militarisation of space. It is also what makes the subject urgent. Speeches on diplomatic stages often insist that space should remain peaceful. Yet satellite jammers are switched on in conflicts. Cyber intrusions probe ground stations. Lasers dazzle sensors. Proximity manoeuvres bring foreign satellites close enough to inspect—or to threaten. Militarisation has already happened. The question now is not whether space will be used for conflict, but how open, restrained, or reckless that conflict will be.

Still, the story is not simply one of rivalry. Space also reveals cooperation in unlikely forms. The same commercial company that sells imagery to a defence ministry might provide maps for climate scientists and drought responders. The same broadband network that links front-line units might also connect remote schools. Often the infrastructure is dual-use because the world itself is dual-use: technology built for peace adapts quickly to war, and technology built for war creeps quietly into civilian life. This blurring of roles can stabilise, or it can inflame. When a single constellation supports hospitals, stock exchanges, and missile batteries, attacking it becomes risky not only for the enemy, but for neutral states as well. Entanglement is both shield and snare.

The central purpose of this book is to make those choices intelligible. Militarisation is not merely a race for superiority; it is an engineering of dependence. Nations are deciding which satellites are expendable and which are sacred. They are designing architectures that either collapse under pressure or degrade gracefully. They are weighing the price of hundreds of small satellites against a few hardened ones. They are debating whether resilience lies in armour or abundance. Many of these debates unfold in technical language, inaccessible to the public. They should not be. Space is now public infrastructure. Citizens deserve to know what their governments are placing overhead, and what risks accompany it.

The book therefore speaks across disciplines. It treats orbital mechanics as policy—because a nation's capabilities are shaped as much by mathematics as by ambition. It examines the tools of disruption, from kinetic interceptors to radio jammers, showing why some are loud and irreversible while others are subtle, deniable, and easily escalated. It reveals how private firms have changed strategy itself, offering governments new agility and new vulnerabilities. It takes an unflinching look at the emerging laws and norms that might tame dangerous behaviour, and at the loopholes that could undo them. It assesses resilience not as a slogan, but as a set of concrete architectures designed to survive stress.

A recurring image threads through these pages: the shadow. Satellites cast no shadows on Earth, but their political presence is immense. The shadow of a reconnaissance satellite can change the timing of a military operation. The shadow of a communications outage can reshape a battlefield. The shadow of a debris cloud can haunt an orbit for decades. In law and diplomacy, the shadow of a capability can matter as much as the capability itself, shaping deterrence through perception and uncertainty. Satellites and shadows: machines and consequences, metal and meaning.

If the topic feels abstract, history reminds us that every strategic frontier begins that way. The sea was once a mystery, then a trade route, then a theatre of war. Airspace followed the same arc. Space is simply the next domain, but with one critical twist: behaviour in orbit leaves fingerprints across the whole planet. A single strategic choice can alter everything from humanitarian relief to the price of crops. Modern societies do not stand apart from space; they stand upon it.

This is why the militarisation of space demands public literacy. Decisions made in launch complexes and mission control rooms are shaping how nations exercise sovereignty, project power, and protect civilians. They determine whether crises escalate silently or remain manageable. They influence whether data is shared, blocked, or manipulated. And they will define what kind of world future generations inherit: one where space remains usable, or one where recklessness turns it into a minefield.

As you move through the chapters ahead, you will see the brute simplicity of orbital physics collide with the messy politics of human ambition. You will encounter strategies that rely not on firepower, but on timing, positioning, and deception. You will see how surveillance satellites read the Earth, how navigation systems synchronise the weapons of modern armies, how communications relays knit continents together. You will examine the logic of anti-satellite weapons, the vulnerabilities of ground stations, the profit motives of private firms, and the uneasy marriage between commercial freedom and national security.

The questions that emerge are disquieting, but necessary. If the world depends on satellites, how should societies respond when those satellites come under threat? If commercial companies control vital infrastructure, who decides when and where it can be used? If protecting orbit requires restraint, how do nations prove their strength without demonstrating their weapons? If proximity becomes intimidation, where is the line between inspection and attack? And if debris from a single strike can linger for decades, who bears responsibility when a future collision destroys something precious and irreplaceable?

Some will argue that space conflict is inevitable, the next logical step in geopolitical competition. Others claim that cooperation will prevail, because destruction harms everyone. Reality will fall somewhere between these poles. What matters is whether citizens, policymakers, engineers, and commanders approach that reality with clarity rather than illusion. The worst outcome is not conflict in space—it is conflict shaped by ignorance.

This book is not a warning of apocalypse, nor a celebration of new weapons. It is a guide to understanding a domain that governs more of life than most people realise. Its ambition is to replace fantasy with comprehension, hype with grounded assessment, speculation with evidence. It offers tools for reading headlines critically: understanding what a launch signifies, what a test implies, what a manoeuvre reveals. And it invites readers to judge proposed laws by their consequences, not their rhetoric.

In the pages ahead, you will find a map—not of geography, but of machinery, incentives, risks, and choices. You will see how states wield satellites as instruments of knowledge, influence, and force. You will learn why some architectures survive hostility and others fold at the first sign of pressure. And you may find that the most important weapons in space are not kinetic at all, but algorithms, antennas, and contracts.

Space has changed warfare, diplomacy, commerce, and daily life. It has become a frontier not of conquest, but of dependence. The struggle is not to hold territory, but to keep the machines running—quietly, invisibly, and all the time. When they falter, the shadows they cast fall across every city on Earth.

The future of space is not written. It will be shaped by decisions taken now, by the values nations choose to encode into their satellites, by the restraint they exercise when conflict looms, and by the rules they agree to uphold. This book offers a clear view of that future, its dangers and its possibilities. The stakes are immense. The lights of orbit may be distant, but they illuminate the world below.

And once you see how power moves in space, you will never look up at the night sky in the same way again.

Chapter 1

The Third High Ground

On a clear night above the Arabian Sea, a cargo vessel moves through dark waters with no lighthouse in sight, no coastline to orient by, and no captain peering through a sextant. Its path is determined by timing signals from satellites thousands of kilometres overhead, invisible threads that knit ocean to orbit. Shift those signals by a fraction of a second, and the ship would drift off course, perhaps into danger. Lengthen the disruption and entire supply chains would feel the tremor. A decade ago, this would have sounded like science fiction. Today it is Tuesday.

Space has slipped quietly into the bloodstream of modern civilisation. The satellites that orbit above us do not resemble the heroic machines in museum brochures; most are small, silent, and profoundly unromantic. They do not carry astronauts. They carry data. Yet from their vantage point in the third high ground, they steer aircraft, anchor financial trades, guide emergency responders, and warn farmers of drought months before cracks show in the soil. The modern state leans on orbit as heavily as it leans on law and electricity. This dependency is not abstract. It is immediate, measurable, and growing.

We are used to thinking of infrastructure as the things we can touch. Roads. Bridges. Wires. But infrastructure has expanded upwards. Space is no longer a theatre of dreams; it is a scaffolding of precision. Navigation satellites grant location. Communication satellites grant reach. Imaging satellites grant foresight. Timing systems grant trust. That last one, timing, is the quiet genius of orbital infrastructure. Banks make trades in microseconds. Power grids rely on synchronised switching. Mobile networks hand calls cell to cell with exquisite rhythm. Every packet of digital life is stamped with time, and time comes from orbit. If the signal falters, the entire edifice begins to wobble. When engineers joke that satellites are the world's most important clocks, they are not being flippant. They are describing the skeleton beneath global finance.

This reliance did not emerge overnight. The first space age was a spectacle of flags and footprints. It was about proving possibility, not delivering utility. Satellites were trophies; missions were theatre. But prestige is a poor long-term business model. What began as competition for symbolic heights slowly became a competition for services. A reconnaissance satellite that once spied on missile silos now monitors shipping lanes, drought zones, and illegal mining. Weather satellites that once tracked storms for national agencies now provide data to insurers, farmers, airlines, and disaster officials. Space technology seeped into commerce and community. It became ordinary. That ordinariness is its power.

The shift from prestige to utility reshaped strategy itself. A nation can ignore a rival planting a flag on the Moon; it cannot ignore a rival controlling the communications backbone that supports its troops. Space infrastructure became the circulatory system of conflict and commerce alike. Every satellite launch added a new artery. Every ground station became a heartbeat. Every lost link was a stroke. When one understands this, headlines that once seemed technical become political. A new satellite constellation may not make front-page news, but it changes who can see, who can speak, and who can strike with precision.

To understand this infrastructure, one must grasp an idea that sounds deceptively simple: orbits are neighbourhoods. They differ in altitude, speed, visibility, and risk. Low Earth orbit, a crowded band of machines a few hundred kilometres up, offers agility and detail: sharp images, low latency, fast passes overhead. It is the realm of broadband megaconstellations and rapid-refresh cameras. Middle Earth orbit, higher and slower, is home to navigation constellations—GPS, Galileo, BeiDou—whose timing signals reach every corner of the planet. Far above them, geostationary satellites hover in lockstep with Earth's rotation, holding position over the same patch of sky. They are the great relay towers of space, broad-footprint guardians of television feeds, military communications, and weather tracking. And beyond, in the quiet expanse between Earth and Moon, cislunar space beckons as the next strategic frontier, a realm sparse today but unlikely to remain so.

Each neighbourhood carries a trade-off. LEO satellites offer speed and redundancy, but they are vulnerable, abundant, and demand constant replenishment. GEO satellites see half the Earth at once, but they are expensive, exposed, and difficult to replace. MEO is a careful balance of coverage and precision. Cislunar space promises opportunity and danger in equal measure. To treat space as a single domain is like treating the ocean as a single depth. Strategy depends on where you float.

Once, the physics of these neighbourhoods were the concern of engineers alone. Now they are tools of diplomacy. A nation may choose LEO to avoid dependency on foreign ground stations. It may choose GEO to monitor an entire region with a single asset. It may place navigational satellites in MEO to guarantee autonomy from foreign timing services. The altitude of a satellite describes not only how it moves, but how a country thinks. Access to launch corridors is itself a geopolitical currency; equatorial states possess natural advantages that others must negotiate, buy, or overcome. Partnerships are written into flight paths and frequencies. Allies can share ground stations. Rivals can crowd orbital slots. In space, distance has politics.

With this infrastructure comes fragility. A single malfunction in a navigation constellation can ripple through banking terminals, transport systems, and military operations. A broken solar array or a corrupted software update can ground aircraft or misdirect supply chains. A frozen attitude control system can send a satellite tumbling, threatening anything that crosses its path. Failures are rare, but rarity is no comfort when consequences are severe. Systems designed for global reach create global exposure.

The modern world, so proud of its resilience, is laced with single points of failure. The clock that keeps a stock exchange honest is no less critical than the wires that power it. Space brings both strength and brittleness. Satellites allow nations to see disasters early, to coordinate responders, to feed and shelter millions. They also invite new vulnerabilities. A hostile actor does not need to strike a city. It can strike the signal that keeps the city functioning.

This, too, is part of the third high ground. Control of orbit is not about raising a flag, but supporting a network that spans continents. A country that loses satellites may lose advantages once taken for granted: precision-guided munitions, secure communications, real-time intelligence. Civilian life feels the loss even faster. Mobile networks slow. Logistics falter. Navigation systems degrade. Cashpoints fail. There are no sandbags or barricades that can guard against such failures; the defence is architectural, not physical.

As space grew more crowded, nations learned to think differently about it. A satellite is not merely a machine. It is a diplomat, a data broker, a watchtower, a courier, an economic instrument. Its orbit suggests intent. Its lifespan suggests commitment. Its frequency allocation hints at alliances. A launch campaign can telegraph a country's priorities years into the future. When a state chooses to build its own navigation system rather than rely on another's, it is declaring sovereignty. When it builds a broadband constellation that blankets friendly nations first, it is engaging in quiet influence. The politics of altitude are precise and cold: neighbours in space can be friends or adversaries, and sometimes both.

Yet the most striking truth about this infrastructure may be its invisibility. People notice a bridge when it collapses. They notice a satellite only when something downstream fails. The vacancy is silent, but the consequences roar. A fleeting timing glitch has frozen airports. Spoofed signals have misled ships into hostile waters. Engineers have sat in darkened control rooms, watching monitors flicker as ground stations lose lock on satellites swaying under space weather. These are warnings, not catastrophes, yet they remind us that the third high ground is unforgiving.

By the end of this chapter, the reader will see space not as a backdrop, but as a living grid beneath everyday life. They will understand why orbits differ, why states cluster satellites at particular altitudes, why redundancy matters more than glamour. They will see how navigation, timing, imaging, and communications form a single fabric, and why a tear in one thread can unravel the rest. They will discover that the most formidable tools in orbit are not always the largest, but those that quietly earn trust: precision clocks, stable relays, agile imagers, robust ground networks. And they will recognise that the infrastructure of space is not owned by governments alone. Commercial operators control constellations that rival national capabilities. Their choices—coverage, prioritisation, data access—can tilt the balance of crises.

The chapter does not ask the reader to admire this system. It asks them to see it clearly. The third high ground is not romantic. It is not even particularly beautiful. It is functional, fragile, and indispensable. Whoever masters its logic governs more than satellites. They govern the infrastructure that makes the modern world coherent.

Some nations have already learned this. Others are learning under pressure. A few still cling to the illusion that space is remote from daily life. They are mistaken. The next conflict will begin with the hum of servers and the silence of lost signals. The next humanitarian crisis will be shaped by which satellites endure and which are blinded. The next peace will be preserved by the networks that continue to operate when everything else is breaking.

In the pages ahead, this chapter pulls back the curtain. It reveals the machinery that keeps the world on time, on target, and in communication. It explains how orbits shape strategy, how fragility breeds caution, and how the politics of altitude define alliances. It shows why space became infrastructure, not scenery—and why there is no going back.

Turn the page, and you will see the map of the sky reimagined as the most important architecture civilisation has ever built. The third high ground is already occupied. The question is who understands it well enough to keep it standing.

Why space became infrastructure, not scenery

A city can lose power without a single lightbulb breaking. It happens quietly: a timing error travels through a network, cascading from substation to substation, tripping protective systems designed to avoid overload. What looks like a local glitch becomes a regional blackout. When engineers trace the fault, they often discover something unnervingly remote—a brief disturbance in a satellite's timing signal, perhaps caused by interference, solar weather, or a misconfigured ground station. No missile struck a power plant. No hacker touched a control room. The failure came from the sky.

This is the strange, faintly disorienting truth of twenty-first-century life: the machines we rarely notice are the machines civilisation depends upon. Satellites were once symbols of national pride, poster children for space agencies. Now they resemble utilities. Invisible, ubiquitous, and indispensable. People imagine them orbiting serenely, like ornaments suspended in an endless void. They are, in reality, part of the plumbing of modern life.

Most citizens never think about timing signals. Why would they? Time, for centuries, has been local. Town clocks, church bells, wristwatches—these organised daily life well enough. That age is gone. Today, markets trade millions of dollars in microseconds, synchronising financial transactions across continents. Power grids stabilise by switching circuits in precise sequence. Mobile networks hand calls from tower to tower with choreography measured in fractions of seconds. If the clock slips, the world stutters. And the most reliable clock humanity has ever built sits not in a vault, but in orbit.

It is almost comic: the global financial system, so meticulously guarded by regulators and cybersecurity teams, ultimately trusts a constellation of satellites flying at thousands of kilometres per hour. These satellites broadcast time produced by atomic clocks, which are corrected by ground stations and cross-checked against one another. Banks, exchanges, and payment networks treat these signals as gospel. The messages float unseen across the atmosphere, caught by antennas that feed servers humming in encrypted basements beneath skyscrapers and data centres. The entire chain, from orbit to algorithm, is delicate yet astonishingly efficient.

Navigation steals more attention, if only because its effects are tangible. A driver follows directions on a phone; aircraft trace invisible corridors above oceans; ships thread through harbours; emergency vehicles race through cities guided by satellites whose signals arrive twenty times a second. Stray a little from accuracy, and the consequences multiply. The captain who once relied on stars now relies on constellations of metal, each satellite spewing precise coordinates into the night. Remove them—even briefly—and the world rediscover chaos.

Yet it is imaging that most clearly alters how humanity sees itself. Modern satellites watch the Earth with a patience no spy, scout, or weather vane ever possessed. They track storms forming over oceans large enough to engulf continents. They follow armies as they mass on borders. They monitor forests, glaciers, and crops. A country can no longer hide a missile factory beneath a tarpaulin or bury fuel trucks behind a warehouse roof. Satellites will see, if not today, then tomorrow, or the next week. What governments once called "secrets" are increasingly just delays—information withheld until the next pass overhead.

But imaging did not remain the preserve of militaries. Commercial constellations now provide pictures to anyone who can pay: journalists, insurers, aid organisations, human rights investigators. Farmers look at fields through infrared bands to discern water stress. Reservoir managers map evaporation. Emergency responders scan floodplains and earthquake zones, planning where helicopters will land and where roads are washed away. The detachment of space is an advantage: satellites cannot be blocked by checkpoints or propaganda. They are impartial witnesses.

Communication completes the quartet. Space gives the world reach. Soldiers in deserts, scientists in Antarctica, fishermen far from shore—all connect through orbit. When undersea cables snap, satellites become temporary lifelines. When wildfires destroy telecom towers, responders rely on terminals the size of suitcases. The cheapness of handsets and the ubiquity of sky coverage mean that the world's most fragile societies often rely most heavily on satellite links. For them, a signal lost is not an inconvenience; it is silence.

Taken together, these services dissolve the old distinction between space and Earth. Space is not separate. It is overhead infrastructure, the unseen layer that keeps the world synchronised, navigable, knowable and connected. The metaphor of scaffolding is useful but incomplete: scaffolding can be dismantled. Space infrastructure cannot be removed without unmaking modernity.

The paradox is that this dependency crept in without fanfare. No global announcement declared satellites part of critical infrastructure. No ceremony marked the transition from scenery to necessity. The transformation occurred because services aggregated quietly, one application stacked atop another, until society forgot how to function without them. A weather forecast became a shipping schedule. A shipping schedule became a commodity trade. A commodity trade influenced markets and governments. An orbital perturbation in a weather satellite can, in rare circumstances, move prices for millions of people. The butterfly effect is no longer a poetic metaphor; it is literal. A signal delayed in orbit can move grain in Kansas and wheat in Karachi.

Because satellites are remote, their fragility is counter-intuitive. They appear invulnerable: no storms, no theft, no earthquakes. Nature cannot reach them easily. But physics is unforgiving. Radiation degrades electronics. Micrometeorites pierce surfaces. Temperature swings strain metal. Solar storms flood sensors with noise. A single faulty component—perhaps sourced from a supplier unaware that their work supports banking systems—can bring down a satellite worth hundreds of millions of pounds.

And satellites do not fail alone. They are nodes in a network. When one goes silent, the rest must compensate. Sometimes they can; sometimes the gap is felt ashore. Engineers build redundancy into constellations precisely because failure is inevitable. The question is not if, but when, and whether people on Earth will notice.

Governments classify satellites as strategic assets. They guard them with secrecy, encryption, and layers of backup systems. Yet many satellites are built and operated not by governments but by commercial firms. This is another quiet revolution. The infrastructure that secures national borders and financial markets may be owned by shareholders in London, Paris, California, Mumbai, or Shenzhen. Firms decide which regions receive service first, how quickly damaged satellites are replaced, and how data is shared or sold. Their business models influence geopolitics. A constellation can favour friendly nations and ignore hostile ones simply through coverage decisions. A communications provider can restrict service in a disputed region. A satellite operator can sell imagery to one side in a conflict and deny it to the other. These choices, sometimes commercial, sometimes political, shape outcomes on the ground.

There is an unsettling aspect to this: sovereignty in space is not neat. Nations depend on assets they do not fully control. If a foreign constellation provides navigation and timing, a hostile government could, in theory, degrade accuracy or restrict access. Such sabotage would not require missiles, only subtle manipulation. A clock shifted by a fraction can scramble the calculations of drones, ships, and stock exchanges. The attack could be deniable, reversible, and devastating. In a world that prizes deniability, that matters.

This vulnerability produces a philosophical tension. Modern societies pursue resilience, yet they cluster risk into orbits that cannot be defended in conventional ways. The electrician can protect a substation with concrete. The network engineer can divide servers across continents. The satellite operator has no such luxury. Once launched, a satellite is far beyond reach, shielded not by armour but by distance and trust. If someone interferes—by jamming signals, spoofing data, hacking control systems, or blinding sensors with lasers—the damage may be invisible until it is already done.

Some observers object to calling satellites "infrastructure." They argue that infrastructure should be tangible: concrete, steel, asphalt. But the definition is outdated. Infrastructure is whatever makes societies function. It is the scaffolding of predictable life. If power grids cannot balance load without precise time, if ambulances cannot route without navigation, if markets cannot trade without universal clocks, then orbit is infrastructure by any serious measure.

The change happened because satellites offered something the ground could not: impartial transmission. Cables can be cut, towers toppled, roads flooded. Satellites look down on all this chaos with indifference. They transmit time regardless of weather. They relay signals regardless of border. They see mountains, oceans, and deserts as trivial obstacles. Their perspective makes them neutral in a way earthly infrastructure never could be.

Yet neutrality can be illusion. A satellite may serve everyone or only those who pay. It may reveal truth or conceal it. Some governments restrict data from Earth-observation satellites, arguing national security. Some manipulate navigation signals. Some jam communications to silence critics or confuse enemies. Infrastructure in space inherits all the politics of the Earth it serves.

The result is a peculiar intimacy: societies are closer to the heavens than they imagine. A bank's servers in Frankfurt and a farmer's tractor in Kenya are both tethered to the same constellation of speeding machines. The chain of dependence is invisible until it breaks.

That fragility does not imply apocalypse. Satellites routinely fail, and society continues. But failures teach. When a navigation satellite drifts off frequency, engineers scramble. Airlines reroute. Surveyors adjust. A power grid operator may shift to backup timing sources. These are small disasters, handled by experts with steady hands. The public barely notices. And yet each incident confirms the same lesson: civilisation has placed trust in orbit.

Some readers will object that humanity lived for millennia without satellites. Surely it could do so again. This is true in theory and misleading in practice. The world built since the mid-twentieth century cannot revert without profound upheaval. The global economy is not a set of independent towns and markets. It is a system of flows, and those flows depend on predictability: knowing where ships are, when aircraft land, where storms strike, how money moves. Precision makes scale possible. Space supplies that precision.

There is a deeper paradox here. The more invisible infrastructure becomes, the more vital it is. People protect what they see: bridges, ports, roads. They ignore what they do not. Satellites sit beyond weather, beyond traffic, beyond public scrutiny. Their disappearance would be catastrophic, and yet their existence rarely crosses public consciousness. Infrastructure used to be physical. Now it is orbital, algorithmic, and silent. That silence is its flaw.

Understanding this shift changes how we view conflict, crime, and catastrophe. A hostile power need not bomb cities if it can interfere with timing signals. A criminal syndicate can spoof a port's navigation data, steering tankers off course. A rogue actor could jam rescue communications during a natural disaster. When space was scenery, none of this mattered. When space became infrastructure, it became a battlefield.

And yet the story is not only one of vulnerability and risk. Satellites also civilise conflict. They provide transparency where secrecy once provoked panic. They allow governments to verify disarmament and monitor ceasefires. They reveal war crimes to the world. They guide humanitarian flights to remote fields. They track emissions, illegal logging, droughts. They make the Earth legible, and legibility can be a force for peace.

It is easy to complain that humans have polluted the heavens with metal, exhaust, and debris. But the complaint misses a deeper point: the world placed its hopes in orbit because orbit offers perspective. Satellites watch without tiring. They serve without fear. They see beyond borders, beyond propaganda, beyond the horizon.

If satellites vanished, humanity would still see the stars. But it would no longer understand the world beneath them.

The question, then, is not whether space is infrastructure. The question is whether we treat it as such—defended, regulated, and respected—or continue pretending the sky is empty.

Somewhere, as you read this, an atomic clock ticks aboard a satellite. A trillion-pound economy depends on it keeping perfect time. The fragility of that arrangement should frighten us. The brilliance of it should inspire us. And the uncertainty of it should compel us to look up, not with nostalgia for rockets and prestige, but with a sober understanding of the machinery that holds civilisation together.

The clock keeps ticking. The signals keep flowing. The world keeps moving—quietly tethered to the sky.

From prestige to utility

On a summer morning in 1969, millions of people sat transfixed before their televisions, watching two men take slow, cautious steps across the lunar surface. The mission was, in scientific terms, modest. No minerals were mined. No permanent equipment was left behind. But the spectacle was irresistible. Flags were planted, footprints pressed into dust, history declared. Space was theatre, and the world observed in wonder. For years afterwards, spaceflight was measured not by what it delivered, but by what it symbolised. The point was not to build, but to prove a nation's daring, wealth, and imagination.

Half a century later, rockets launch without guaranteed spectatorship, and satellites quietly begin work long before the press notices. The symbolism has drained away. Spacefaring nations no longer ask who can plant a flag; they ask who can maintain a service with uptime measured in years. What counts today is not the drama of landing but the dull miracle of persistence. A satellite that remains functional for a decade is more valuable than a dozen breathtaking missions that achieve nothing lasting. Space has become ordinary because its utility has become extraordinary.

The shift began with reconnaissance. Early spy satellites returned physical film capsules parachuted into the sea or desert, where retrieval teams waited with nerves of steel. They were instruments of national power but not of daily use. Today, imaging satellites deliver digital files to analysts, journalists, and disaster responders within hours. A typhoon forming in the Pacific is tracked as precisely as a missile convoy rolling across a border. The same cameras that once searched for silos now watch ice shelves, agricultural yields, and illegal fishing fleets. Governments may still fund sophisticated imaging spacecraft, but commercial constellations, built at a fraction of the cost, update maps daily and sell customers slices of the Earth.

Utility eroded prestige because prestige could not scale. A single lunar landing inspired awe, but it changed nothing for farmers in Kenya or commuters in São Paulo. A reliable satellite weather forecast, by contrast, can save lives and livelihoods. When Cyclone Phailin approached India in 2013, improved satellite monitoring allowed early warnings and mass evacuations. Fewer than fifty people died—a staggering reduction compared with past storms of similar force. Satellites did not make headlines; they simply worked.

Modern agriculture is built on this quiet competence. A farmer deciding when to irrigate or when to harvest no longer relies solely on intuition or inherited wisdom. Weather satellites track cloud movements, soil moisture, and temperature gradients. Some systems scan crops in infrared, detecting water stress invisible to the human eye. Insurance companies use satellite data to assess crop failures, reducing fraud and accelerating payouts. Food supply chains depend on knowing what will grow, when, and in what volume. Without orbital eyes, global markets would revert to guesswork and volatility.

Disaster planning has changed as profoundly. After the 2004 Indian Ocean tsunami, emergency workers relied on fragments of information, rumours, and delayed reports. Today, satellites map flooded zones, collapsed bridges, and trapped populations in near real-time, guiding helicopters and relief convoys. Earth-observation companies can task sensors to monitor a region every few hours, even in cloudy weather using radar imaging. The world no longer waits for official statements; it watches from above.

Navigation followed a similar path. The United States built GPS as a military tool, but its civilian value overwhelmed its original purpose. Taxi drivers, hikers, cargo pilots, cruise ships—all navigate by satellite. Even mundane services, like food delivery and ride-sharing, are quietly orchestrated from orbit. The technology's power lies in its banality: it is used constantly, invisibly. If the signal vanished, modern cities would appear haunted. Ambulances searching for unfound homes. Ships drifting uncertainly. Supply chains snapping. Some nations built their own systems—Russia's GLONASS, Europe's Galileo, China's BeiDou—not because flags matter, but because sovereignty does. When navigation becomes infrastructure, outsourcing feels dangerous.

Communications satellites underwent the same transformation. The first geostationary platforms were marvels: television relays linking continents. Today, they are simply utilities, like undersea cables in the sky. A miner in Western Australia, a doctor in the Amazon, a journalist in northern Syria—each can send a message to the world through orbit. Broadband satellites deliver internet to remote schools and disaster shelters, connecting people far beyond the reach of fibre. Again, the miracle is not in the hardware but in the routine: dishes pointing skyward, networks humming, packets travelling through vacuum and atmosphere with barely a pause.

Even the glamour of launch faded. Reusable rockets land on barges with a grace that would have stunned the space pioneers of the 1960s, yet the spectacle has become repetitive. The headline is not the ascent but the payload: a dozen broadband satellites, a weather radar, a navigation augmentation module. Spaceflight is no longer theatre. It is logistics.

This shift unsettles those who remember the age of glory. They ask: where is the romance? Where is the exploration? Why trade poetry for practicality? The answer is both mundane and profound: because utility changes lives, while symbolism fades. A flag on the Moon proves prowess. A satellite warning a coastal village of a coming cyclone saves children from drowning. Which legacy endures?

Yet the pivot from prestige to utility is not purely altruistic. States discovered that influence came easier through services than spectacle. A nation offering free navigation signals builds soft power. A company providing communications to militaries gains leverage. Weather forecasts are diplomatic tools; countries share data to build trust, and sometimes withhold it to apply pressure. The infrastructure of space, though silent, is political.

There is a philosophical depth here. Human beings chase glory, but they live by routine. Once the novelty of spaceflight faded, societies demanded reliability. They wanted satellites that never slept, clocks that never drifted, cameras that never blinked. Prestige is episodic; utility is continuous. And continuous systems must be built, maintained, and defended. Space became infrastructure because civilisation needed it to be.

But utility has a price. When satellites became indispensable, they became targets. Military planners study how to disable navigation, blind radars, jam communications. Intelligence analysts track foreign launches, not because they fear flags, but because they fear services that tip the balance in war. A reconnaissance pass can reveal troop movements; a communications relay can empower insurgents; a weather satellite can guide an invasion fleet. The same infrastructure that supports relief supplies can support missile strikes. This ambiguity is not a flaw—it is the essence of dual-use technology.

Meanwhile, commercial players entered the scene, accelerating the trend. Companies build constellations of hundreds or thousands of satellites, designed to provide uninterrupted coverage. Their motives may be profit, not prestige, but the outcome is the same: satellites become utilities, priced per gigabyte or per square kilometre of imagery. They serve customers from small farms to multinational corporations. Their algorithms predict crop yields, traffic flows, and shipping delays. Space is no longer the domain of governments. It is a marketplace.

Some critics lament this shift as a diminishment of imagination. They see space as a place of exploration, not commerce. Yet the truth may be more interesting. By embedding space into daily life, society has woven exploration into existence itself. The wonders of orbit are not diminished by ubiquity; they are made more profound. A child video-calling a parent across oceans is using space. A researcher modelling a hurricane is using space. An aid worker navigating a destroyed city is using space. The frontier is no longer distant. It is overhead, constantly in motion, constantly serving.

And because space became useful, it became urgent. The incentives changed. Nations poured money into resilience, redundancy, and autonomy. They learned that prestige cannot keep satellites functioning during a solar storm. Practicality demanded engineering excellence. A constellation must survive single-point failures, cyberattacks, maintenance outages, and hostile interference. This is why space technology advanced so rapidly: not to impress, but to endure.

There remains a tension between the two eras. The prestige age produced awe but little permanence. The utility age produces permanence but little awe. Yet there is beauty in quiet success. When a navigation satellite is replaced without interruption, when a radar spacecraft maps a flooded plain for rescuers, when a weather system detects a cyclone early enough to evacuate half a million people—that is humanity's better self at work.

Still, the pivot is not complete. Nations still dream of Moon bases and Mars crews. Private firms speak of asteroid mining and orbital tourism. Exploration continues, but the psychology has changed. The goal is persistence, not flags; sustainability, not spectacle. The true revolution of space is not that humans left the Earth for moments, but that satellites make every moment on Earth more predictable.

Perhaps that is the most profound shift of all. Space no longer represents escape from the planet, but stewardship of it. The satellites launched today are less about conquering distance and more about understanding home. They watch oceans warming, forests shrinking, storms intensifying. They help humanity measure the consequences of its choices. Prestige never asked what comes next. Utility always does.

And beneath this transformation lies a question that will only grow louder: if space is now woven into the fabric of civilisation, who decides how it is used? Who owns the satellites that feed data to farmers, soldiers, and stockbrokers? Who controls the signals that guide ships and ambulances? What happens when profit collides with the public good, or when war disrupts the infrastructure of peace?

The age of flags gave simple answers. The age of utility demands better ones.

Orbits as neighbourhoods

A satellite is not merely above the Earth; it lives in an address. Engineers speak of altitude, inclination, and period, but the terms hide a deeper truth: space is organised. It has lanes, crowds, quiet suburbs and dangerous intersections. Some neighbourhoods teem with traffic, others are sparse enough to feel frontier-like. Strategy begins with understanding those differences, because an orbit shapes what a satellite can see, how quickly it can respond, and how easily it can be attacked. A nation may launch one spacecraft into the void, but it joins a community the moment it arrives.

Consider a simple image: a farmer in Cameroon checks a weather forecast on a smartphone. The data he reads came from satellites that passed overhead minutes earlier, capturing cloud movements and heat signatures. Those satellites travel in low Earth orbit, whipping around the planet every ninety minutes. The same layer hosts broadband constellations, Earth-imagers, and scientific sensors. If one of them falls silent, another will pass again within hours—or even minutes—depending on how many satellites populate the constellation. That rapid revisit rate makes LEO agile, but it also makes it crowded, fragile, and geopolitically competitive.

Low Earth orbit, usually defined as altitudes below 2,000 kilometres, is where most operational satellites now reside. Its popularity stems from physics: the closer a satellite is to Earth, the sharper the pictures, the lower the latency, the easier the tracking. Signals arrive quickly, allowing video calls from mountaintops and time-sensitive military communications from desert convoys. But the very qualities that make LEO attractive make it turbulent. Gravity drags satellites downward; atmospheric drag slowly erodes altitude; collisions are more likely because everything moves fast and the population is dense. Orbital debris is a constant threat. A fragment the size of a screw could disable a satellite worth hundreds of millions of pounds. And every destroyed satellite generates more fragments, each another projectile in a crowded lane.

LEO is therefore both opportunity and hazard. Commercial operators adore it. Governments rely on it. Militaries monitor it obsessively. But the neighbourhood is noisy. Satellites race overhead in shifting geometries, their paths crossing in ways that require perpetual vigilance. Operators issue collision warnings daily, occasionally firing thrusters to dodge incoming objects. To build a large constellation in LEO is to accept continual maintenance, constant manoeuvring, and the knowledge that a single reckless launch could endanger the rest. It is dynamic, democratic, and disorderly: a marketplace, not a fortress.

Travel higher—about 20,000 kilometres up—and the neighbourhood changes. Here lies medium Earth orbit, slower-moving, sparser, and critical. Navigation satellites inhabit this band: GPS, Galileo, GLONASS, BeiDou. Their purpose is timing, not spectacle. They sing atomic time to Earth, broadcasting signals that synchronise aircraft, ATMs, power grids and guided munitions. Unlike LEO satellites, which must be replaced frequently, MEO satellites enjoy longer lifetimes. Their altitudes grant broad coverage: a handful can watch the entire planet with redundancy to spare.

Yet MEO has its own strategic quirks. It lacks the glamour of LEO imagery and the permanence of geostationary stations. A malfunction in this neighbourhood is subtle but profound. If a navigation satellite drifts off frequency, centimetres become metres, then kilometres; farmers planting crops and captains steering supertankers feel delays and inconsistencies long before the public does. MEO must be precise. A tiny error compounds through every receiver, every aircraft autopilot, every automated port. The neighbourhood appears calm, but the stakes are enormous. If LEO is a busy marketplace, MEO is the quiet backbone that keeps society orderly.

Far above both lies geostationary orbit—GEO—at 36,000 kilometres, where a satellite circles Earth once every twenty-four hours and appears frozen in the sky. From the ground, antennas point towards a single spot without ever needing to track motion. This stability is GEO's defining advantage. One satellite can cover a third of the planet, casting a wide electronic footprint across continents and oceans. Communications networks rely on this permanence. So do weather forecasters, broadcasters, intelligence agencies and remote communities. GEO satellites are grand, expensive, long-lived machines: the broadcast towers of space.

But nothing in space is free of trade-offs. GEO's height brings latency; signals must travel 72,000 kilometres round-trip. For phone calls, the fraction of a second delay is tolerable. For high-frequency trading or drone piloting, it is crippling. GEO satellites also sit in predictable positions—an attacker knows exactly where they are and which frequencies they use. Jamming becomes easier. Directed energy attacks become plausible. And because these satellites are few, each one is strategically priceless. If a constellation of thousands in LEO offers resilience through abundance, GEO offers capability through concentration—and concentration is vulnerable.

Then there is the quiet expanse beyond GEO: cislunar space, the enormous region between Earth and the Moon. For decades, it was empty. Only scientific probes and the occasional deep-space mission passed through. Now militaries and commercial firms eye it with curiosity and ambition. Why? Because cislunar space offers vantage points where satellites can loiter, observe, and position themselves for manoeuvres that are hard to track from Earth. Objects stationed near the gravitational balance points—the Lagrange points—can watch Earth and Moon with minimal fuel. An adversary could hide a vehicle there, invisible to most ground radars, then drift toward GEO without warning. Cislunar space is not yet crowded, but like any frontier, its emptiness is temporary.

Thinking of space in layers illuminates strategy. A satellite's altitude is a declaration of purpose. A government that invests in LEO wants agility, responsiveness, and constant refresh of information. A government that favours GEO wants stability, reach, and long-duration control. Those that build navigation systems in MEO are declaring sovereignty—timing is too precious to outsource. And those who explore cislunar space are signalling long-term intent: protection of GEO, lunar exploitation, and deep-space situational awareness.

The trade-offs between neighbourhoods echo familiar human dilemmas. Live close to the ground and everything is vivid but noisy. Live at altitude and life is calmer but communication lags. Live farthest away and freedom grows, but so does isolation. Space mirrors these choices. Engineers do not choose an orbit merely to launch something; they choose to live in a neighbourhood that constrains every future decision.

Coverage is the first trade-off. A single GEO satellite can serve a multinational region. A LEO constellation may require thousands of satellites to avoid coverage gaps. MEO sits in between: robust, predictable, and ideal for global timing systems. When demand demands universality—navigation for ships, planes and smartphones—MEO is king. When demand requires sharp imaging and low latency—battlefield communications, high-resolution cameras—LEO wins. When demand calls for permanence across continents—television, strategic communications, weather tracking—GEO takes precedence.

Latency is the second trade-off. A broadband signal sent from LEO returns quickly. Video calls feel natural. Drone operators receive real-time feedback. Emergency responders in wildfires can coordinate without delay. Move the same service to GEO and the lag becomes noticeable, even frustrating. That is why terrestrial internet firms fret about every millisecond—they count losses in fractions. Space magnifies these concerns. A millisecond in fibre is trivial. A quarter-second in space is maddening.

Vulnerability is the third trade-off, and perhaps the most politically charged. In LEO, satellites are hard to hit reliably. They move too fast, change position constantly, and are numerous. A missile fired at a single satellite might succeed, but destroying an entire constellation would require dozens or hundreds of intercepts—an act so provocative and debris-generating that it could cripple all nations, not just the target. In GEO, by contrast, a single strike can blind a continent's communications or remove a critical weather satellite. The altitude makes replacement slow and costly. GEO is stable, but the stability has a price.

Cislunar space deepens the dilemma. It is far, but not protected. A spacecraft stationed there has months of warning before reaching GEO or LEO—but so does a hostile object. The vast distance means tracking is harder. Sensors on Earth struggle to spot objects in deep space unless they reflect sunlight. An attacker could hide in shadow or drift behind the Moon, emerging when least expected. As states test new rendezvous vehicles and propulsion systems, strategic planners watch the cislunar region with growing unease. It is an unregulated neighbourhood, and history teaches that empty frontiers rarely stay peaceful.

Thinking of orbits as neighbourhoods also clarifies politics. When countries share LEO through commercial constellations, the market moderates behaviour. Everyone benefits from a clean environment; no one wants debris. But when states build bespoke GEO or MEO systems, cooperation shrinks. They guard frequencies, orbital slots, and ground stations jealously. Allies negotiate access. Rivals contest overflight rights. The International Telecommunication Union arbitrates orbital claims like a global zoning board. The process is technical, but the stakes are national: lose a slot and a country may lose the chance to broadcast across entire populations.

There is also the matter of visibility. In LEO, manoeuvres are obvious. Ground sensors track every pass. Analysts watch satellites shift or linger near others. Suspicion is easy to arouse, accusations easy to level. In GEO, the neighbourhood is quieter. Satellites drift slowly, making proximity operations stealthier. A small inspector spacecraft nudging close to a foreign satellite can alarm militaries: is it conducting maintenance, surveillance, or preparation for attack? The ambiguity breeds anxiety. In cislunar space, ambiguity becomes near-imperceptibility. A spacecraft could shadow another for months before ground radars detect the pattern.

These concerns are not theoretical. Nations have tested co-orbital rendezvous in both LEO and GEO. Some satellites approach others under the guise of inspection, refuelling, or repair. Others have suspicious or secretive trajectories. Diplomats complain of "unprofessional" behaviour in space, but there is no universally accepted code of conduct. If the neighbourhood lacks laws, residents invent their own. The absence of policing heightens mistrust.

Yet space is not a battlefield by default. Most satellites serve peaceful purposes, and the neighbourhoods coexist because cooperation provides mutual benefit. Communications relays serve continents, not flags. Navigation systems guide foreign ships. Weather satellites offer warnings to coastal states regardless of alliances. Space, paradoxically, can ease geopolitical tension by producing common knowledge. A nation confronted with evidence from orbit—floodplain risks, illegal logging, military buildups—cannot dismiss the information as rumour.

Still, the strategic logic is inescapable: whoever commands the neighbourhood commands the service. Those who can defend GEO protect half the world's communications. Those who can sustain LEO constellations own the future of broadband, imaging and intelligence. Those who monitor cislunar space will see threats long before others. These are not abstract arguments. Satellites define the tempo of modern life. The neighbourhoods where they reside determine whether they endure.

There is an intellectual elegance to this architecture, mirrored by philosophical weight. For millennia, humanity looked to the sky for mystery. Now it looks to the sky for reliability. The heavens have become predictable. Fixed. Mapped. And yet the neighbourhoods above us are anything but settled. Population expands. Debris accumulates. Militaries experiment. Firms launch by the thousand. The quiet order of MEO, the refined permanence of GEO, the thriving chaos of LEO, the uncertain frontier of cislunar space—all coexist uneasily.

This is the uncomfortable ending: the neighbourhoods of orbit were not designed. They evolved, improvised by engineers and policymakers responding to technology, profit and fear. The next decades will decide whether these neighbourhoods remain navigable or drift towards disorder. The sky is not limitless. It has lanes, choke points, scarce real estate and shared vulnerabilities.

And if the future of security, communication and knowledge depends on these neighbourhoods, one question lingers: will nations learn to live as responsible neighbours—or as rivals separated only by altitude?

Fragility and dependence

On a winter evening in northern Europe, commuters queued at cash machines, tapping cards and waiting for screens that never loaded. Petrol stations refused payments; trains sat idle at platforms; supermarket tills stalled. The outage lasted only minutes, yet the disruption echoed for hours. Engineers traced the fault to an invisible culprit: a brief disturbance in the timing signals that synchronised financial networks. No server farm burned, no data centre flooded. A single glitch in a satellite's broadcast was enough. That is the fragility of dependence. The modern world rests on infrastructure that cannot be touched, cannot be seen, and cannot be easily replaced.

Most people imagine satellites as rugged symbols of technological power—armoured machines soaring through a vacuum untouched by weather or war. Yet orbital systems are simultaneously mighty and delicate. A spacecraft can survive radiation and micro-meteoroids for years, but a corrupted software patch or a misfired thruster can render it blind, mute, or tumbling. Its failure may appear trivial: one vehicle lost among thousands. But networks are webs, not chains. The pressure of one snapped strand redistributes across the rest, sometimes gracefully, sometimes catastrophically.

Navigation systems demonstrate this tension with painful clarity. Global Positioning System satellites, and their counterparts in Europe, China and Russia, provide precise timing signals that underwrite global commerce. Every bank transfer, every stock exchange algorithm, every encrypted communication depends on clocks synchronised to billionths of a second. If a timing signal drifts, it does not announce itself dramatically. No alarms ring. Instead, errors accumulate quietly in spreadsheets and databases. A fraction of a second becomes a mismatch in certificates, a failed transaction, a frozen server. Power grids, which balance supply and demand through exquisitely timed switching, suddenly misread load. Protective systems trip. Sections of the grid disconnect to save themselves, triggering rolling blackouts.

Engineers build redundancy to prevent this cascade. Satellites cross-check one another; ground stations validate updates; atomic clocks switch to backups. Yet redundancy can mask fragility. When the United States lost a GPS satellite in 2016, the immediate effects were modest—phone maps behaved strangely, some radio transmissions flickered—but a deeper unease spread among those who knew how close the system had come to a wider outage. A full denial of timing would cripple markets in seconds. Few infrastructures are so vital, so hidden, and so brittle.

The same paradox haunts communications. A geostationary satellite may relay television broadcasts for dozens of nations, serve military headquarters and remote hospitals, and handle emergency traffic during natural disasters. It is a single point of reliance suspended thirty-six thousand kilometres above the equator. If its transponders are jammed or its solar array fails, the region beneath it grows silent. There is no cavalry to dispatch. Repairs are impossible. Replacement takes months, and only if a spare exists on a launch pad. For militaries, whose command-and-control systems depend on secure links, a lost satellite can slice through strategy like a knife through fabric. Battles are not won by firepower alone; they are won by coordination. Without communications, coordination dissolves.

Low Earth orbit avoids this concentration by multiplying satellites—dozens, then hundreds, now thousands. A damaged spacecraft simply retires while others take its place. But abundance carries its own hazards. When one satellite in a constellation suffers a malfunction, the network must reorganise instantly. Software routes traffic across remaining nodes, antennas retune, ground terminals shift beams. If a second or third satellite falters, the margin narrows. A sufficiently large failure—perhaps triggered by a solar storm or cyber intrusion—can overwhelm the system. Unlike GEO, where each satellite is a fortress, LEO constellations resemble swarms: resilient, agile, but susceptible to sudden exhaustion if too many wings break at once.

This fragility is not limited to machines. The dependence reaches into human systems: supply chains, emergency services, diplomatic communications, even cultural expectations. Consider aviation. Commercial aircraft now assume satellite navigation. Pilots still know how to fly without it, but airports, air-traffic controllers and automated routing software do not relish the prospect. A navigation outage would force widespread diversions, stack planes in holding patterns, and ground flights across entire continents. The industry has become so efficient, so optimised, that the margin for manual reversion has shrunk. Efficiency breeds vulnerability.

Or take maritime trade. Container ships traverse narrow straits guided partly by GPS and partly by radar. Spoof a ship's position—feed it a false signal—and it may believe it is on a safe course while edging towards shoals. Port authorities have faced suspicious GPS anomalies near conflict zones and smuggling hotspots. The truth is uncomfortable: navigation signals can be hijacked. Modern piracy may not involve boarding ladders and rifles; it may involve laptops and antennas.

Weather sensing reveals a different flavour of dependence. Meteorological agencies rely on satellites to track storms across oceans. Without them, hurricanes would strike with little warning and cyclones would make landfall blind. The cost in lives and property would be astonishing. Satellite imagery is woven through insurance models, disaster planning, and casualty forecasts. A prolonged outage during monsoon season or hurricane season would not merely inconvenience civilians; it would change the outcome of catastrophes.

Yet the most poignant examples often occur far from headlines. In rural communities, satellites provide the only lifeline during floods or earthquakes. When communications go dark, survivors wait longer for help. Aid convoys navigate more slowly. Medical evacuations stall. In parts of the world where roads wash away and mobile towers collapse, orbital links carry the only voice that matters: "We are alive. Send help."

Infrastructure is not defined by glamorous machinery. It is defined by the failure that follows its absence. Electricity is invisible until the lights go out. Navigation is ignored until a ship runs aground. Timing is unnoticed until cashpoints freeze. Space systems are no different. Their fragility is tolerated because their benefits are immense. But tolerance is not preparedness.

Defence planners understand this acutely. A modern military assumes uninterrupted access to navigation, imaging and communications. Artillery officers calculate trajectories through satellite time. Drones receive commands via relays in orbit. Surveillance analysts fuse data from radar satellites and infrared sensors. A single blackout can unravel command hierarchies. That is why attacks on satellites—whether through cyber intrusion, jamming or kinetic destruction—are not acts of science fiction but instruments of strategy. They disable the spine of a force without touching a soldier.

Even reversible interference can sow chaos. During regional conflicts, satellite signals have been jammed to obscure troop movements or disrupt drone flights. The attacks are temporary, deniable, silent. No explosions, no smoke. Only confused receivers and frustrated operators. When militaries rely on commercial networks—which they increasingly do—their fortunes rest partly in the hands of private firms. A corporate decision to throttle service, reassign capacity, or comply with sanctions can alter a battlefield as surely as a missile strike.

This vulnerability raises a philosophical tension. Society celebrates efficiency, but efficiency eliminates slack. Space systems are efficient because they centralise capability: one satellite replaces hundreds of ground stations; one constellation serves millions. But centralisation concentrates risk. When a single point supports a vast system, its failure becomes systemic. Power grids learned this lesson a century ago, the financial system learned it in 2008, and space may yet learn it at scale.

Some argue the answer lies in redundancy: more satellites, overlapping constellations, cross-compatible services. It is a start. But redundancy alone cannot solve fragility if systems share common vulnerabilities. A solar storm hitting Earth could flood sensors across multiple fleets. A sophisticated cyberattack might compromise shared software. Space debris could scatter through a popular altitude band, forcing evasive manoeuvres and burning scarce fuel. The hazard is not one failure but correlated failure.

Others suggest sovereignty: build independent systems so no nation relies on another's satellites. Europe built Galileo partly for this reason. China developed BeiDou. The logic is intuitive—control your own destiny. But independence is expensive, and global interdependence has its advantages. Shared networks create shared incentives for stability. The tension between sovereignty and cooperation remains unresolved.

Beyond technical remedies lies a more human question: why does fragility in space feel abstract when its consequences are intimate? Perhaps because the sky has always been distant, a place of stars and gods, not circuitry and risk. People do not see satellites as they see bridges or dams. They do not feel their vibration or hear their hum. Fragility without visibility breeds complacency.

This complacency is dangerous. The modern world has built a quiet cathedral of dependence, its pillars of precision timing, global communications and real-time observation all rooted above the atmosphere. Every year, those pillars carry more weight. Autonomy, supply chains, financial markets, climate science—they lean on orbit relentlessly. But the cathedral has no caretaker. Space governance is fractured, space traffic control is embryonic, and norms for responsible behaviour are aspirational at best.

Engineers can design satellites to endure radiation and micrometeoroids, but they cannot design away political conflict, negligence, or hubris. The fragility lies not only in the machines but in the society that trusts them without knowing their limits.

Somewhere tonight, a satellite will fail. It may be small—a power module glitch, a thruster misfire—but the network around it will shiver. The signals will reroute, the software will adjust, and life will go on. Yet every failure is a reminder. We are climbing ever higher on ladders we did not build to withstand a storm.

The question is not whether the world can live without satellites. It is whether it can bear the shock of losing them suddenly, without warning, in the middle of crises that demand calm, clarity and connection.

The fragility is real. The dependence is total. And the next chapter in space power will be written not by those who build the strongest satellites, but by those who learn how to keep civilisation steady when one of them goes dark.

The politics of altitude

On the coast of French Guiana, where the rainforest meets the Atlantic, a rocket leans against a pale morning sky. The countdown is quiet; engineers speak in clipped phrases, the air trembling with heat and tension. When the engines ignite, the vehicle does not simply rise—it steals momentum from the Earth itself. Because the launch site sits near the equator, the planet's rotation lends a free push of hundreds of metres per second. A nation with such geography can loft heavier satellites for less fuel, transform launch economics, and negotiate from a position of advantage. Space begins on Earth, and altitude begins with latitude.

Few publics think of orbital politics in such earthy terms. Satellites seem to float above terrestrial drama, unbothered by borders or treaties. Yet every orbit is a signature of power, privilege, and diplomacy. To choose an altitude is to choose a geopolitical stance: who can see you, who can interfere with you, who must share the lane beside you. Every height has a patron, a rival, a price.

Countries without equatorial territory know this well. Some rent foreign launch pads. Others carve out partnerships—Russia leases sites in Kazakhstan; the United States launches from island possessions; China builds coastal spaceports. The trade is straightforward: strategic access for money, security guarantees, or political alignment. But there is always leverage. A host nation that controls a launch range can delay or deny a mission, demand concessions, or shift allegiance. Geography becomes currency.

Altitude carries similar bargains. Low Earth orbit, the chaotic alley where thousands of satellites race at breakneck speed, is theoretically open to all. But capacity is not infinite. Frequencies, orbital slots, and tracking channels crowd quickly. Powerful spacefaring nations shape these rules through international bodies and bilateral deals. New entrants must negotiate or accept suboptimal paths. The language is technical—inclinations, conjunction warnings, station-keeping windows—but the outcome is unmistakably political. Access is managed by those who arrived first.

Medium Earth orbit is calmer but no less political. Navigation satellites—the silent custodians of global timing—must maintain precise spacing. A country that controls its own navigation constellation does not merely claim technological prowess; it claims autonomy. Galileo frees Europe from reliance on American signals. BeiDou gives China a backbone for military and commercial independence. When signals become infrastructure, dependence becomes vulnerability. Nations that lack their own systems must trust others not to restrict, degrade, or manipulate timing during conflict.

Geostationary orbit is even more contested. It is a narrow belt, a ring of scarce real estate. Each satellite occupies a slice of longitude and a carefully tuned frequency band. A GEO satellite can broadcast across continents, relay military traffic, or monitor weather patterns for entire hemispheres. It is influence made visible. The International Telecommunication Union allocates these slots through a complex blend of technical requirements and political negotiation. Small states guard their rights obsessively; large states sometimes shadow those rights by launching satellites "at risk," daring others to object. The geopolitical weight of a GEO slot can exceed that of embassies or treaties.

Because altitude determines influence, states build alliances around it. When a country hosts a ground station that uplinks to a GEO satellite, it becomes part of the satellite's protection network. A station in Australia that tracks a European weather satellite may rely on European investment, training, and diplomatic support. Conversely, a government that expels a ground station can strand a spacecraft, forcing it to operate blindly. Control of dirt gives control of space.

Altitude shapes surveillance, too. A satellite in polar LEO orbits the Earth from pole to pole, scanning every latitude. Nations favouring global reconnaissance—watching oceans, ice shelves, missile silos—choose these trajectories. A constellation in mid-inclination LEO focuses on populated belts: the Americas, Europe, Asia. The choice reveals intent. A state that purchases imagery from polar LEO but launches its own satellites into mid-inclination LEO is signalling priorities: perhaps espionage outsourced, but domestic surveillance internalised. Analysts read these patterns the way historians read letters.

No altitude is apolitical, but geostationary orbit might be the most transparent testbed of power. To sit motionless above the equator is to claim a seat at a celestial table. Yet the equator passes over no major Western power. Instead it crosses South America, Africa, and the Pacific. For decades, European and American launchers sought equatorial advantage abroad. It was cheaper, faster, safer. But those arrangements also meant vulnerability to local governments. Political revolutions, protests, or unilateral renegotiations could threaten entire launch calendars. Some nations responded by developing polar launch corridors or new offshore platforms. Others deepened diplomatic ties to secure the ground beneath their rockets.

Cislunar space introduces a more unsettling politics. It is vast, dark, and poorly monitored. A spacecraft stationed near a Lagrange point can watch Earth with patience, unseen by most sensors. It can drift towards GEO over months, altering its path minutely. Rival states accuse one another of placing "mysterious" payloads in deep space—objects that cannot be identified easily, whose missions are opaque. In this frontier, altitude is secrecy. And secrecy, as always, breeds suspicion.

The politics of altitude also governs risk. A nation with most of its communications in GEO is exposed differently than one relying on LEO constellations. Striking a GEO satellite is a single, precise act; disabling a LEO network requires a barrage. Thus, states with concentrated GEO assets gravitate towards diplomatic norms and deterrence—they want predictability. States with sprawling LEO fleets favour resilience and rapid launch—they accept attrition and plan to outrun it. The altitudes chosen today hint at the wars states expect tomorrow.

History offers subtle warnings. When the first navigation satellites entered service, no one imagined they would underpin financial markets. When the first geostationary broadcasters launched, no one predicted they would carry encrypted military command channels. When the first commercial imagers flew, governments dismissed them as toys. Altitude turns frivolous toys into strategic instruments. The change is rarely announced; it simply happens, and the world adjusts.

This is why negotiations over space traffic management are so fraught. Assigning responsibility for manoeuvres sounds technical: collision avoidance, tracking accuracy, debris warnings. In reality, it is a question of sovereignty. If a major power issues a directive telling another country to move its satellite, is that coordination or coercion? If a smaller nation lacks fuel to manoeuvre, and its satellite poses a risk to a larger constellation, should the constellation move instead? Who pays for the lost fuel? Who assumes liability if one object strikes another? These questions are answered by physics, but enforced by power.

Altitude even influences law enforcement. Radiofrequency interference from a GEO satellite can disrupt communications across borders. Nations accuse one another of hosting "rogue" broadcasters that hop between frequencies. Investigating such incidents requires access to orbital telemetry, ground-based tracking, and technical expertise. Some states can produce evidence; others must rely on claims and counterclaims. In a courtroom, altitude becomes narrative: who had motive, who had access, who had control?

Perhaps the deepest political tension is between openness and control. The idealists argue that space should remain a shared commons—equal access, peaceful use, scientific collaboration. The realists counter that nations will protect their orbital assets with the same fervour they protect borders. Both sides are partly right. Satellites offer global public goods—weather forecasts, climate monitoring, search-and-rescue beacons—and yet are owned by particular governments or corporations. When a company in the United States sells high-resolution imagery to an ally, it strengthens that ally's intelligence capability. When it refuses to sell to a hostile nation, it shapes geopolitics. Market decisions become strategic decisions.

And so altitude becomes an instrument of diplomacy. A country offering hosted payloads in GEO is selling influence, promising coverage in times of crisis. A country inviting others to co-finance LEO constellations is binding partners to shared infrastructure. Joint launches create shared risk. Shared risk creates alliance.

There is no perfect altitude. Each one encodes vulnerability, ambition, and alliance. LEO thrives on numbers; GEO thrives on scarcity; MEO thrives on precision. Cislunar space thrives on opacity. Nations choose depending on what they fear and what they seek. A state that expects conflict will disperse satellites. A state that seeks status will anchor itself in GEO. A state dreaming of lunar industry will plant its sensors in cislunar space and wait.

The public rarely sees these choices. They see only a rocket rising, a headline announcing success, perhaps an artistic rendering of a satellite against blue-and-black horizons. But the real story is quieter: orbital filings, diplomatic cables, transponder leases, ground-station rights, secret agreements to share tracking data. The sky is not lawless. It is governed by a bureaucracy of frequency plans and coordination notices—paper shields with geopolitical consequences.

The politics of altitude is the politics of dependence. Choose a height, and you choose who can protect you, who can abandon you, who can threaten you. A navigation system might require foreign ground stations to maintain precision. A GEO satellite might depend on tracking radars in another hemisphere. A LEO constellation might rely on shared debris monitoring. No nation is alone above the Earth, however powerful its rockets.

And this dependence cuts both ways. A state that hosts a foreign ground station gains prestige, technical training, and sometimes cash. But it also inherits targets. If war breaks out, that ground station may be struck. Satellites make neighbours of nations that never touch. Altitude erases distance.

Somewhere tonight, a diplomat will draft a memorandum about orbital coordination. The language will be technical, the tone sterile, the audience small. Yet buried in those pages will be the shape of future alignments. Which nations share weather data? Which share timing? Which share launch pads? Alliances once built on troops and treaties are now built on altitude.

There is an uncomfortable question beneath these arrangements. Space was meant to free humanity from Earth's politics. Instead, it has become a mirror—reflecting ambition, hierarchy, and fear. If satellites are the new high ground, altitude is the new territory, and territory has never been neutral.

What happens when the most valuable regions of orbit fill up, or when cislunar space becomes contested? Who decides who may launch, who may station-keep, who may inspect another's satellite? The world is building an invisible geography above its head, piece by piece, without a shared map.

And the higher states climb, the harder it becomes to pretend that altitude is merely physics. It is strategy. It is leverage. It is power wrapped in vacuum and silence. The politics of altitude has only begun.

Chapter 2

Physics as Policy

At a missile range in the Pacific, a general once demanded that a reconnaissance satellite be retasked urgently: "Put it over the target within the hour." The engineer beside him stared in disbelief. "Sir," he replied, "it's in orbit, not on wheels." The satellite could not swerve like a jet or sprint like a drone. Its path was dictated by the brute geometry of its orbit—silent, invisible, inescapable. This is the unspoken truth of space power: leaders may posture, diplomats may negotiate, but a spacecraft's behaviour is decided first by the laws of motion. The fastest way to move a satellite across the sky is often to wait.

That waiting has reshaped strategy. A satellite circling the Earth at eight kilometres per second is both a marvel and a prisoner. It will not hover over a city unless placed thirty-six thousand kilometres high. It will not see every battlefield unless launched into a polar orbit. It will not provide seamless video calls unless joined by a constellation of siblings, fanning across the sky in regimented formation. Space is full of political ambition, but ambition must negotiate with physics.

This chapter follows that negotiation. It shows why orbital mechanics, not speeches or doctrines, draw the boundaries of power. It explains why delta-v—the precious ability to change speed or direction—is often more politically important than payload mass. Why some satellites glide past every latitude while others remain fixed over a narrow belt. Why a thousand tiny nodes in low Earth orbit can outmanoeuvre a single glorious flagship in geostationary space. And why, in a world where fragments of scrap metal can travel faster than bullets, even debris has become a strategic actor.

To grasp this world, start with the tyranny of orbit. A satellite's path is a loop of inevitability. Want to watch every country every day? Place sensors in polar orbit, slicing through Earth's rotation so the planet turns beneath them. Want constant coverage of a specific region? Use equatorial orbits, trading global sweep for local persistence. These decisions are not aesthetic;

they are iron rules shaped by altitude, inclination, and the cold arithmetic of revisit rates. A spy satellite circling every ninety minutes may cross a warzone repeatedly, but it cannot linger. Its enemy knows the rhythm and hides between passes. A geostationary platform, staring endlessly at a hemisphere, enjoys patience—but sacrifices detail, latency, and surprise.

Most people imagine space weapons or dazzling technologies when they think of power. In truth, power often looks like maths. Analysts speak about delta-v budgets as if they were defence budgets, because they are. A spacecraft with fuel to manoeuvre—just a little—can dodge debris, alter track, or rendezvous with a friendly satellite. A spacecraft without fuel is a hostage to its orbit, waiting for the inevitable decay that pulls low satellites back to Earth or the slow drift that leaves high satellites deaf and blind. Alliances are forged not only between nations, but between satellites sharing the ability to adjust when events demand it.

Then comes the matter of latency, coverage, and cost—the holy trinity of modern constellation design. Civilian users demand internet that works on mountains, in deserts, on oil rigs, and aboard ships. Militaries demand communications that survive jamming, storms, cyberattacks, and missile strikes. The easiest answer is to place satellites closer to Earth, reducing round-trip signal time. But physics punishes simplicity. Low altitude means narrow footprints: one satellite can only watch a small patch, so thousands must be launched to blanket the globe. Constellations become logistical enterprises. Rockets fly weekly. Ground stations multiply. Software orchestrates traffic between satellites as if conducting a choir. Each node is cheap alone, powerful together, and at constant risk of collision, burnout, or interference.

High altitude flips the equation. A single giant satellite in geostationary orbit can relay television, intelligence feeds, and emergency communications across continents. Its coverage is magnificent. But signals are sluggish. When a user speaks, half a second passes before the reply arrives, stretched by the sheer distance of the journey. For broadcasters and meteorologists, this trade-off is acceptable. For financial traders, drone pilots, and tactical operators, it is intolerable. Hence the split: telecom firms hedge bets across both regions, and militaries supplement their grand GEO birds with nimble LEO fleets that can be replaced after losses.

Here, survivability by design emerges as the invisible philosophy of spacefaring. Satellites cannot build armour like tanks or hide in forests like infantry. Their survival comes from dispersion, autonomy, and redundancy. A proliferated LEO constellation spreads risk across hundreds or even thousands of small satellites. Destroy one and the network heals. Destroy ten and service degrades, not collapses. In such systems, capacity is sand, not stone. The era of single-point failure—one satellite providing the only service—has given way to something more organic: swarms that adapt, regenerate, and refuse to present a single target.

Yet even swarms can be trapped, not by weapons, but by debris. A fragment the size of a coin, travelling seven kilometres per second, carries the force of an artillery shell. When nations test anti-satellite missiles, they do not merely destroy a target; they litter the orbital lane with shrapnel. Each piece becomes a wandering threat, capable of slicing panels, puncturing fuel tanks, or crippling solar arrays. These fragments can take decades to fall. They create no border, speak no language, and swear allegiance to no flag, yet they alter manoeuvre plans, reroute satellites, and raise insurance premiums. Debris is becoming a geopolitical asset—sometimes wielded deliberately, sometimes unleashed through carelessness. A cloud of fragments in a useful orbit is a silent veto on who dares travel there.

And so strategy adapts. Satellites move cautiously, conserving fuel to dodge hazards. Operators issue warnings, negotiate orbits, and argue liability when collisions occur. Diplomats talk of "responsible behaviour," while military planners quietly study how a well-timed destructive test could deny an altitude band to rivals without ever firing on their satellites directly. Space, once imagined infinite, is proving territorial in practice.

But raw destruction is rarely the first choice. Signals matter as much as steel. A satellite need not be blown apart to be neutralised. Jamming can blind it. Spoofing can deceive it. Cyberattacks can hijack control or corrupt data. These soft-kill tools are cheap, reversible, and deniable. A jamming burst during a tense border crisis can be attributed to weather, solar activity, or "technical malfunction." A corrupted timing signal can scramble aviation routes or bank transactions without leaving shrapnel. In a world that fears escalation, soft-kill methods are seductive: they wound without blood. Yet their ambiguity is dangerous. If a navigation system malfunctions, is it sabotage or accident? If a satellite drops offline, is it software failure or hostile action? Misinterpretation becomes a path to miscalculation.

Across all of this, one idea binds the chapter: physics is not a backdrop to policy; it is policy. The laws of motion predetermine what leaders can promise, what militaries can threaten, and what diplomats can negotiate. Strategy in space means designing within constraints, not imagining beyond them. A politician may wish for surveillance "on demand," but an orbital pass must still obey Kepler. A corporation may plan global internet coverage, but latency and launch cadence will dictate the architecture. A general may demand wartime resilience, but resilience comes not from rhetoric, but from fuel reserves, cross-links, error-correcting codes, spare satellites, and ground stations in friendly territory.

The significance is larger than engineering. On Earth, power often flows from will: build a fleet, raise an army, declare a border. In orbit, power flows from mathematics. Nations can lie to each other about intentions, but they cannot lie to the laws of mechanics. A satellite's orbit is a declaration written in gravity: where it can look, how often, and for how long.

This chapter offers more than technical insight. It shows how orbital mechanics becomes strategy, how trade-offs in latency and coverage become commercial empires, how survivability becomes architecture, how debris becomes deterrence, and how invisible beams of interference replace missiles as instruments of coercion. It argues that space is becoming a theatre where the most decisive battles are waged not with explosions, but with equations—where victory belongs to those who master the quiet art of designing networks that cannot be easily broken.

Somewhere tonight, a politician will give a speech promising dominance in space. The engineers listening will smile politely. The satellites already know what is possible. They glide in paths set decades ago, obeying a physics indifferent to ambition. The future of space power lies not in louder speeches, but in better orbits, better constellations, and better mastery of the delicate mechanics that rule the sky.

And as thousands more satellites rise on columns of flame, the question hangs unanswered: when physics sets the boundaries of power, who will learn fastest—and who will discover too late that policy cannot defy gravity?

The tyranny of orbital mechanics

In 2020, during a tense standoff in a disputed border region, analysts watched satellite images arriving in newsroom after newsroom. Each pass revealed subtle shifts—artillery dug in deeper, airstrips reshaped, convoys edging towards mountain roads. Yet the updates did not arrive every hour, or even every afternoon. There were gaps. Journalists begged for fresher views. Governments wanted timelier intelligence. The satellites, indifferent to politics, continued their silent circuits. They would pass again when orbital mechanics allowed—not before. The planet spun beneath them; the cameras rode their fixed loops; the world waited.

For all our talk of space-age innovation, satellites remain obedient servants of gravity. They cannot loiter, hover, or reverse on command. They can pivot their cameras, but they cannot magically appear above a crisis. The, hardest lesson of modern space power is that physics—not ambition—draws the boundaries of action. A general may demand constant surveillance of a battlefield, yet a satellite in low Earth orbit will inevitably vanish beyond the horizon, leaving troops beneath an unblinking sky. The only remedy is more satellites, precisely choreographed. The sky becomes theatre, but the scripts are written by Kepler.

Delta-v—short for change in velocity—is the ration book of orbital life. To alter a trajectory, evade debris, rendezvous with a target, or shift to a fresh orbital plane, a spacecraft must consume fuel. Every manoeuvre subtracts from a finite supply, measured not in litres but in metres per second. Designers agonise over every gram of propellant, knowing that a spacecraft with limited delta-v is a prisoner of its initial orbit. A satellite with a generous budget is a different creature entirely: it can adjust its altitude to sharpen images, dodge hazards, or frustrate inspectors shadowing it. Operators can hide intentions behind graceful sweeps and gentle drifts. The spacecraft becomes unpredictable, and unpredictability is leverage.

Inclination—the tilt of an orbit relative to Earth's equator—adds another constraint. Most surveillance satellites favour polar or near-polar orbits, slicing north-to-south on every pass. As the planet rotates beneath them, each loop reveals a fresh slice of terrain: Siberian forests at dawn, Pacific fleets at noon, Middle Eastern deserts at dusk. That global reach is priceless for weather agencies, reconnaissance units, and environmental scientists. But it comes at a cost. A satellite in polar orbit spends much of its time over oceans and uninhabited regions, its sensors pointed at emptiness. It is global, but not persistent.

By contrast, equatorial orbits deliver focus. A spacecraft circling above the equator sees the same band of latitudes again and again. Its revisit rate for equatorial nations is high; its value for higher latitudes is minimal. Users in northern Canada or southern Chile receive sparse coverage, while regions around the equator enjoy repeated attention. This raises an uncomfortable strategic truth: orbital architecture embeds political geography. Decide to prioritise equatorial passes, and you implicitly devalue polar interests.

Deploy a polar fleet, and you neglect the equator. States notice. Allies question priorities. Rivals exploit the gaps.

Then there are sun-synchronous orbits, finely tuned lanes that allow satellites to cross the same spots at the same local time each day. Shadows fall in predictable angles. Analysts compare images precisely—before and after, week by week, pixel by pixel. This orbit birthed the art of change detection: discovering new missile silos as pale scars in the desert, studying illegal logging in remote jungles, monitoring glacial retreat. But sun-synchronous paths impose their own rigid schedule. If a tank battalion moves at night, the satellite will miss it until the next morning. If a wildfire erupts hours after a pass, responders must wait for the next window or call on a different sensor. The orbit is loyal to the Sun, not to human urgency.

Every orbit has a revisit rate—a measure of how quickly it will return to view the same patch of ground. Policymakers speak of "persistent surveillance," yet persistence is expensive. One satellite in low Earth orbit revisits at intervals of hours or days. Ten satellites may cover a whole region hourly. Hundreds may border on continuous observation. The mathematics are unforgiving. To shorten delays, you must multiply spacecraft, lease fresh ground stations, and coordinate immense volumes of data. This creates a new tyranny: logistics. Satellites are not just objects in the sky; they are participants in a vast choreography of antennas, algorithms, and operators.

No state escapes these laws. Even the most advanced powers struggle. The United States once wanted a space radar constellation that could map every corner of the Earth continuously. The price spiralled into fantasy: too many satellites, too many launches, too much data. Designs were shelved. Ambition met physics, and physics won. More recently, commercial firms have revived the dream—smaller satellites, cheaper launches, cloud processing—but even their claims of "real-time" coverage stretch the truth. The time between passes may shrink to minutes, but orbital gaps persist.

When crises erupt, politicians often ask why satellites could not respond faster. The answer is orbital planes. A satellite's path is a ring around the Earth. To reposition it over a distant longitude may require a costly plane change—one of the most fuel-intensive manoeuvres in celestial mechanics. In most cases, it is cheaper to launch a new satellite than to twist an old one into a drastically different orbit. Strategy, then, requires foresight. You place satellites where you expect to need them, not where you hope never to.

Delta-v shapes diplomacy as much as physics. A spacecraft running low on fuel cannot evade a suspicious neighbour or dodge a threatening approach. It becomes a soft target—predictable, inert, vulnerable. Nations invest in fuel margins not merely for longevity but for political signalling: a satellite that can manoeuvre is a satellite that can refuse inspection or pursue it.

The tyranny also governs life expectancy. Solar storms can swell the upper atmosphere, increasing drag on low satellites and draining their orbits. Operators must boost altitude, spending delta-v they never planned to lose. A storm lasting weeks can accelerate decades of decay. Those who can manoeuvre survive; those who cannot burn up silently, uncelebrated.

Yet for all this constraint, orbital mechanics also shapes ingenuity. If one satellite cannot linger, three can stagger their passes. If three are insufficient, thirty provide a mosaic. Constellations stitch together half-glimpses into continuous knowledge. A vehicle in distress might be invisible to one sensor, but another, minutes behind, can catch the plume of smoke or the ripple of movement. In effect, states and companies build synthetic persistence—a patchwork of intermittent eyes that feel omnipresent to those on the ground.

The most telling proof that physics governs power lies in behaviour during conflict. When satellites pass over hostile territory, forces learn to hide between orbits, scatter equipment, or time redeployments. The art of camouflage has become temporal as well as spatial. Armies read orbital predictions as carefully as weather forecasts. A brigade will move at 02:17, knowing the next imaging pass arrives ten minutes later. They gamble on speed, darkness, and orbital blind spots. Intelligence officers learn to fuse imagery from multiple constellations—military and commercial—to close these gaps. The battle is not just on Earth; it is waged against time.

There is philosophy buried in this physics. Orbital mechanics is a reminder that power cannot bend nature indefinitely. Leaders boast of dominance, yet their satellites are chained to ellipses drawn by gravity. They boast of global awareness, yet the planet's rotation hides and reveals with indifference. The heavens do not care for strategy. The heavens care only for force and motion.

Still, human creativity tests the limits. Small satellites with electric propulsion can stretch their fuel for years, trimming orbits delicately. Agile imagers slew rapidly, capturing fleeting targets. Synthetic aperture radar satellites see through clouds and night, denying weather the final word. But no technology escapes the geometry. To observe constantly, you must deploy many. To manoeuvre often, you must carry more fuel. To patrol globally, you must launch in polar or inclined planes. Every choice carries price.

Even nations that dream of lunar outposts and Martian colonies must first bow to this tyranny. Their spacecraft will take weeks to adjust course, months to reach new destinations, years to return. Every miscalculation compounds over vast distances. The mathematics tolerates no excuses.

Perhaps that is why space expertise is quietly sobering. Engineers speak without bravado. Astronauts recount near misses with humility. Operators tracking debris describe objects screaming past each other with a few kilometres of separation—cosmic proximity, lethal if anything strays. They know how thin the margins are. They know that a satellite is not a symbol of dominance but a delicate arrangement of vectors and propellant.

Meanwhile, the public sees impressive images and assumes all-seeing omnipresence. They ask why satellites did not prevent a terror attack or predict a coup. They do not realise that satellites glide on predetermined rails. A window of opportunity might be minutes wide. The world spins, clouds gather, and the chance is gone.

This is not cause for despair. It is cause for respect. Orbital mechanics teaches restraint. It punishes impatience and rewards planning. It forces collaboration, because no state has enough satellites to watch everything always. Even rivals quietly exchange tracking data. The sky is too crowded, too dangerous, for secrecy alone.

Yet one unsettling truth lingers. As constellations multiply and ambitions grow, the tyranny tightens around new questions. Who can afford the thousands of satellites needed for persistence? Who controls the launch pads that feed them? Who will provide the fuel for rendezvous missions, the bandwidth for downlinks, the algorithms for coordination? Physics draws the boundaries, but politics crowds the interior.

If strategy is the art of bridging desire and reality, orbital mechanics is the reality. It speaks without rhetoric, without mercy. A satellite will be where the equations say it will be, no matter how loudly Earth shouts. And as space becomes the backbone of modern civilisation, society will find itself negotiating not just with rivals, but with gravity itself.

The question that hangs in the air is deceptively simple: when the next crisis erupts and leaders demand immediate answers from orbit, will their satellites be watching—or already gone beyond the horizon, obeying the ancient geometry that no nation can command?

Latency, coverage, and cost

A trading firm in London, chasing microseconds of advantage on transatlantic markets, does not care where its data travels—only how fast. A surgeon guiding a remote robotic instrument in a disaster zone cannot tolerate even a fractional lag. A drone squadron, relying on satellite control links, must react in synchrony with threats on the ground. Yet a child on a remote island simply hopes that a video call will not freeze. These needs are wildly different, but all lean on an invisible equation of latency, coverage, and cost. And space, with its grand distances and unforgiving geometry, sets the terms.

Satellite internet once meant tolerating delay. Signals travelled from a dish on Earth to a satellite parked 36,000 kilometres overhead, then back down again. The round trip took a quarter of a second. For broadcast television, that was fine. For live conversations, it felt awkward. For real-time control of machinery or trading systems, it was intolerable. Physics had placed a ceiling on performance, and for decades it seemed immovable. Then engineers asked a radical question: what if satellites did not live so high?

Low Earth orbit slashed latency. Signals reached satellites in tens of milliseconds, not hundreds. The difference sounds trivial, but for modern applications it was transformative. Pilots, gamers, traders, emergency responders—everyone noticed. A fleet of small satellites closer to Earth could give rural schools the same access as cities, fishing vessels the same capacity as downtown offices. The promise was universal connectivity, fast and unconstrained by geography.

But physics wrote the bill. A single geostationary satellite can watch a continent; a low-orbit satellite sees only a narrow slice of the planet before racing over the horizon. To keep the signal seamless, the network must hand users off from one satellite to the next. Hundreds, even thousands of satellites must work in concert. Rockets must launch not yearly, but monthly. The ground segment—antennas, data centres, fibre routes—must keep pace. Every satellite has a lifetime measured in five to ten years, after which replacements must rise. The sky begins to look less like a majestic expanse and more like a conveyor belt.

Coverage, too, is uneven. High-latitude regions—Alaska, Scandinavia, the Southern Ocean—benefit from certain orbital geometries, as satellites spend more time above those areas. Equatorial nations see leaner coverage unless satellites are tuned to their latitudes. There is no free solution. Design choices privilege some users over others, and those users often notice. Access becomes geopolitical: who gets high-speed service, who waits for upgrades, who is stuck with ageing infrastructure?

To complicate matters further, payloads shrink as satellites descend. A platform in low orbit must be lightweight enough to ride cheaply and often. It carries smaller antennas, less fuel, and reduced redundancy compared to a bus-sized geostationary titan. Its processing power may be modest, its links narrower. To overcome these limitations, operators push capability into ground infrastructure: optical terminals, phased arrays, cloud routing. The network becomes hybrid: light spacecraft above, heavy computation below.

This division of labour has consequences. The more you rely on ground stations, the more vulnerable you are to terrestrial politics. A ground site in a friendly nation may stay online; one in a turbulent region may be shut down, attacked, or expropriated. As a result, companies stitch together a patchwork of leases, partnerships, and sovereign approvals. Connectivity becomes not merely engineering, but diplomacy.

Cost threads through every decision. A geostationary satellite is expensive but singular; it may serve millions for decades. A low-orbit constellation costs more cumulatively: dozens of launches, constant replenishment, relentless coordination. Yet the economics flip when the customer base is global. If thousands of subscribers, aircraft, ships, and governments pay for service, the model works. If not, the system burns cash faster than rocket fuel. Investors can measure the health of a constellation not by its satellites, but by its launch cadence and subscriber count.

For defence and intelligence agencies, the same equation dictates architecture. High-altitude satellites deliver broad coverage for strategic communications, nuclear command links, and meteorology, but they are tempting targets: predictable, unprotected, irreplaceable. Low-orbit fleets are harder to kill. They offer redundancy, stealth in numbers, and rapid refresh. But they demand data management at planetary scale. Militaries accustomed to protecting a handful of exquisite spacecraft must now harden thousands of small nodes, each linked to ground gateways, each vulnerable to interference.

Some nations seek hybrids: medium orbits, highly elliptical loops, orbits frozen over high latitudes. These compromise between latency and coverage, but inherit the weaknesses of both. The physics allows no perfect solution. Instead, operators mix layers—LEO for speed, GEO for reach, MEO for navigation stability. The result is a multi-orbit ecosystem, complex and constantly adjusting.

What is easy to overlook is how profoundly launch cadence defines strategy. When satellites were rare, a lost spacecraft meant years of disruption. Now, reusable rockets fly weekly. A constellation can be replenished rapidly, damaged nodes replaced within months or even days. But only for those who own or can purchase launch capacity. For nations without rockets, dependency becomes acute. A constellation is only as resilient as its access to orbit, and that access is concentrated among a few countries and companies. In space, sovereignty is measured in payload mass and launch windows.

The same trade-offs shape civilian life. A rural hospital connecting to specialists in a capital city relies on low latency. An oil platform monitoring storms needs persistent wide coverage. A maritime rescue operation must communicate through clouds, fog, and polar darkness. Different altitudes serve these needs differently, and so operators tailor their fleets: radar sats for all-weather imaging, optical sats for detail, communications sats for command and coordination. Space becomes an orchestra, with each instrument tuned for a distinct task. The score is global, the tempo relentless.

Yet there is an ethical undertone. If the cheapest way to serve remote communities is a constellation of small satellites, who ensures that those communities are not priced out? If the most profitable routes run between financial hubs and shipping lanes, who protects the rest? The intersection of latency, coverage, and cost is not only technical—it is social. The digital divide can be widened or narrowed from orbit.

As constellations multiply, operators wrestle with a new fear: congestion. Too many satellites demanding too many hand-offs, over too few radio frequencies, with too much debris. Who grants permission to launch the next thousand? Who arbitrates priority when networks overlap? Signals may interfere; navigation may drift; regulators may flee the complexity. The sky could become not simply expensive, but chaotic.

And looming behind it all is the quiet arithmetic of fuel. Each satellite must station-keep, dodge debris, and compensate for atmospheric drag. As fleets grow, propulsion budgets expand. The drive to reduce cost pushes innovations: electric thrusters sipping xenon, solar sails making gentle corrections, autonomous systems predicting collisions. A constellation that cannot manoeuvre is a constellation that will die young.

The harsh truth is that latency is not merely about physics—it is about power. High-performance networks shape finance, warfare, disaster response, remote medicine, and international trade. Nations that master low-latency coverage wield an influence that rivals old naval chokepoints and fibre backbones. Those who cannot afford it become dependent customers in a marketplace they do not control.

And so the equation tightens. Lower orbits promise speed, but demand numbers. Higher orbits promise reach, but cost time. Every kilo of payload competes with every kilo of fuel. Every new satellite competes with every scrap of debris. The future will belong to those who can choreograph vast orbital fleets without letting cost spiral into absurdity.

It leaves a final, uncomfortable question. If universal connectivity requires thousands of satellites and persistent launch cycles, what happens when rockets falter, supply chains tighten, or debris forces operators to abandon key orbits? Does the dream of seamless global coverage endure—or does the sky become another critical infrastructure, taken for granted until the day it stutters?

Survivability by design

In 1998 a communications satellite over the Pacific behaved strangely. First it wobbled, then it drifted, then its signals began to stutter. Engineers on the ground panicked: tens of millions of receivers relied on that single node. Television feeds blinked out across countries. Radio links collapsed. Navigation networks suffered cascading timing errors. For a few hours, much of the Western hemisphere felt the absence of a single satellite—a reminder that power in orbit had once been built around singular instruments, grand and fragile. They were crowns: impressive, expensive, and breakable.

The twenty-first century has no patience for crowns. The lesson of that failure—and of countless near-misses, solar storms, collisions, jamming attempts and software faults—is brutally simple: a space system that depends on a handful of exquisite satellites is a space system waiting to fall. Modern networks are built to survive. They are dispersed, redundant, and increasingly autonomous. They behave less like palaces and more like forests: many trunks, intertwined roots, constant renewal. Lose a tree, the forest lives.

At the heart of survivability is dispersion. When satellites lived high above the equator in geostationary orbit, they were few, oversized, and irreplaceable. A missile test against one could cripple whole regions. A debris cloud aimed at that orbital lane might hobble communications for nations that owned nothing in low orbit. Today, commercial and military operators scatter capability across vast constellations: hundreds, soon thousands, of spacecraft working in concert. Each is small. Each is cheap. Each carries only a sliver of the total capacity. Destroy one, and the network shrugs. Destroy ten, and the gap is patched through rerouting. Space is becoming a domain where single-point failure is a design sin.

The philosophy behind this shift is not new. The internet was built to survive nuclear war by rerouting around damaged nodes. Cloud computing learned that resilience comes from replication, not from fortress servers. Now space follows the same logic. A proliferated constellation behaves like a living organism: self-healing, flexible, impossible to decapitate. A missile cannot hit a thousand targets. A cyber-attack cannot compromise every link at once. An adversary that fires upon a swarm risks revealing intent without gaining decisive effect.

Yet dispersion alone is not enough. Satellites must talk to one another in orbit, passing data through intersatellite links when ground stations are disrupted or under attack. Some constellations are stitching webs of optical cross-links, beams of invisible light carrying traffic from spacecraft to spacecraft. If a gateway on Earth goes dark—whether from weather, power outage, cyber sabotage, or missile strike—the swarm routes around it. Autonomy rises from necessity: the system must think for itself when humans cannot reach it.

Redundancy amplifies dispersion. Old generation satellites tried to pack multiple transponders, antennas, and sensors onto a single chassis. When one subsystem failed, others compensated. But redundancy within one satellite is limited by mass, cost, and complexity. Redundancy across satellites is the new model: many units performing overlapping roles. If an imaging satellite burns up in the upper atmosphere, another with a similar orbit passes minutes later. If a communications node goes silent, adjacent satellites expand their coverage footprints. The network behaves like water filling the cracks in rock.

Military forces have taken notice. Space was once a strategic trophy: destroy the enemy's "eye in the sky," and blind their forces. But how do you blind a thousand eyes? How do you silence a network whose nodes are manufactured on assembly lines, launched weekly, upgraded by software? A proliferated LEO constellation denies adversaries the satisfaction of decisive strike. It shifts war in space from single blows to attritional campaigns—and attrition favours those who can build faster than they can be killed.

Autonomy is the quiet revolution beneath this architecture. Human operators cannot micromanage hundreds of satellites manoeuvring through crowded orbits. Nor can they respond fast enough when debris fragments streak across predicted paths. Onboard systems now detect hazards, calculate escape burns, and dodge automatically. They negotiate operational space with one another, exchanging telemetry to avoid collisions. Once, manoeuvres required days of planning and clearance. Now, satellites may shift orbit in hours, or minutes, without waiting for human permission. The constellation becomes a choreography of machines, graceful and uncomplaining.

But autonomy has deeper implications. A spacecraft in a contested theatre may lose contact with ground control. It might be jammed, its antennas blinded, its data pipelines severed by cyber interference. If it cannot think, it dies. If it can decide, it lives. Increasingly, satellites carry not just sensors but algorithms—onboard processing that compresses images, detects targets, encrypts links, and reshapes priorities. Some can re-task themselves, switching from maritime monitoring to wildfire detection as needs shift. Survivability is not just a matter of hardware; it is a matter of intelligence.

There is a philosophical discomfort here. We are building constellations that behave like digital organisms, capable of making decisions faster than any command centre. They are not sentient, but they are independent. The more intense the threats in orbit—debris, jammers, cyberattacks, co-orbital inspectors—the more freedom satellites must have to defend themselves. The line between automation and autonomy blurs. In future crises, machines may manoeuvre long before diplomats can discuss what happened.

Still, survivability is not only about warfare. It is about weather. Solar storms can drench satellites in charged particles, shorting circuits and swelling the atmosphere so that low-orbit objects face sudden drag. Satellites with no fuel or autonomous reboost systems fall. Survivable fleets maintain propulsion margins, hardened electronics, redundant power. Those that do not are memorials, tumbling in silence until incinerated. Space weather, not enemy action, may become the greatest destroyer of fragile fleets.

There is also the risk of silent corruption. A satellite does not need to explode to be ruined. Faulty firmware, a miscalculated manoeuvre, an onboard computer glitch—any one of these can strand a spacecraft. That is why resilient systems layer redundancy at every level: two star trackers, backup gyroscopes, fault-tolerant processors. But the most powerful redundancy is systemic: if one satellite goes dark, the others pick up the load. A distributed architecture treats failure as routine, not catastrophic.

For commercial operators, survivability is economics. A single malfunctioning node in a network of thousands may go unnoticed by customers. A fault in a monolithic system triggers legal claims and international headlines. Insurance markets reflect the shift: underwriters increasingly reward proliferation and penalise fragile architectures. Investors prefer businesses that can lose satellites without losing service. Space has become a numbers game, and resilience is a metric of maturity.

There is a paradox at the heart of all this: the more satellites we launch to ensure resilience, the more crowded and dangerous space becomes. A collision between two small craft may spray debris into neighbouring orbits, threatening the very networks that rely on proliferation to survive. Resilience demands numbers; numbers raise risk. Designers counter with autonomous collision avoidance, debris tracking, rapid end-of-life disposal. But the margin for error tightens as the sky fills. The future could be a stable swarm—or a minefield.

Alliance politics seep into this arena. Nations with friendly launch providers, spare manufacturing lines, and domestic tracking networks gain resilience not just in hardware, but in logistics. Those without must rent capability, sometimes from rivals. A nation may own a constellation, but if it cannot replace satellites at pace, its resilience is temporary. Sovereignty in orbit is not just about satellites in the sky; it is about the industrial capacity beneath them.

The military implications are stark. If a country depends on a small number of high-value satellites, an adversary can disable them with a few well-placed strikes or cyberattacks. If a nation fields thousands of small satellites, an adversary must choose between ineffective harassment and an escalation so large it looks like war. Survivability becomes deterrence: the more dispersed and redundant a system, the less tempting it is to attack.

A proliferated constellation whispers a warning: *you can hurt us, but you cannot stop us.*

And yet, dispersion is not invincible. Ground stations remain choke points. Radio frequencies remain finite. Software bugs scale. Supply chains break. A resilient space network must extend its philosophy to Earth: distributed antennas, mobile ground terminals, cloud-native processing that does not care where the data enters the system. True survivability is holistic. It is orbital and terrestrial, hardware and software, physics and policy.

The most profound shift is conceptual. Space power is no longer about spectacle. It is about endurance. Leaders once pointed to majestic satellites as symbols of national prestige. Now they point to launch logs, production rates, and replacement cycles. The winning architecture is messy, iterative, constantly replenished. It is less a monument and more a bloodstream.

Which raises a final question, hanging like a shadow across every new launch: if satellites must think for themselves, fleets must replace themselves, and networks must heal themselves, how much human control remains? In building constellations that survive attack, neglect, weather, and accident, we are building something with momentum of its own. One day, an operator may look up at a sky full of resilient machines and realise the simplest truth of all: survivability by design is not only about enduring threats. It is about shaping a world where space infrastructure, once fragile, learns to outlast us.

Debris as a strategic actor

On a cold morning in January 2007, a missile launched from central China streaked upward and smashed into an ageing weather satellite. The blast was invisible from Earth, yet what followed was anything but silent. Radar stations soon lit with thousands of new objects—shards, plates, bolts, splinters—each travelling faster than a rifle bullet. The original target was gone in an instant; its pieces will haunt orbit for decades. Airlines had to reroute spacecraft. Operators scrambled to revise manoeuvre plans. Insurance markets twitched. A single destructive act had changed the geometry of low Earth orbit. The satellite was dead, but its ghost multiplied.

This is the paradox of debris. It is passive matter with active consequences. It has no propulsion, no computer, no mission. Yet a metal fragment weighing a few grams can puncture solar arrays, crack optical lenses, or cripple guidance systems. A shard the size of a coin can break a satellite costing hundreds of millions. Operators spend fuel avoiding particles they cannot see. Militaries rethink tactics. Diplomats argue responsibility. Everyone fears the cascade—the nightmare where one collision creates fragments that trigger others, until a whole orbital lane becomes unusable. Space, once imagined infinite, turns into contested real estate fenced by shrapnel.

Debris is more than rubbish: it is strategy in physical form. Nations study it, exploit it, complain about it, but rarely stop producing it. Each new fragment forces operators to burn delta-v for avoidance. Each burn reduces life expectancy. Each shortened mission inflates replacement costs. In a world crowded with low-orbit constellations, debris changes the balance of power. A fleet that can dodge lives longer than a fleet that cannot. A satellite with excess propellant for manoeuvre has advantage over a heavier, more sophisticated competitor. Physics creates hierarchy where law remains silent.

In the early days of spaceflight, debris seemed inconsequential. Orbits were sparse, satellites were few, and most craft burned up naturally after re-entry. Engineers worried more about cosmic rays than leftover screws. That illusion evaporated with the first major collision. In 2009 an American commercial satellite, long defunct, drifted unsuspectingly into the path of an active communications spacecraft belonging to Iridium. They hit at a closing speed of some eleven kilometres per second. Two dead objects became thousands. Radar networks tracked the fragments; operators braced for secondary strikes. Suddenly debris was not an abstraction but a weapon nobody intended to fire.

Insurance firms reacted first. Premiums rose. Underwriters demanded manoeuvre capability, shielding, end-of-life disposal plans. A satellite with no propulsion became a liability. A bus with poor situational awareness was uninsurable. The market, not diplomacy, forced some responsibility onto the industry. Yet insurers cannot solve the physics. Fragments too small for radar still travel fast enough to penetrate. Hundreds of thousands of microscopic particles swarm unseen, scraping surfaces like cosmic sandpaper. A satellite rarely dies from one big hit; it is damaged gradually, performance eroding until a system quietly fails. Operators rarely announce the cause. The public simply hears a euphemism: "unexpected anomaly."

Debris changes manoeuvre options in subtler ways. Imagine a reconnaissance satellite needing to shift orbit for a new mission. Its flight path crosses a region polluted by fragments from a long-ago rocket explosion. The operators must either burn more fuel to skirt the region or accept elevated risk. Either option reduces mission efficiency. In military theatres, where agility matters, debris becomes a strategic tax—levied unpredictably, collected relentlessly. A nation whose satellites sit in cleaner orbits enjoys capability others lack.

This has frightened diplomats into action, but not enough. No binding global treaty bars debris-generating anti-satellite tests. Some nations have declared unilateral moratoriums. Others remain silent. Behind the scenes, analysts whisper a darker possibility: a state could deliberately create a debris belt in a crucial altitude band, denying that orbit to rivals while maintaining access for itself with hardened, shielded spacecraft. No shots fired; no treaties breached; yet an orbital lane rendered hazardous for a generation. It is coercion disguised as pollution.

Debris also complicates attribution. When a satellite dies in a crowded orbit, who is responsible? Was it a stray fragment from a decades-old rocket stage? Was it an intentional interference masked as accident? Nations may blame each other, but proof is elusive. A tiny shard carries no flag. Its origin may be unknown, its trajectory unrecorded. In such ambiguity lies danger. Misinterpretation breeds escalation. An outage could be sabotage—or merely bad luck—but the victim might assume hostility either way.

Operators try to catalogue the growing cloud. The United States, Europe, Russia, India, Japan, and commercial firms track objects larger than a few centimetres. They publish warnings. But tracking is not protection. A predicted risk may still turn catastrophic if manoeuvre options are limited. Sometimes there is not enough time or fuel. Sometimes burns risk placing a satellite in the path of other debris. Sometimes jamming or cyber interference prevents safe control. Space traffic management is moving from polite coordination to a high-stakes air-traffic control problem—except the aircraft travel fifteen times faster and cannot change altitude with ease.

Commercial constellations suffer most. Hundreds of satellites in low Earth orbit navigate a cluttered environment while sharing frequencies, crossing orbital planes, and exchanging crosslinks. Each one must dodge hazards without colliding with siblings. Autonomy helps, but autonomy is imperfect. The more densely populated the orbit, the more chaotic the avoidance. A single piece of debris can force dozens of satellites to adjust, rippling disruption through weeks of carefully planned schedules. In effect, debris wields veto power over the intentions of billion-dollar companies.

And then there is the legal labyrinth. Under existing space law, the state that launched an object retains liability for it—even long after control is lost. A rogue fragment from a rocket fired fifty years ago remains legally attached to the nation that fired it. If that fragment cripples a satellite today, the victim may demand compensation. But how do you prove which fragment struck? How do you prove whose explosion created it? Courts require evidence; orbits offer uncertainty. The law remains aspirational.

Some firms are developing debris removal technologies: nets, harpoons, grappling arms, or tugs that push dead satellites downward to burn in the atmosphere. It sounds heroic, like cosmic housekeeping. Yet these same technologies can serve as weapons: any vehicle that can de-orbit a dead satellite can de-orbit a live one. Thus removal tools are dual-use by design, and most nations treat them warily. Cleaning the sky risks appearing as preparation for attack. The simplest acts in orbit acquire political shadow.

Debris also shapes insurance portfolios in subtler ways. Premiums are not only higher in polluted orbits; they are volatile. After every major collision or anti-satellite test, insurers recalculate risk. A firm planning a constellation faces uncertainty: a launch may be affordable this year, ruinous next. Investors examine orbital cleanliness when choosing business models. In this way, debris influences commerce, investment, and innovation. It is not merely a physical hazard but an economic one.

Yet debris has a moral dimension seldom discussed. Space is shared. A fragment created today may injure someone else's spacecraft twenty years from now. It is pollution that outlives its polluter. Future generations of engineers and astronomers will inherit whatever mess we leave. Unlike carbon emissions, which can be reduced gradually, debris cannot be vacuumed by policy alone. Each fragment demands individual intervention. The sky accumulates history.

Philosophers might say debris reminds us that power leaves residue. Nations chase prestige, deterrence, advantage—but rarely account for the aftermath. Blowing up a satellite demonstrates capability; it also handcuffs future missions. A state that wants to impress the world may find itself trapped by the legacy of its own demonstration.

Engineers know this and speak cautiously. They talk of "conjunction warnings" and "close approaches", phrases that sound technical but signify fear. When a predicted conjunction falls within a few hundred metres, operators plan burns. When two fragments approach each other, surveillance intensifies. The effort is constant, like sweeping a battlefield without end. In private, some wonder if space will suffer the tragedy of the commons: a domain used freely until it becomes unusable.

There may come a moment when a crucial mission—disaster relief, climate monitoring, military reconnaissance—cannot fly a safe orbit because debris blocks its path. Insurance will refuse to cover it. Launch companies will balk. Politicians will learn that strategic behaviour decades earlier has created an invisible minefield. Then debris will no longer be a quiet topic of scientists and insurers; it will become headline news.

Even now, nations compete to publish debris guidelines, hoping their preferred standards gain legitimacy. The true prize is not moral authority but regulatory influence. Whoever sets the standards shapes future industry. If a state's satellites are designed for crowded environments, they may welcome tighter rules that penalise less advanced operators. Debris regulation becomes economic strategy.

And yet the problem remains unsolved. New constellations launch weekly. Old satellites linger without functioning propulsion. Upper stages decay slowly. Explosions from ruptured fuel tanks spawn fresh clouds of chaos. We are filling orbital lanes faster than we are cleaning them. Debris is no longer a legacy issue; it is a present one.

The strategic question is uncomfortable to voice: could debris become a deliberate tool of conflict? A covert explosion, carefully timed, could seed fragments in a rival's key corridor while appearing accidental. A state could feign ignorance. Attribution would be murky. The burden of manoeuvre would fall on the victim. A hostile actor might never fire at a live satellite—merely "accidentally" pollute its orbit. In a world fearful of open warfare, such silent aggression becomes tempting.

Even peaceful nations hesitate to confront this reality. To acknowledge debris as a weapon is to admit the fragility of everything in orbit: navigation, weather forecasting, communications, financial timing, national security. Civilisation stands on glass.

Debris asks a final, unnerving question. If fragments dictate manoeuvres, undermine insurance, reshape alliances, and limit access, who truly governs space? The governments who sign treaties? The companies who build satellites? Or the physics of tens of thousands of untracked shards, drifting without permission or purpose?

In the growing shadow of those fragments lies the dawning recognition that humanity may lose parts of its sky without ever fighting for them.

There will be no flag, no treaty violation, no announcement. Just orbits that quietly become too perilous to use. And when those lanes close—when satellites must reroute or surrender altitudes once thought permanent—people on Earth will learn that the most dangerous actors in space are sometimes the ones we never intended to create.

Signals versus steel

In 2018, flights over the eastern Mediterranean began reporting bizarre navigation behaviour. Aircraft autopilots flicked into warning mode. GPS receivers placed jets where they clearly were not—sometimes tens of kilometres away, occasionally over water when they were firmly over land. Pilots checked instruments twice, then a third time. Crews swapped stories through informal channels. Something invisible was tugging at the digital map. No satellites had been destroyed, no radars jammed into silence, yet the sky had been subtly booby-trapped by radio waves. The satellites still shone above; the signals beneath them had been bent.

This is the quiet face of modern space warfare. A missile is unmistakable; a fake signal is not. A kinetic strike produces debris, headlines, and accusation. Spoofing produces doubt. And doubt travels faster than any rocket.

For decades, the popular imagination cast space conflict as a contest of steel—missiles launched, satellites shattered, fragments cascading through orbit. Kinetic destruction is cinematic and simple: one object strikes another; its absence becomes victory. But those who study the craft know that the cheaper, deniable, and strategically elegant path often lies not in hitting satellites, but in blinding or deceiving them. Space warfare has become a contest of signals, not shrapnel. The weapon is not a warhead but a waveform.

Jamming is the bluntest tool. By flooding a receiver with noise, an attacker can drown out the signal a satellite sends. Civilian GPS receivers are especially vulnerable; their signals are faint, easy to overpower. A truck-mounted jammer on the ground can knock out navigation for nearby aircraft, ships, and drones. The effect is reversible: turn the jammer off and the world snaps back to normal. Importantly, the target satellite remains unharmed. There is no destroyed hardware to mourn, no debris cloud to sweep, no treaty breached. It is interference without blood.

Spoofing is more cunning. Instead of silencing a signal, it replaces it. A receiver believes it is receiving authentic data from a satellite, when in fact the attacker is feeding false coordinates, false timing, false telemetry. The victim does not lose service—it trusts the wrong service. Spoofing has nudged oil tankers off course, confused unmanned aerial vehicles, and triggered costly diversions of commercial flights. A pilot who sees a blank screen knows something is wrong. A pilot whose instruments lie must second-guess everything.

This ambiguity is the key. If a satellite stops responding, its owner may suspect attack. If a pilot merely notices navigation oddities, blame can be scattered: software glitch, hardware failure, atmospheric anomaly. Nations can deny involvement with a straight face. No fragments to photograph, no strike to confirm, no forensic trail burnt into an orbital lane. In a diplomatic culture that demands proof before punishment, plausible deniability is a strategic weapon of its own.

To be clear, kinetic weapons have not vanished. The ability to destroy a satellite with a missile, a co-orbital interceptor, or a kamikaze drone remains a deterrent. But they are tools of last resort. They change the physics of orbit in a single violent moment, adding debris that might later injure the attacker's own spacecraft. Even a victorious strike may poison the very altitude one seeks to dominate. Jamming and spoofing, by contrast, leave no permanent scar. When the conflict cools, frequencies can be cleared and services restored. Cyber packets disappear; steel remains.

Cyber intrusion adds a further wrinkle. If an attacker can seize control of a satellite's command link, they may silence it, misorient it, or force it into safe mode without ever touching its hardware. A hacked satellite can be blinded, deafened, or even deorbited with no visible violence. Such attacks blur the line between espionage and warfare. A compromised ground station on Earth can have consequences in orbit. Digital sabotage becomes orbital sabotage by proxy.

Cost drives much of this logic. Developing and launching an anti-satellite missile requires advanced rocketry, precision tracking, and political tolerance for the fallout. Building a portable jammer requires a power source, an antenna, and a technician. A few thousand dollars versus hundreds of millions. A student hacker might disrupt a satellite's service; only a small club of nations can shoot one down.

The economics change the strategy. If a state wants to harass an adversary without provoking open conflict, it can jam border regions, spoof shipping lanes, or flood satellite communication channels with noise. The victim may complain, but retaliation is tricky. Attribution is murky. A jammer can be switched off before inspectors arrive. A spoofing signal can be broadcast from international waters, or through leased commercial equipment. Responsibility becomes a shadow play.

Civilian systems are particularly soft targets. Remote farmers rely on satellite-guided tractors. Stock exchanges depend on satellite timing. Airlines trust GPS for navigation and geofencing. Most of these systems have minimal protection against deliberate interference. In 2022, small jammers sold on online marketplaces interfered with airport operations in several countries. Each device was the size of a cigarette packet. None of the users intended to wage war; they simply wanted to block tracking of their vehicles. Yet the side-effects cascaded into commercial aviation. A tiny transmitter on a motorway can have consequences hundreds of kilometres away.

A military planner studies these events with cold interest. If accidental jamming can disrupt vital infrastructure, imagine what deliberate, coordinated interference could achieve. A blackout of navigation across a coastline. A fleet of cargo ships forced into harbour. Drones grounded. Banking transactions frozen. All without firing a shot, without harming a single satellite. Soft-kill effects can achieve hard results.

There is also the question of escalation. Destroying a satellite is a public act. Nobody doubts the intent. It invites retaliation—perhaps against the attacker's own spacecraft, perhaps on Earth. Jamming, by contrast, is a nuisance. Spoofing is a trick. The injured party may hesitate to respond aggressively, unsure of the attacker's identity or intent. In deterrence theory, ambiguity is often a disadvantage; in space warfare, it is an asset. States can signal displeasure, impose cost, or test defences without crossing the red line of kinetic destruction.

Yet soft-kill is not without risk. A spoofed receiver might direct an aircraft into danger. A jammed rescue helicopter might lose navigation mid-mission. If civilian casualties occur, the political costs could outweigh any strategic gain. For this reason, sophisticated states often aim their interference at military channels or strategic assets. Even then, the boundaries blur: many civilian systems piggyback on military signals, and vice versa. A frequency jammed for security might inadvertently undermine farming, shipping, or emergency response.

In this crowded spectrum, resilience matters. Modern satellites experiment with encrypted signals, directional antennas, and frequency hopping. Some constellations build redundancy into their architecture: if a few satellites are jammed, others route around the interference. Ground stations learn to detect spoofing patterns, triangulate jammers, and adjust algorithms. Yet defence is never perfect. The physics are unforgiving: a satellite 20,000 kilometres above Earth transmits a signal no stronger than a household lightbulb. Almost any deliberate interference on the ground can overwhelm it. Power favours the attacker.

This imbalance has philosophical implications. The dream of satellite technology was pure utility—navigation for all, communication for all, weather insight for all. But a system that is globally useful is also globally vulnerable. Space infrastructure thrives on openness; warfare thrives on exploitation. The same transparency that allows a smartphone to find its route allows a hostile jammer to find its target.

Signals versus steel also alters diplomacy. Nations can quietly test jammers or spoofing methods during peacetime, gauging adversary reactions without risking war. Stealth trials creep across borders: ships lose GPS in harbour, drones drift off course, survey equipment reports phantom coordinates. Each incident is small enough to ignore but large enough to signal capability. It is deterrence by inconvenience.

Companies face the dilemma too. A broadband constellation might suffer widespread jamming. No satellites die, so insurers refuse payouts. Customers complain. Revenues collapse. The operator suspects state-sponsored interference but cannot prove it. Legal recourse is limited. The victim bears the loss. As in cyber warfare, attribution becomes the hardest part of justice.

And all the while, the weapons improve. Software-defined radios make jammers more agile. Machine learning refines spoofing patterns. Ground-based antennas become steerable, pulsing energy into narrow beams that blind specific craft without drawing attention. A future conflict may involve fleets of autonomous jammers, sailing international waters beneath deniable flags. The satellites they attack will never fall from the sky—they will simply lose their voice.

Some strategists quietly ask whether kinetic strikes will become rare relics of a crude past. Steel is effective, but messy. Signals are elegant. In a domain where every fragment is a hazard, the clean kill is the one that leaves nothing broken. A silent temporary blackout achieves much of the same purpose with none of the eternal consequences. And if the interference goes too far, it can be lifted in a heartbeat. Reset the spectrum, and the world forgets—until the next outage.

There is a darker scenario still: a state might combine both approaches. A few select satellites could be destroyed to send a message; the rest could be jammed to control escalation. The victims would lose capability yet have no incontrovertible casus belli. Power would be asserted, deniability maintained.

In this strange theatre, steel feels almost honest. A missile announces its allegiance. Hard-kill attacks carry signatures that even amateurs can trace: trajectory, radar tracks, debris patterns. By contrast, a spoofed navigation grid can torment a nation long before it identifies the culprit.

Thus, space warfare is evolving into something more psychological than physical. The target is confidence itself. If a state stops believing in its satellites—if it fears that coordinates are false or communications unreliable—those assets lose strategic value without ever breaking.

Somewhere, right now, a satellite is broadcasting truth into a sky filled with lies, and a small transmitter on Earth is trying to make the world look the other way. In the coming decades, the quiet duel between signals and steel will define which nations command the high ground and which merely stare at it, uncertain whether what they see is real.

Chapter 3

Eyes, Ears, and Relays

At first light, a fishing crew off the Horn of Africa began hauling in nets. Nothing unusual: the sea was calm, radios crackled, gulls barked over the swell. Fifty miles away, a destroyer altered course. Hundreds of miles beyond that, an analyst in a quiet room studied a series of satellite radar frames that showed faint blips trailing a commercial tanker—shadows on the water that were not waves and not whales. The net closed, not through a dramatic chase, but through a constellation of silent watchers in orbit. By midday, authorities intercepted vessels suspected of smuggling weapons. The fishing boats never knew that their morning routine unfolded beneath a web of sensors. Up above, nothing shimmered, nothing flashed. Yet the sky had been listening.

We often speak of satellites as if they are eyes alone—cameras peering down from the heavens—but that cliché sells them short. They are eyes, ears, timekeepers, and telegraph lines, all at once. They witness, synchronise, whisper, relay, and corroborate. In space, sensing and communicating blur. A picture is not only a picture; it is a coordinate for a missile battery, a warning for a farmer, a dataset for an oil trader. A whisper of timing becomes a synchronised strike or a stock trade executed a fraction of a second sooner. Every signal has consequences far beyond its photons.

A modern satellite might look unimpressive on the ground: a metal cylinder, some panels, a dish. But in orbit it becomes an instrument of perception, tuned to wavelengths your eyes will never see. Electro-optical cameras capture sunlight reflected from land and sea. Synthetic aperture radar pierces clouds and darkness, watching ships move beneath storms. Infrared sensors notice heat where no heat should be—engines warming on hidden airfields, missiles breaking through cloud. Together, these orbiting sentinels create a mosaic of the world more complete than any single telescope.

Their effect is subtle yet profound. Cargo ships that once vanished between ports are now tracked continuously, even when they "go dark". Military units dispersing through woodlands leave signatures invisible to human scouts but bright to satellites that sense thermal contrast. Weather systems, once guessed through sparse observation, now reveal their swelling guts in high-resolution imagery. A storm that destroys food crops or halts aircraft does not surprise us: the sky's eyes warned us days in advance.

But sensing alone is not the story. Information isolated in orbit is worthless. It must be timed, interpreted, shared, fused. Precision timing, broadcast from satellites, is the quiet miracle that keeps the modern world stitched together. Without those pulses of atomic time, securities markets fall apart, mobile networks fall out of alignment, and guided munitions miss their mark. The same clock that directs aircraft also guides tractors sowing crops in perfect parallel lines. The same constellation that allows a driver to navigate to the nearest bakery also enables a fighter pilot to strike a moving target at night. This duality—simple convenience intertwined with strategic precision—is what makes space infrastructure so strange and so powerful. Its gifts cannot be separated from its dangers.

Communication satellites take this dependency further. They form the hidden backbone of distant command. A strategic submarine does not rise near the surface every hour to telephone home; it whispers to orbit. A special operations team pushing through mountains cannot rely on a mobile mast; they reach upward. When a wildfire burns telephone poles, when earthquakes topple cellular towers, when war shatters fibre cables, space preserves the connection. And because modern constellations can stitch a mesh across the sky, even moving units—vehicles, aircraft, ships—can form networks on the edge of conflict, without revealing their position through radio chatter that enemy sensors might intercept. The satellite becomes both shield and amplifier.

There is a quiet choreography behind this: many satellites, many ground stations, many beams of radio and laser light dancing across continents. Every hop carries risk of interception, jamming, misalignment. Yet without these links, modern warfare collapses into blind groping. The precision strike becomes the indiscriminate blast. The coordinated manoeuvre becomes chaotic retreat. Armies that cannot talk are armies that cannot win.

Still, raw data is insufficient. A single satellite photograph can be ambiguous. A radar sweep reveals motion, not identity. A thermal signature shows heat, not intent. The real art lies in fusion: combining observations from many sensors—space-based, airborne, maritime, terrestrial—to produce a coherent picture. A commercial imaging firm might notice new earthworks near a border. A signals-intelligence satellite might register encrypted radio bursts from a nearby brigade. An academic researcher might see fuel deliveries rising at a remote depot. When stitched together, these fragments become the story of a mobilisation, a supply build-up, a threat. Intelligence agencies are no longer the only ones interpreting this tapestry. Today, public volunteers, journalists, and think-tank analysts comb commercial satellite feeds with forensic patience. Open-source intelligence, once dismissed, now shapes headlines and policy. Space has democratised surveillance.

This is the chapter's heart: satellites have become not just witnesses, but arbiters. They do not merely record history; they actively influence it. In some conflicts, commercial imagery has exposed mass graves, mapping atrocities faster than governments could claim innocence. In others, satellite phones have connected civilians trapped by siege when terrestrial networks collapsed. These services are sold on subscription, like music streaming or cloud storage. A government at war might not own the satellites supporting its troops. It might rent them.

This rental logic changes strategy. A state cannot silence a constellation simply by bombing a ground station; the operator has backups, and other nations might share ground access. In a crisis, a government can request higher-resolution imagery or wider coverage, and commercial fleets can retask themselves accordingly. Private companies have become part of national defence, whether they wish to be or not. Their satellites carry civilian broadband one week and encrypted military traffic the next. Their imagery feeds scientific research by day and targeting software by night. Dual use is not a buzzword; it is the condition of the orbital age.

The moral questions thicken. If a commercial satellite is used to guide a missile, is it a civilian asset or a military one? Does the attacker have the right to jam it? Destroy it? Courts and treaties lag behind reality. Insurance firms now debate what constitutes a loss in space. Academics build models to predict how close a "peaceful inspection" satellite can approach a rival craft before it becomes provocation. Every dataset has geopolitical weight.

Yet the power of these constellations is not merely about conflict. They tell farmers when to irrigate. They monitor wildfire fronts. They connect Arctic schools. They help map humanitarian corridors after earthquakes. The same network that coordinates artillery also finds survivors beneath rubble. This asymmetry—technology that serves both mercy and war—runs throughout modern geopolitics. But in orbit, the contradiction is starkest. The satellite that forecasts a cyclone can, a moment later, enable a cruise missile to thread a canyon.

In the chapters behind and ahead, space has revealed itself as infrastructure, then as contested terrain, and now as perception itself. To see is to act; to hear is to decide. Nations that once fought blind now fight with maps so precise they can pinpoint an enemy's water supply or fuel dump. Allies share data in near-real time. And adversaries know they are being watched.

Space no longer counts tanks; it counts intentions. Every new satellite launched extends the human ability to measure the world, and measurement is power. A country that can track the movement of every ship, every night, in every weather condition holds strategic advantage even without firing a bullet. A country that can guarantee timing to within billionths of a second controls coordination, logistics, and markets.

But perception has a dark reverse: deception. If satellites see, others try to hide. Camouflage, decoys, electronic blinds—an ongoing duel of reveal and conceal. Some nations spread inflatable tanks across fields, hoping to flood sensors. Others paint their warships in patterns that confuse radar. Still others build deep underground shelters and flood tunnels to hide movement. Space sees much, but it does not see everything.

This chapter will follow these tensions closely: the miracle of orbital sensing, the fragility of its signals, the dependence of societies on timing, the vulnerability of fleets to surveillance, and the creative countermeasures of those who do not wish to be seen. It will show how satellites turn the Earth into a kind of annotated manuscript: every movement dated, every change logged. It will show how shipping routes, troop convoys, and container terminals can be mapped like circuits on a board. And it will show how every new sensor creates incentives to deceive, disrupt, or saturate.

Eyes, ears, and relays: three functions, inseparable. To listen is to prepare; to speak is to coordinate; to see is to decide. In the pages ahead, the satellite becomes not an icon in a museum, but a living nerve in the body of global affairs. Those who command it do not merely observe the world—they choreograph it. Those who lose it do not simply go blind—they forfeit time, coordination, and truth itself.

Imaging from orbit

On a winter night in the North Atlantic, a storm swallowed the sea. Waves twisted like black metal, radar on the destroyers flickered, and aircraft diverted rather than gamble with ice and wind. Yet hundreds of miles overhead, a satellite watched the darkness as easily as if it were noon. Its synthetic aperture radar threw pulses through cloud and gale, painting a ghostly map of ships that could no longer see one another. Crews huddled below, deafened by weather. The satellite was unbothered. It did not blink.

That is the quiet power of imaging from orbit. Space-based cameras are not cameras in the cinema sense. They are instruments stitched to physics: light, radio waves, and heat, each tuned to reveal a different truth. The old notion of a spy satellite peering down like a telescope is far too simple. Modern constellations gather layers of reality—colour, texture, warmth, movement—in wavelengths no human eye can register. The result is a portrait not of what the world *looks* like, but of what it *is*.

Electro-optical imagery is the closest to what our senses understand. Sunlight bounces off roofs, vehicles, runways, coastlines, and returns to the sensor. High-resolution satellites can pick out tyre tracks, earthworks, and changes in vegetation that suggest trenching or camouflage. Militaries have used electro-optical systems since the Cold War to watch missile silos and armoured divisions. Today, commercial companies sell images so sharp that one can see the shadows of aircraft on tarmac. When a warship leaves port, analysts halfway across the world sometimes publish annotated images before the ship's crew have finished breakfast.

But electro-optical imagery has a tyrant: the weather. Clouds interrupt the picture; darkness erases the detail. Nations learned quickly that adversaries can hide convoys beneath overcast skies or move armour at night. Nature became a shield.

Radar stripped that shield away. Synthetic aperture radar—SAR—does not wait for the sun. It emits bursts of radio energy and measures their echo. With clever processing, those echoes reveal shape, motion, even subtle surface changes. A tank hidden beneath camouflage netting may vanish to the human eye, but SAR can detect the hard edges of the metal. A fleet may claim to be at anchor; SAR exposes the wake of a ship pretending to be still. In the open ocean, SAR has become the great leveller. Storms that ground aircraft barely perturb radio waves from orbit. A smuggling flotilla, a clandestine tanker, a submarine on the surface: none of them can count on bad weather anymore.

Where electro-optical imagery shows *what* is there, SAR often shows *what it is doing*. Ships leave patterns in the water. Vehicles compress earth. Buildings shift under load. even minute changes in terrain—bridge strain, runway collapse, groundwater pumping—appear as interference in the radar signal. Engineers have used SAR to map landslides and earthquakes. Militaries use it to detect tunnelling or fortification. Intelligence agencies use it to track cargo ships that switch off their transponders in contested waters. Clouds, darkness, deception—the radar is indifferent.

Then there is heat. Infrared satellites track the glow of engines, the warmth of factories, the combustion of rockets. A missile launch is a roaring flare of infrared light. Aerospace designers have tried to hide these signatures, but the laws of thermodynamics are unforgiving. Even stealth aircraft, wrapped in radar-absorbing materials, glow in infrared. Satellite infrared sensors stare across continents, warning of launches within seconds. Some of these systems, built for missile defence, see heat from over the horizon, sensing ballistic arcs long before they crest.

Infrared does not merely warn. It diagnoses. When fuel depots heat unevenly, analysts infer usage. When blast furnaces dim, industrial output has shifted. During humanitarian disasters, infrared reveals burning villages when smoke hides the ruins. During war, it tracks artillery flashes, tank engines, even the heat of bodies massed in trenches. A satellite can count troops without seeing a single face.

No single modality tells the full story. A tank decoy carved from wood can fool electro-optical imagery. A net strung across a river might disrupt radar. Engines can be cooled before movement. But fusion defeats the trick. When electro-optical imagery confirms a silhouette, SAR measures the ground it presses, infrared senses the heat of its machinery. When adversaries set up inflatable decoys, infrared notices their cold hollowness. In the most telling cases, satellites can spot the tracks leading *to* a decoy even if the object itself fools the eye.

Civilian uses are equally transformative. Weather forecasters rely on multispectral satellites to see water vapour spirals and wind shear. Farmers study vegetation health through reflectance in narrow bands invisible to humans. Disaster agencies map floodplains hour by hour, directing rescue teams where the waters rise fastest. In recent years, wildfires that once overwhelmed firefighters became navigable through thermal overlays of burning fronts. From volcanic ash to locust migrations, orbiting sensors have turned uncertainty into evidence.

Yet what makes orbital imaging strategically potent is not just what satellites see—it is what they make visible about geopolitics. Consider how coastal patrols used to work: hours of flight time, expensive fuel, human fatigue, and blind spots. Now, a single radar satellite sweeping a coastline can produce a catalogue of vessels: size, heading, speed. When ships turn off their AIS beacons—the maritime equivalent of calling out their name—their shadows remain. A smuggler cannot jam the ocean surface.

In land conflict, high-resolution electro-optical imagery maps trenches, artillery positions, and supply depots. Before satellites, commanders sent scouts, risking ambush. Now, one constellation pass can expose entire logistics networks. Nations study satellite images to infer intent: tank parks swelling, fuel trucks lining roads, airbases cleared of civilian traffic. Mobilisation leaves fingerprints.

Perhaps the most extraordinary shift is public transparency. For much of the twentieth century, only states possessed satellites. Secrets were traded behind closed doors; the public heard nothing until decades later. Today, a university student with a laptop can purchase imagery, annotate it, and publish analysis read by millions. Governments have found themselves cornered by proof they do not own and cannot discredit. Mass graves, scorched villages, hidden prisons—satellites have stripped plausible deniability from dictators. Truth has altitude.

And still, we are only at the beginning. New satellites capture not just images but change. They fly the same route every few hours, comparing one picture to the last, detecting what shifted. Did trucks arrive? Did tanks leave? Did someone pave a runway overnight? Machine learning combs through endless frames, flagging anomalies: a new shack, a missing pipeline segment, a ship loading cargo after midnight. Space becomes a ledger of movement.

Where humans cannot go, satellites glide. They watch disputed borders through snows and monsoons. They track illegal fishing fleets dodging coast guards. They map refugee camps swelling after conflict. Every image becomes an argument: this is happening, here, now.

Of course, militaries have learned to respond. Camouflage is an art reborn: infrared-suppressing nets, radar-absorbent foams, decoy heat sources. Engineers reshape vehicles to blur their outlines. Ships scatter chaff to confuse radar interpretation. On land, armies build fake airfields and inflatable armour to lure analysts astray. The duel between watcher and watched is constant, sophisticated, and strangely intimate.

But deception has limits. A wooden tank may fool a single sensor for a single moment. It cannot fool a network that sees, measures, and calculates across spectra. In the First World War, reconnaissance aircraft gave generals a new vantage. In the Second, radar showed them beyond the horizon. Today, space grants omnipresent context. "We did not know" is no longer credible.

The philosophical consequence is profound: power no longer rests only on the ability to act, but on the ability to be *seen acting*. The satellite archive is a memory that nations cannot erase. A massing army cannot swear it was never there; a burning oil field cannot hide behind storm clouds. A government can deny a rumour. It cannot deny a photograph taken from orbit.

Yet the inverse is also true: dependence on orbital imagery creates fragility. If satellites are blinded by lasers, jammed, spoofed, or simply clouded with debris, the world grows opaque again. Militaries accustomed to seeing everything might suddenly be blind. A navy that relies on radar imaging to track adversaries could wake to empty maps. The hunter would become uncertain. The strategist would be forced to guess. That is the unsettling tension: the clearer our vision from space, the more catastrophic the loss of it might become.

And beyond that looms a troubling future. If satellites can image every object bigger than a car, what becomes of privacy? If governments can track any ship, what becomes of neutral commerce? If analysts can watch humanitarian corridors form and fail in real time, what excuses remain for inaction? A world of perfect visibility is not a world of perfect justice—it is simply a world without shadows.

Somewhere, at this very moment, a satellite passes over a coastline. Its SAR system paints an invisible portrait of ships that think themselves hidden. A tanker loads fuel under cloud cover. A patrol vessel shadows it silently. Cameras on the ground cannot see through the storm. The satellite does. When the images download, analysts will trace the path of the ships frame by frame. By morning, the sea's secrets will be documented, timestamped, archived.

Imaging from orbit has made the planet legible. Whether that legibility protects us or exposes us depends on who holds the images—and who they decide to show them to.

Timing and navigation

In the spring of 2019, dozens of crop sprayers rolled across wheat fields in Kansas, guided not by the eyes of their drivers but by invisible pulses from orbit. Each nozzle opened and closed to the exact centimetre, spreading fertiliser only where soil needed it, avoiding waste and run-off. A thousand kilometres away, a precision-guided munition spiralled towards a desert test range, its avionics reading those very same pulses. One nourished grain; the other steered explosive steel. Two acts, separated by politics and morality, united by the same celestial clock. The paradox is both unsettling and profoundly ordinary: satellites synchronise bread and war.

People often assume satellites tell us where we are. In truth, they tell us *when* we are. The navigation part is almost incidental. Your phone works out its position by comparing the arrival times of signals from different spacecraft, each carrying an atomic heartbeat. Because space is a realm where light itself is slow enough to measure—just under 300,000 kilometres per second—nanoseconds matter. If your device misreads those blinks of time by even a millionth of a second, you will be kilometres from where you truly stand. Navigation is, at its core, precision timekeeping written into geography.

This is why militaries care so fiercely about timing. To synchronise strikes, aircraft, artillery, cyber operations, and logistics, commanders need shared clocks more reliable than any wristwatch or phone network. Missile defence systems calculate where a threat will be, not where it is, and they must perform those calculations faster than a human can blink. Without absolute timing, a missile launched from a submarine might miss its retaliatory window; an interceptor might arrive seconds too late. In a world where milliseconds decide whether a city lives or dies, the clock is a weapon.

Yet the civilian world depends on that same weapon. Financial markets price assets by the microsecond. High-frequency traders synchronise servers with satellite time to ensure that buy and sell orders execute in the correct sequence. If timestamps drift, billions of dollars can evaporate in legal disputes. Energy grids rely on timing to balance power flows across vast distances; without it, transformers overload and breakers trip. Mobile networks use timing pulses to align signals between towers; lose those pulses and calls drop, messages vanish, ambulance dispatch systems stall. A power outage in one city, a communications blackout in another—timing errors cascade quickly.

This fragility is not theoretical. In 2016, a software glitch propagated through part of the GPS constellation and several satellites began broadcasting faulty time. The error lasted less than a day. Yet across the world, some telecom systems faulted, digital radio services went dark, and scientific instruments reported anomalies. No war, no sabotage—just a fault in a handful of satellites. The world felt the tremor.

Every satellite navigation system—GPS, Galileo, GLONASS, BeiDou—carries atomic clocks more precise than any master clock on Earth. They drift by nanoseconds across a day. The physics is almost absurd: to correct for relativity, engineers adjust for the fact that time flows differently in orbit. Without those relativistic offsets, timing errors would snowball until navigation was useless. Einstein is an unseen engineer in every car and combine harvester.

Precision agriculture might seem far removed from geopolitics, yet it illustrates the stakes. Tractors guided by satellites plant and harvest with mechanical exactness. They optimise fuel, water, chemicals, and labour. If timing signals vanish, those tractors can revert to manual operation—slower, less efficient, more costly. If the outage lasts days during planting season, yields plummet. A hostile actor does not need to strike a granary to wound a nation's food supply. It can disrupt timing.

In coastal waters, fishing fleets depend on satellite navigation for safety. A trawler misreading its coordinates might cut across a reef or stray into foreign territorial seas. Shipping giants use satellite timing to coordinate port arrivals, crane operations, and automated logistics. A glitch ripples outward: ships stack offshore, cargo delays multiply, supply chains stall. The clock becomes an economic circulatory system.

That circulatory system also governs emergency response. When earthquakes topple towers and slice cables, satellite timing restores order. Ambulances navigate wrecked streets by GPS; firefighters triangulate positions by satellite coordinates; helicopters land where dust clouds smother visibility. If those coordinates drift, responders risk landing on debris, missing victims, or crashing in smoke. Lives depend on clocks.

The military demands a harsher threshold. Guided munitions deviate if timing shifts. Artillery shells using satellite corrections can miss by hundreds of metres. Soldiers relying on encrypted positioning signals might lose situational awareness. Intelligence analysts tracing vehicles could follow ghosts. Without trustworthy time, the modern battlefield dissolves into uncertainty.

Because timing is so central, nations compete to control it. The United States, the European Union, Russia, and China each maintain global navigation constellations, guarding autonomy against dependence. Some allies agree to share military-grade signals under treaty; others build parallel systems to hedge against sanctions or sabotage. A state that loses access to satellite timing in wartime faces not just battlefield confusion, but national paralysis. The drive for sovereignty is not abstract: it is survival.

And so the politics of navigation become a quiet rivalry. Ground stations must remain secure. Satellites must resist jamming, spoofing, and cyber interference. Radio receivers must discriminate between legitimate and fraudulent signals. Even a crude jammer—sold online for a few pounds—can cause havoc near airports or seaports. A nation skilled in deception can broadcast counterfeit signals, leading ships astray or nudging drones into the wrong valley. No explosion, no debris—only confusion.

Governments are not blind to the risk. Some invest in terrestrial backups: eLoran radio beacons, fibre-based timing networks, inertial navigation systems on vehicles and missiles. But redundancy is uneven. Many sectors—transportation, finance, agriculture—barely think about the fragility beneath their feet. They assume the sky will keep time. They do not budget for the day it stops.

The irony is that navigation satellites were never designed to be linchpins of civilisation. Early systems aimed to guide missiles and submarines. Civilians received the leftovers. But as the signals matured, billions of receivers bloomed: phones, watches, tractors, ships, drones, financial servers, seismic sensors, stock exchanges, smart meters, ride-sharing apps. If time is money, space has become the mint.

There is a philosophical tension in this dependence. Humans once measured time by the sun, then by mechanical clocks, then by quartz oscillations. Now we borrow our sense of "now" from machines orbiting the Earth at thousands of metres per second. We anchor our reality to distant atoms vibrating in vacuum, waiting for pulses we cannot hear. A society that cannot navigate without space is a society orbitally tethered.

If those tethers fray, what remains? Militaries drill for GPS-denied environments. Pilots train with dead reckoning. Artillery batteries revert to older targeting. Yet the harsh truth is that modern warfare—precision, coordination, speed—assumes satellite timing. A naval fleet spread across hundreds of kilometres must coordinate manoeuvres to the second. Cyber operations aimed at disabling air defences must align with missiles and drones in perfect sequence. Without shared clocks, the choreography collapses.

The same collapse haunts markets. If financial exchanges lose synchronisation, trade order becomes chaos. Traders exploit arbitrage created by timing drift. Some exchanges would freeze to avoid legal disaster. Others would push through corrupted data. Even a brief outage could shake confidence in a currency. In the digital economy, time is trust.

Trust, of course, is the ultimate strategic currency. Allies trust that shared timing gives them a common battlespace map. Civilians trust that aircraft will not collide, that ambulances will arrive, that cash machines will not spit out fatal errors in the dead of night. Engineers trust that the pulse arriving from orbit is true. Somewhere above them, a hydrogen atom oscillates. Somewhere below, a city breathes in rhythm with it.

It is easy to imagine satellites as intangible abstractions, but their vulnerability is painfully concrete. A kinetic strike on even a handful of navigation satellites would shower debris across critical orbital lanes. But an adversary does not need to break anything. Jamming devices can drown out signals; spoofers can project counterfeit ones. A ship that suddenly "believes" it has drifted might slow, turn, or reroute. If enough vessels act on distorted coordinates, ports jam and trade chokes. In war, altered coordinates could scatter convoys, confuse artillery, or misdirect precision weapons. Errors become weapons.

Governments therefore obsess about encrypted signals, anti-spoofing receivers, directional antennas, and fallback timing modes. Satellites carry redundant clocks and software patches. Ground stations constantly correct drifts. Engineers test for relativistic quirks: time circulates differently at altitude and speed. Physics is a constant adversary.

Yet the private sector adds complexity. Commercial fleets of low-Earth-orbit satellites now broadcast positioning signals alongside broadband. Their timing may one day compete with state systems. Tech firms already experiment with hybrid receivers blending GPS, Galileo, inertial sensors, and mobile network timing. As redundancy increases, so does the attack surface. More clocks mean more points of failure, more vectors of deception. The world gains resilience and vulnerability in the same breath.

Some argue that humanity has surrendered too much autonomy to space. Others counter that precision timing is the foundation of prosperity. Neither is entirely wrong. What matters is recognising that every supermarket supply chain, every air corridor, every bank transfer depends on pulses from machines that could, in theory, be silenced.

Somewhere tonight, a missile test will be simulated. A war game will model what happens when navigation signals fade across a theatre. Generals will watch icons jitter, missiles veer, logistics collapse. Somewhere else, a harvester will turn soil with astonishing efficiency, its tyres guided by the same satellites. The farmer will not think of defence ministries or nuclear submarines. The soldier will not think of wheat. Yet their worlds orbit the same clock.

One day, the clock may stutter. It might be accident or malice. It might be brief or prolonged. The question is not whether society *can* endure such a moment, but whether it realises that the moment is possible at all. When civilisation forgets that its time comes from the sky, it risks being blind not in space, but on Earth.

Communications backbones

In the early hours of February 24, 2022, as armour rolled across the Ukrainian border and missiles arced through the night, something unexpected happened. Amid collapsing cell towers, severed fibre lines, and jammed radio bands, a handful of portable terminals pointed their dish-shaped faces towards the sky. Within minutes, Ukrainian commanders were speaking to dispersed units, drones were transmitting video feeds, and government ministries were still reaching the world. A satellite signal—quiet, cold, unimaginably distant—pierced the fog of war. It did what terrestrial systems could not: it created a lifeline above the battlefield.

This was not the first war to rely on space for communications, but it was the first where a commercial low-Earth-orbit network acted as a tactical mesh for ground forces. Soldiers in armoured vehicles, volunteers in pickup trucks, and drone pilots in garages used the same constellation to talk, coordinate, and share imagery. A system once imagined for rural broadband became a military backbone overnight. The line between civilian infrastructure and wartime capability blurred.

Satellites carry messages where fibre cannot run and radios cannot reach. They bridge continents in seconds, stitch together navies, and allow aircraft to talk across oceans. In the Cold War, strategic satellite links enabled early-warning radars, nuclear command-and-control, and diplomatic hotlines. Today, those strategic channels remain—the hidden arteries of deterrence—but they share orbit with tactical constellations that serve platoons, police, cargo ships, oil rigs, and refugees.

A satellite is not simply a floating repeater. It is a node in a global system: spacecraft, ground stations, mobile terminals, software, encryption, spectrum licences, insurance, fuel reserves, spare satellites, launch contracts. When one soldier presses a push-to-talk radio linked to a satellite terminal, thousands of components conspire to turn vibration into data, data into pulses of light, and pulses of light into coordinates for orbiting machines that relay it back to Earth. The complexity is invisible. The effect is simple: the right message reaches the right person at the right moment.

Strategic militaries maintain dedicated SATCOM constellations for command-and-control. These spacecraft are often in geostationary orbit, staring at the same region of Earth and providing persistent coverage. Their beams carry encrypted orders to submarines hiding beneath the waves, to bomber crews circling above cloud cover, to ships patrolling shipping lanes. In crisis, geostationary links sustain nuclear deterrence: leaders cannot retaliate if they cannot communicate.

But geostationary orbit is not enough. Its distance—36,000 kilometres above Earth—adds latency. For many applications, that delay is tolerable. For others, it is crippling. A drone swarm does not want half-second lag. Remote pilots correcting a drone's flight path in a narrow canyon cannot tolerate sluggish control loops. Soldiers fighting in hills, forests, or rubble need mobile terminals that fit in rucksacks and lock onto satellites that skim the sky rather than hover in eternity.

Low-Earth-orbit constellations answer that need. Thousands of satellites orbit a few hundred kilometres above Earth, passing overhead every minutes, creating a shifting web of connectivity. Ground terminals track them automatically, handing signals from one spacecraft to the next. Latency drops. Bandwidth rises. Cars in deserts, freighters in the mid-Pacific, hikers in avalanche zones—anyone with a terminal sees the world again.

This agility produces new forms of warfare. A reconnaissance drone can fire compressed video through LEO satellites to analysts hundreds of kilometres away. A platoon can call artillery support beyond the horizon. Unmanned vehicles at sea or on land can be piloted from safe distances. Information becomes weapon, shield, and fuel.

Yet LEO connectivity is both miracle and nightmare. Thousands of satellites must launch, replace, and coordinate. Their ground segment requires gateways, antennas, site permissions, integration with terrestrial networks, and cybersecurity. Protecting this fabric is a challenge. A state can jam uplinks, hack gateways, or cut power to remote ground stations. A constellation may survive in space but die on Earth.

Many governments are learning from commercial models. Defence ministries buy capacity from private operators, share terminals across units, or place military payloads onto commercial spacecraft. In some cases, commercial firms offer encrypted channels and priority switching for governments. In others, militaries insist on sovereign constellations. The divide is not purely technical; it is political. Reliance on foreign networks raises uncomfortable questions: what if the provider is sanctioned, compromised, or pressured? What if the network operator chooses neutrality or withdrawal in wartime?

The flip side is resilience. Commercial operators often build far larger fleets than any single government would. A proliferated LEO constellation can lose dozens of satellites without collapsing. Mesh routing, laser inter-satellite links, and automated collision avoidance make these networks flexible. In effect, the commercial world has built space-based communication infrastructure that no wartime planner could ever have justified on defence budgets alone.

Strategic SATCOM remains distinct. Ultra-secure geostationary satellites with hardened electronics, anti-jam waveforms, steerable beams, and classified payloads channel the most sensitive traffic. These craft are expensive, few in number, and indispensable. But they are not immune to disruption. If an adversary blinds a satellite's sensors, spoofs its command link, or attacks its ground station, the silent void that follows can be strategically decisive. National leaders increasingly see threats to SATCOM as threats to sovereignty.

At the tactical edge, communications define tempo. Infantry units with satellite terminals coordinate in mountains where radios fail. Humanitarian teams restore internet access after hurricanes. Merchant vessels using SATCOM dump sensor data to shore, helping ports schedule berths and customs inspections. In remote mines, automated trucks send status reports via satellites. Every message prevents a delay, a collision, a misread, a panic.

This connectivity changes accountability. War crimes filmed by drones and uploaded through satellites become global evidence within hours. Civilians document mass graves, shelling, and refugee flows. Activists in authoritarian states bypass censorship by beaming encrypted data beyond national borders. A constellation becomes a civil rights tool.

But communication is not just transmission; it is control. Satellites route data differently depending on priority, encryption, and spectrum. They might throttle content, restrict regions, or grant emergency access to hospitals and rescue crews. In some designs, spacecraft talk directly to each other through lasers, bypassing Earth entirely. This architecture creates shadow networks that are harder to jam and harder to spy upon.

Those who cannot afford geostationary terminals—too heavy, too power-hungry—can now carry backpack-sized flat antennas that track LEO satellites electronically. These antennas reshape beams without motors, following spacecraft like invisible eyes. Special forces on patrol quietly message each other through the sky. Journalists in blackout zones file reports minutes after atrocity. Doctors in field hospitals sync patient records. Every field with a view of the heavens becomes a temporary command centre.

This diffusion of power unsettles generals. If civilians can access wartime-grade communications, so can insurgents, pirates, cartels, and hostile states. Encryption arms criminals as efficiently as soldiers. A militia with satellite messaging can ambush convoys, coordinate propaganda, and evade surveillance. The backbone is neutral; its users are not.

Diplomats face dilemmas. Should governments regulate commercial SATCOM as critical national infrastructure? Should they subsidise domestic terminals to reduce reliance on foreign networks? If a private constellation is targeted by a missile or cyberattack, does a state have the right—or duty—to retaliate? The law lags behind the orbit.

Meanwhile, engineers confront physics. Every satellite needs spectrum—scarce, contested, and policed by international regulators. Too many constellations in similar bands cause interference. Ground terminals compete for clear skies in cities thick with radios. Signals bounce off buildings, scatter in storms, and fade in polar twilight. All the redundancy in orbit is meaningless if interference on Earth ruins reception.

And then there is space traffic. Thousands of satellites mean thousands of collision risks. A single smash-up could sever a constellation's backbone, fragmenting communication for soldiers and civilians alike. Operators must dodge debris, manoeuvre spacecraft, and constantly update trajectories. Every course change eats fuel. Every fragment of junk carries menace.

In the shadows, military planners test jamming. Powerful ground transmitters can flood satellite receivers with noise. Spoofers can imitate friendly signals, tricking terminals into silent compliance. More subtle attackers slip malware into ground gateways, corrupting routing tables, injecting false coordinates, or stealing encryption keys. No kinetic explosion is required to silence a battlefield.

Not all attacks are hostile. Solar storms can fry electronics, distort signals, degrade solar panels. Engineers build shielding and redundancy, but the cosmos has a mindless hostility that respects no treaty. When a geomagnetic outburst struck Earth in 2022, dozens of newly launched satellites died in atmosphere before then could raise orbit. Communication backbones are fragile because space itself is not gentle.

Yet societies keep pouring capacity into orbit. Why? Because the alternative is unimaginable. Fibre can snap. Towers can burn. Submarines may cut cables. Nations that hope to keep cities running, fleets sailing, stock markets trading, and armies coordinated require a communications safety net immune to terrestrial chaos. Space is that net.

The irony is that the more constellations spread, the more every nation and corporation becomes hostage to orbital stability. Rivals who might once have risked attacking satellites now think twice: to blind one opponent is to blind themselves. Every commercial network carries multinational customers. Every military payload shares orbital lanes with civilian craft. The backbone is shared, and shared assets create shared caution.

But caution is not certainty. Somewhere, planners still sketch scenarios where LEO satellites vanish in showers of debris, where geostationary birds fall silent, where ground stations are overrun, where a digital desert descends. The question that lingers is no longer whether satellite communications can survive war—it is whether modern life can survive without them at all.

Targeting the invisible

On a grey morning in the South China Sea, a tanker cut its transponder and vanished. Its digital identity—name, flag, cargo—simply winked out. On paper, it ceased to exist. Yet the ocean does not erase steel so easily. Hours later, analysts spotted a faint wake in synthetic-aperture radar imagery: a thin white line against an indifferent sea. Days later, infrared satellites picked up warm exhaust plumes from engines that officially were not running. Hours after that, a commercial electro-optical satellite captured a grainy hull silhouette—just enough for maritime authorities to recognise a sanctioned vessel attempting to sneak oil to a forbidden port. Three kinds of satellites, three kinds of sensors, one hidden ship. The ocean had not given up the secret; data had.

Space turns invisibility into a temporary condition. It does not matter whether the ship turns off its transponder, the smugglers change painted identifiers, or night masks the deck crews. Somewhere, a sensor is watching. Somewhere else, an algorithm is listening. Signals bounce, reflections echo, heat radiates. The modern surveillance system is not a single eye; it is a constellation of eyes, ears, and inferences, each imperfect on its own, but formidable in combination. The invisible can be tracked. The question is how, and by whom.

For most of history, disappearance at sea was easy. A vessel that slipped over the horizon entered a private world. When storms or wars claimed it, families waited without answers. Governments guessed. Commerce prayed. Today, a ship's location is not merely a curiosity—it is a choke point in sanctions enforcement, a test of naval deterrence, a key to insurance, a safeguard against environmental crime. In global politics, knowing where an object is matters as much as knowing what it carries. Space-based detection and data fusion make that knowledge possible, and no state can afford to ignore it.

Detecting what does not want to be found is both science and strategy. Different sensors perceive different truths. A radar satellite sees structure and movement regardless of daylight or clouds. An electro-optical satellite sees colour, shape, and shadow, but needs sunshine and clear skies. Infrared systems see heat—engines, fires, missile launches, warm bodies on cold ground. Radio-frequency collection hears the chatter: radar pulses, communications bursts, navigation beacons. Each sensor is flawed; together, they are encyclopaedic.

A single satellite pass rarely provides certainty. A radar image might show a bright speck on dark water. Is it a ship? An iceberg? A strange reflection from waves? A second satellite, tuned to infrared, might show a plume of heat. A third, in optical mode, might catch a geometric hull form hours later. Once these images are fused—layered, aligned, and timed—they reveal a vessel that pretends not to exist. In maritime security, this fusion is everything. It transforms fragmentary evidence into actionable truth.

What is true of ships is true of armies, missile batteries, mobile command posts, even individual vehicles hiding beneath camouflage nets. A radar satellite can see metal under cloud. An infrared satellite can see warm trucks parked in forests long after drivers switch off headlights. High-resolution optical spacecraft can pick out tyre tracks, tent shadows, and runway repairs. Signals-intelligence satellites can hear encrypted bursts from radios that soldiers believe are silent. The world is opaque to people but transparent to physics.

And yet, invisibility fights back. Militaries disperse equipment, deploy decoys, disguise hulls, scatter radar-reflective chaff, switch frequencies, or hide in civilian traffic. They spoil satellites' attempts to build a clear picture. A radar operator on Earth might see one large target, one medium one, and one small one. In reality, the large target might be a decoy balloon, the medium a fishing trawler, the small a missile boat. The contest is no longer about hiding a single object; it is about confusing a network of sensors.

But deception has limits. A decoy does not heat like a real engine. A fishing trawler does not emit the same radar signature as a missile boat. A missile battery pretending to be a barn might fool an optical sensor, but infrared satellites will see heat from power generators. Even silence betrays: when communications vanish across a region, analysts suspect jamming, disruption, or secret movement. Space does not merely watch activity; it watches absence.

The most powerful system is not a sensor at all—it is analysis. Data fusion brings together streams of imagery, thermal readings, radio signals, shipping databases, weather reports, port logs, and social-media clues. A photo of a vessel's flag on Instagram can validate a radar trace. A port schedule can explain a sudden turn at sea. A traffic jam near a military depot may indicate an impending deployment. Satellites provide the canvas; intelligence paints the pattern.

Increasingly, those analysts are not governments. They are non-profits, universities, investigative journalists, commercial tracking firms. When a tanker offloads oil illegally, a university lab might detect it before a navy does. When a dictatorship buries mass graves, independent researchers using commercial satellites might find them. When Russian troops massed near Ukraine in 2021, the evidence did not begin with classified intelligence. It began with open-source imagery. Citizens could watch the build-up day by day. Invisibility no longer protects the powerful from scrutiny. It protects no one.

This civilian transparency unsettles states. Intelligence monopolies crumble when private satellites can surveil missile silos or submarine pens. Public pressure mounts when citizens see what their governments preferred to hide. Diplomats lose plausible deniability when NGOs publish satellite evidence of atrocities. Invisibility used to be a privilege of the strong; now it is a temporary illusion contested by many.

Yet fusion is not simple. Volume overwhelms. A radar constellation can generate terabytes per day. Optical fleets multiply that. Signals collection adds oceans of radio noise. Analysts drown unless software filters the torrent. Machine-learning tools now detect patterns faster than humans: unusual ship movements, vehicles assembling at bases, trucks dispersing into hills, roads freshly graded. The software does not "understand" war, but it understands anomalies. And war is defined by anomalies.

Still, software is fallible. Rainstorms distort radar. Cloud shadows trick optical models. Sandstorms hide convoys. Objects fused incorrectly generate false targets. A country might accuse a rival of deploying missiles based on a misclassified satellite image. A misinterpretation can turn a quiet border into a crisis. Ambiguity breeds paranoia. Decision-makers want perfect vision; space provides powerful vision, but never perfect.

This imperfection has consequences. States adopt doctrines that assume they are always being watched. They hide equipment underground, rotate units constantly, and camouflage logistics. Armies practice deception as seriously as manoeuvre. Submarines remain the last great source of invisibility—not because satellites cannot see steel underwater, but because physics protects them with depth. Space shapes strategy even below the waves.

And yet, invisibility still matters. A missile launcher that remains hidden long enough to fire changes the balance of deterrence. A clandestine satellite in a strange orbit can operate undetected until it performs a hostile manoeuvre. A cyber operation that spoofs maritime signals can fabricate fleets out of nothing. The invisible has not disappeared; it merely competes with a far more observant sky.

The race is becoming brutal. States invest in hyperspectral imaging that can detect buried mines, hidden crops, and chemical signatures on roofs. They launch radar constellations with global revisit rates measured in minutes rather than days. They build telescopes in orbit that spot other satellites quietly approaching. They fuse satellite data with drones, aircraft, underwater sensors, and ground networks. The goal is dominance: to see without being seen, to track without being tracked, to anticipate without revealing intent.

Commercial players join this arms race unintentionally. Oil firms track tankers to prevent theft. Logistics firms track cargo vessels to refine routes. Environmental groups track illegal fishing fleets. Their data becomes intelligence when war erupts. During conflicts, militaries buy emergency subscriptions to commercial imagery. Analysts merge these civilian feeds with classified sources. In effect, war now recruits the global economy as an intelligence system.

There is a darker side. If satellites can find a hidden ship, they can find a hidden refugee boat. If they can track a sanctioned fleet, they can track dissidents fleeing a regime. In authoritarian hands, space-based fusion becomes an instrument of repression. The same images that expose war crimes can be used to hunt those who documented them. Technology magnifies moral choices.

And then there is insurance. If a ship crosses a high-risk zone undetected, insurers lose visibility. When fusion improves, insurers adjust premiums based on verified behaviour: speed, route, proximity to embargoed ports. Space data polices commerce as much as it polices war. Corporations steer by satellites because banks and regulators demand it.

In the far future, fusion may operate automatically. A missile launch detected by infrared satellites triggers radar satellites to search for mobile launchers. Optical satellites capture fleeing vehicles. Electronic intelligence listens for retreating radio chatter. Drones swarm, linked through LEO constellations, to relay live video. Human analysts become editors, not hunters. The system hunts itself.

Yet uncertainty remains. Even the best fusion cannot see inside a nuclear submarine, inside a sealed container, behind a mountain, beneath dense canopy. To target the invisible is to live with doubt. War is fought in that doubt. Diplomacy is negotiated in that doubt. Decision-makers must decide whether to trust imperfect data or risk catastrophe. One blurred pixel can change history.

As sensors proliferate, invisibility becomes a precious commodity. Some states invest in stealthier ships, quieter missiles, deception campaigns, decoy constellations. Others accept visibility, betting that open tracking deters escalation. Some secretly hope that the abundance of satellites will expose every lie and punish every crime. Others fear that the flood of data will simply create more narrative battlefields, where truth and falsehood compete in real time.

Somewhere tonight, another ship will kill its transponder. Somewhere above, satellites will search for the wake, the heat, the radio whisper. Machines will argue over pixel brightness and Doppler shift. Analysts will stitch fragments into meaning. But the ocean remains wide, the night deep, and the game endless. The invisible still moves—but space has made running out of places to hide.

Civil data, military sense

A decade ago, a retired schoolteacher in Wales discovered that he could track war. Not through leaks or secret sources, but with a laptop, a modest internet connection, and images bought legally from commercial satellite companies. He watched convoys assemble, missile batteries relocate, and airfields bustle in countries he would never visit. His findings, posted to public forums, sometimes preceded official statements by days. Intelligence, once the guarded craft of governments, was quietly becoming a public activity.

That quiet shift has changed the nature of power. For centuries, armies, spies, and states relied on monopoly: they saw what others could not. Now, a journalist or student with access to commercial imagery can watch armour columns creeping across borders in near real time. When thousands of Russian troops massed near Ukraine's frontier in 2021, the first images to circle the globe did not come from secret satellites hidden in classified budget lines. They came from commercial constellations whose primary customers were farmers, insurers, and shipping firms. Within hours, analysts on social media mapped tent cities, artillery positions, and vehicle parks. The world did not need to take a government's word for anything. It could *see*.

This inversion—civil data creating military sense—upends old assumptions. Public information was once a distraction from statecraft, something diplomats managed and generals tolerated. Now, open-source intelligence sits alongside classified reporting, sometimes shaping it. Governments read the same satellite images that activists pore over. Military planners monitor the same maritime feeds as energy traders. The boundary between civil and military sight has dissolved.

What gave the public access to the sky was not ideology but economics. As launch prices fell and small satellites became cheap to build, companies began offering imagery as a commodity. Some sold pictures to agribusinesses monitoring crop stress; others sold to mining companies tracking excavation; still others built markets for insurance firms checking wildfire damage. But satellites cannot choose to avoid borders. A constellation that images vineyards in France will also image armoured brigades in Belarus if they cross its path. Commercial customers pay for resolution and revisit rate, not geopolitics. The result: the same camera that helps a vineyard optimise irrigation gives a researcher evidence of troop movements.

In war, this neutrality becomes leverage. During the early weeks of the Russian invasion of Ukraine, commercial satellite firms captured long columns of vehicles stretching across highways, rockets launchers tucked into woodlands, and destroyed bridges along key supply lines. These images circulated globally, reshaping diplomatic debates and informing humanitarian organisations planning corridor routes. It was not military secrecy but public transparency that set the world's narrative. When foreign ministries demanded clarifications, the rebuttals often came with annotated satellite maps shared openly online.

And it was not just imagery. Radio-frequency satellites listened for ships that turned off transponders, identifying illegal oil transfers on dark seas. Infrared sensors tracked missile launches. AIS and ADS-B data, originally designed for civil shipping and aviation, revealed surprise naval deployments and sudden airbase evacuations. What once required spies and reconnaissance flights now requires little more than API access.

The dual-use nature of these systems was always inevitable. Digital life produces data, and data leaks into military analysis. A logistics company's satellite ground station becomes a resource for tracking containers that double as military cargo. A weather-imaging network designed to serve agriculture becomes vital for forecasting cloud cover before airstrikes. Even mapping software—intended for construction and city planning—can show where trenches appear and fortifications expand.

For states, this transparency cuts both ways. On the one hand, open-source intelligence reduces uncertainty. When a rival claims it has withdrawn troops, analysts can check. When a missile test is denied, infrared satellites can confirm the launch. Public evidence defuses misinformation, gives journalists proof, and forces governments to justify their statements. Democracies use it as a tool of accountability.

But authoritarian regimes find that the sky erodes control. They can silence reporters, censor newspapers, and jail witnesses—but they cannot switch off commercial satellites owned abroad. Their secrets belong to physics, not propaganda. When they move prisoners, bulldoze villages, or build clandestine bases, someone somewhere sees it. They cannot predict who will interpret the images, post them, or assemble them into a story.

Yet openness creates vulnerability. If anyone can watch troop movements, so can adversaries. The same commercial imagery that helps a small nation verify a superpower's deployments can also help a hostile militia plan an ambush. When weather satellites show clear skies over a battlefield, ground forces expect drone attacks. When broadband constellations guarantee connectivity, electronic-warfare units design new jamming plans. Transparency is not a moral good; it is a strategic condition.

Some militaries respond by integrating open-source data into their doctrine. They buy commercial imagery on subscription, fuse it with classified feeds, and deliver it to field units. Instead of waiting for a high-end spy satellite to pass every few days, they get hourly updates from private constellations. A single reconnaissance satellite might take a picture of a missile base once every week. A proliferated commercial network might capture the same site several times per day. Precision comes from abundance, not exclusivity.

This abundance produces new forms of intelligence. Analysts no longer treat single images as revelations. They study patterns: how often trucks enter a fuel depot, how quickly a runway is repaired, how many ships loiter in a harbour at dusk. When Sudan's civil conflict intensified in 2023, commercial satellites documented scorched villages and refugee flows long before diplomats acknowledged the scale. Images debunked propaganda, confirmed eyewitness claims, and forced international agencies to act.

In this world, data becomes diplomacy. Nations publish satellite images to shame rivals, rally alliances, or justify sanctions. Firms release emergency imagery after earthquakes or floods, showing damage before governments admit it. Insurers use satellite data to argue that states mismanaged relief operations. Citizens watching from phones become auditors of state performance. No conflict is purely domestic when the world can watch from above.

The commercial firms providing this visibility did not intend to shape geopolitics. Their profits depend on agriculture, logistics, and climate monitoring. Yet conflict increases demand. Governments under pressure buy imagery faster. Defence ministries request priority tasking. Multinationals want route security. A business that planned to map wheat fields becomes a de facto intelligence vendor overnight.

This raises uncomfortable questions. Should a private firm choose which country receives imagery first during a crisis? Should it release pictures of mass graves, knowing dictators may retaliate against witnesses? Should it comply with government requests to delay publication? Commercial power introduces moral complexity. Shareholders do not always share the values of nations. Sometimes they do; sometimes they do not.

And yet, without these firms, the world would be blind again. Human-rights investigators rely on satellite archives to document destroyed villages, torched crops, or secret prisons. Environmental activists track illegal logging and fishing fleets. Journalists reveal missile bases hidden in mountains. Citizens prove that governments lied about accidents, pollution, or war crimes. Civil data becomes public conscience.

But reliance is not without risk. If a powerful state pressures companies to withhold imagery, open-source intelligence weakens. If firms offer exclusive access to paying governments, transparency fractures. If data pipelines are hacked or manipulated, analysts may mistake fabricated patterns for real ones. The integrity of public vision becomes a battlefield.

There are already signs of strain. Some companies blur certain sites, citing safety or regulation. Others sell high-resolution imagery to only a select group of nations. Metadata can be censored. Tasking queues can be prioritised quietly. In theory, commercial satellites democratise sight. In practice, money and politics influence who sees what and when.

Yet the genie is out of the bottle. Thousands of satellites, operated by firms in dozens of countries, feed data into the global network. Even if a major supplier restricts access, another fills the gap. Citizen analysts—some professionals, some amateurs—scrutinise every new feed. When one company hides a missile launch, another captures it. When a government denies responsibility for a bombing, open-source investigators match crater size, angle of entry, and blast radius to weapons inventories. Truth becomes a technical exercise.

And technical truth is difficult to silence. Images can be mirrored, archived, copied, downloaded, and redistributed. Once published, they belong to the world. This terrifies regimes that depend on secrecy. It reassures societies that distrust official statements. It complicates militaries who must assume their every movement may be observed within hours.

But what happens when adversaries flood the same channels with fabricated evidence? When manipulated images circulate faster than verifiable ones?

Deepfakes are coming for satellites too. Synthetic imagery that appears real—ships that never sailed, tanks that never moved, fires that never burned—may pollute public analysis. The very openness that empowers truth also invites deception.

When that day comes, civil data will require civil trust. Analysts will need to show their methods, reveal their raw files, and defend their interpretations. The crowd will demand proof, not assertion. Intelligence will become a public debate, not a secret pronouncement. And governments—long accustomed to controlling the narrative—will find that narrative contested by strangers with laptops.

Yet perhaps the deepest consequence is philosophical. Intelligence no longer belongs to kings, generals, or clandestine elites. It belongs to anyone curious enough to look. War becomes visible to those who pay attention. Crimes cannot easily hide. A farmer in Argentina can analyse a battlefield in Asia. A student in Nairobi can debunk a government in Europe. Truth crosses borders even when people cannot.

Somewhere tonight, a satellite will photograph a convoy under cloud. Another will detect engine heat through darkness. A third will capture the same road at dawn, revealing fresh tyre tracks. On a laptop far away, a researcher will line up the images, cross-check a database, and send a report. Civil data will become military sense. The world will learn something governments preferred to keep quiet.

And tomorrow, something else will vanish from view—another tank column, another ship, another secret flight. It will not stay invisible for long. The sky has witnesses, and those witnesses no longer wear uniforms.

Chapter 4

Private Rockets, Public Aims

On a cold California morning, a crowd gathered on a beach to watch what looked like a trick of physics: a rocket returning to land upright, flames cushioning its descent, the hull trembling but controlled, the vehicle lowering itself onto concrete as if spaceflight had become as repeatable as a bus timetable. Children cheered, engineers wept, and investors recalculated their forecasts in real time. In that moment, the space launch market ceased being a realm of spectacular, disposable fireworks and became something unsettlingly routine. A rocket that can fly again is not a novelty; it is a business model.

Routine changes power. When rockets cost hundreds of millions and flew a few times a year, states controlled the skies by default. But when launches become weekly and prices fall by orders of magnitude, access to orbit stops being a privilege and starts becoming an option. Small nations, universities, start-ups, hedge funds, and humanitarian groups can lift sensors, relays, and experiments into space. The bottleneck is no longer aspiration but scheduling. Reusable boosters land, refuel, and fly again. Small-sat rideshares throw dozens of payloads to orbit in a single manoeuvre. The bottleneck of cost has shifted to a bottleneck of imagination.

This transformation is not just technological; it is political. Private launch providers now operate as infrastructural giants, holding the keys to orbit. Governments that once owned the ascent now negotiate it. The shift echoes the transition from state-run telephone monopolies to global telecom giants: the physical backbone is private, the usage is strategic, and the consequences of failure or refusal are geopolitical.

What drives this new world is cadence. Militaries once assumed that a satellite loss meant years of replacement. Today, a damaged constellation can be replenished within weeks. A nanosatellite destroyed in orbit might be replaced before the debris cloud expands. Defence planners speak of attritable space assets—expendable nodes cheaper to swap than to defend. That logic only works when rockets are affordable and frequent. Reusability and rideshares provide the throughput. A war that damaged space infrastructure used to be a catastrophe; now it may be a logistics challenge.

This has created a commercial race not just to launch, but to launch more often. Firms compete on turnaround time, pad efficiency, and integration speed. A company that can manifest a payload in ten days becomes a strategic partner. One that takes six months becomes irrelevant. States have begun reserving launch capacity the way supermarkets reserve delivery slots—anticipating surges, hoarding time, and paying premiums for priority. Launch manifests are becoming strategic resources.

Above the launchpads, constellations are multiplying. Where the twentieth century imagined a handful of enormous satellites, the twenty-first built swarms. Earth observation fleets map floods, track trains, and forecast crop yields. Broadband constellations beam internet to warzones and villages alike. What began as commercial convenience has become strategic leverage.

Constellation capitalism rests on a simple truth: if you can provide persistent connectivity or persistent imagery, you own attention. A broadcaster with orbital reach can bypass censored ground infrastructure. A logistics firm can track its fleet across oceans invisible to radio towers. A defence ministry can buy global situational awareness without owning a single satellite. But profits and geopolitics collide. A broadband operator whose satellites cover a battlefield may choose—or be compelled—to prioritise one side's traffic. An imagery provider may sell daily passes to a humanitarian group but give preferential tasking to a national government. During crises, the business model becomes a political instrument.

Governments have noticed. Instead of commissioning bespoke satellites, defence ministries now subscribe to services. They purchase imagery feeds, communications bandwidth, and tasking rights. A contract may no longer produce hardware; it produces access. This changes procurement from a decade-long engineering effort to a quarterly negotiation. It also changes power: a small defence ministry that cannot build satellites can still buy near real-time pictures. A country without an aerospace industry can still deploy secure communications to troops. Capability is divorced from manufacture.

The shift ripples through bureaucracy. Military logisticians accustomed to decades-long programmes now sign service-level agreements. Mission planners ask for API endpoints instead of tracking stations. The state becomes a customer rather than a builder. Support contracts now blend engineers with lawyers: uptime guarantees, coverage obligations, legal indemnities, and data-retention rules become as strategic as rocket thrust.

Interoperability becomes the hinge. For a constellation to serve many buyers, it must speak many languages: standardised telemetry, cloud-integrated ground stations, shared antennas, and modular payloads. A ground antenna in Norway may receive data from an American satellite one hour and a Japanese radar satellite the next. An operations centre in Singapore may downlink SAR data on behalf of a dozen clients, each with different encryption keys and tasking rights. The sky becomes an exchange, with satellites visiting ground stations like aircraft visiting airports. Open interfaces make this possible; proprietary lock-in hinders it. States must decide whether they want flexibility or control.

The infrastructure of space is being rebuilt around software. When satellites become nodes in a cloud architecture, the line between aerospace and computing blurs. A tasking request travels through web services. Storage sits in commercial data centres. Downlink scheduling merges with distributed computing. Security teams treat orbital assets like network endpoints. The battlefield of the future may be managed through dashboards familiar to civilian IT operators.

All of this sets the stage for a new kind of statecraft. Once, diplomacy worked through treaties, ambassadors, and summit declarations. Now, it can work through terms of service. A satellite firm can geofence coverage around a disputed region, intentionally or not. A broadband provider can throttle traffic to ground stations in a contested port. A data company can suspend civilian access when foreign militaries misuse its products. These actions are not negotiated in Geneva; they are flicked in control rooms or toggled in software updates. A corporation can impose consequences faster than a government can draft a speech.

The unsettling question is who decides. Private executives now make choices that shape battlefields, humanitarian corridors, and refugee communications. Their first duty is often to shareholders, not citizens. Yet their products carry moral weight. When a broadband network keeps hospitals connected during shelling, its operator becomes a lifeline. When coverage is withdrawn—whether for safety, liability, or profit—it can change the fate of towns.

Some states respond by demanding sovereignty: national launch vehicles, national constellations, national ground stations. Others embrace interdependence, believing redundancy offers resilience. Yet even the most sovereign systems rely on global supply chains, commercial components, and launch windows negotiated with private firms.

The old image of space power—a rocket on a military pad, a general watching from a bunker—no longer defines reality. Instead, space power may look like a boardroom deciding whether to prioritise a medical charity's bandwidth request over a military drone feed. It may look like a rideshare manifest where civilian satellites sit beside defence payloads, each owned by different nations but launched together. It may look like an API key revoked after suspicious activity.

And somewhere in this complexity lies the new balance of power. Rockets that land themselves, satellites that launch by the dozen, companies that blur the line between infrastructure and policy. Governments still matter profoundly, but they share the stage with firms that can accelerate or frustrate national ambitions through spreadsheet logic rather than missile silos.

A century ago, the great infrastructure of geopolitics was railways and ports. Today, it is reusable boosters, cloud-linked ground stations, and subscription-based access to the sky. The state owns less; the market owns more. But the stakes are higher than markets alone can handle. Orbit has become a place where private rockets serve public aims—and where public aims may depend on private will.

The question is no longer who can reach space. It is who controls what happens once you get there, and whether those decisions answer to citizens, to customers, or to no-one at all. The answer will write the next chapter of power above the Earth.

The rise of launch platforms

A few decades ago, launch day looked like theatre: a single, gleaming rocket, an army of technicians, and the quiet knowledge that this was a once-only machine. If a flight ended in flames, the hardware simply ceased to exist. Every mission carried the psychological weight of a one-off experiment, not an industrial process. Yet on a coastal pad in Florida and another in California, something quietly revolutionary has unfolded: rockets come home. They tip back through the atmosphere, fire their engines, and touch down on landing pads or drone ships as though this had always been the obvious way of doing things. Spaceflight, once an extravagant spectacle, has begun to resemble logistics.

Reusability is not a gimmick. It is compounding economics in motion. When a booster flies ten times, the marginal cost of those flights converges towards fuel, refurbishment, and operations. That shift turns what used to be national prestige projects into commercial infrastructure. The more often a rocket flies, the cheaper it becomes to launch. The cheaper launches become, the more satellites reach orbit. And when access to orbit is no longer scarce, strategy changes with it.

Small-sat rideshares further accelerate this shift. Instead of booking an entire rocket, operators now purchase space—literally—in cubic increments. University payloads sit beside commercial imagers, military prototypes, and venture-funded experiments. A single launch deploys dozens of satellites into multiple orbits using adapters that look like celestial vending machines. For some customers, the alternative used to be waiting years for a national launch slot. Now they may wait weeks.

The consequences are immediate for space-reliant industries. Earth observation companies once built a handful of large satellites and lived with gaps between replacements. The new model sends up many smaller craft: cheaper, more agile, and far easier to replace. Broadband operators building constellations in Low Earth Orbit rely on a perpetual rhythm of launches. Satellites retire, degrade, or collide with debris; the fleet is replenished in batches. The sky becomes a living network, constantly refreshed.

For militaries, this cadence rewrites expectations. During the Cold War, losing a satellite meant years of lost capability. Modern constellations break that dependency. If a node is jammed or destroyed, another can be lofted within days. A nation that controls rapid launch has insurance against on-orbit attrition. Replenishment becomes part of war-planning: a logistics pipeline through the stratosphere.

This does not diminish the grandeur of launch; it simply buries it beneath utility. Reusable boosters are trucked to hangars, inspected like aircraft, rolled out again. Engineers obsess over turnaround time, not spectacle. A fast-cycling launch platform becomes a strategic asset akin to a naval port or an oil terminal. Where once states competed for the biggest rockets, now they compete for the busiest.

The shift to reusability shifts responsibility too. Privately operated launch fleets are subject to weather, financing rounds, regulatory approvals, and factory throughput. Governments accustomed to owning the hardware must accept that, in many cases, they are leasing space on privately maintained vehicles. The symbolism is uncomfortable for some defence establishments: national security riding atop corporate engineering.

Yet the market logic is unignorable. Private launch firms price aggressively to fill manifests. As utilisation rises, costs fall further. A satellite manufacturer with five customers waiting can pressure a launch provider to add rideshare slots. A telecoms firm with hundreds of spacecraft in production can demand bulk rates. In a competitive market, launch capacity becomes a commodity.

This introduces a paradox. Access to space has never been more democratised, yet control over launch infrastructure is increasingly concentrated among a few firms. If a single provider commands the lion's share of reliable reusability, nations become dependent on its cadence. A maintenance setback can ripple through dozens of planned missions. A regulatory dispute can leave satellites on factory floors. A cashflow crisis can stall fleets.

States respond in different ways. Some pursue indigenous launch systems to guarantee sovereignty, irrespective of cost. Others take the opposite route: diversify across multiple commercial providers. Europe, Japan, South Korea, and India all seek to ensure they are never hostage to a single pad or platform. Even the United States—home of the most aggressive commercial launch innovators—hedges its bets, retaining government launch vehicles as strategic backups.

Small nations, meanwhile, gain agency they never had. A state with no historic aerospace programme can afford to orbit a climate sensor, a maritime tracker, or a communications relay. The capital barrier collapses. Once a satellite is deployed, its data can serve farmers, coastguards, intelligence agencies, and insurers. The gap between satellite-owning nations and satellite-dependent nations narrows.

The pace of launch also alters how satellites are designed. When rideshares are plentiful, size becomes negotiable. CubeSats—once academic curiosities—now conduct serious scientific and commercial missions. Advances in on-board processing, miniaturised radar arrays, and electric propulsion have made small spacecraft capable far beyond their volume. Fewer components, less mass, lower insurance, faster replacement. Space ceases to be a cathedral of engineering perfection and becomes a workshop of iterative development.

Mission designers talk in terms borrowed from software: agile deployment, rapid prototyping, constellation scaling. A sensor that fails in orbit might be superseded within a quarter, not a decade. Early movers in launch platforms have effectively speeded space into a near-continuous development environment, where fleets evolve while deployed.

Rapid replenishment does not just mitigate losses. It encourages experimentation. Defence customers can trial new payloads, communications links, or imaging modes knowing they can swap hardware quickly. Commercial operators can A/B test satellite designs. When time to orbit shortens, innovation accelerates.

There are trade-offs. Fast launch cadence increases congestion. More rockets mean more spent upper stages, more fairings, and more potential debris. Regulators debate how to enforce responsible disposal. Insurers demand proof of de-orbit plans before underwriting payloads. Reuse mitigates some waste; it does not eliminate it. A world of frequent launches must become a world of disciplined stewardship.

There is also strategic nervousness. If commercial launch infrastructure is essential, sabotage need not target satellites; it can target factories, propellant depots, tracking systems, or logistics chains. A state might weather the destruction of ten satellites, but not six months without launch. The chokepoint shifts from the heavens to the ground.

And in the background lies a deeper question: does the rise of private launch constrain or expand state power? Governments gain capabilities at lower cost, but lose monopoly over access. They gain launch capacity in peacetime, but risk vulnerability if commercial providers withdraw in wartime. They gain speed, but sacrifice exclusivity.

Still, the trajectory is set. Launch is becoming infrastructure. Rockets are assets, not artefacts. Their reuse marks a philosophical shift from "reach the sky" to "operate routinely". As reliability increases, demand grows. As demand grows, economies of scale intensify. Space becomes a domain that responds to market signals as much as national strategy.

The next frontier is cadence so high it becomes invisible: weekly launches, daily launches, multiple launches per day. A constellation that refreshes itself continuously, satellites expiring like components in a supply chain. The sky filled not with grand monuments but with machinery in motion.

At that point, a peculiar inversion occurs. The world will have become reliant on orbital services, yet barely notice the rockets that sustain them. Launch, once the public face of space power, becomes background infrastructure—like undersea cables or power lines—essential but unseen.

When rockets land themselves and fly again, sovereignty shifts. When satellites are replaced in weeks, deterrence changes. When launch slots are traded like commodities, diplomacy acquires an economic dimension. The question will not be who can reach orbit, but who can stay there, replenish there, and adapt there faster than anyone else.

The planet has begun to build an orbital supply chain. It is no longer a dream of explorers, but a business plan, a military contingency, and a diplomatic bargaining chip. The rise of launch platforms marks the quiet moment when space stopped being a destination and became an operating environment—one in which access is currency, cadence is power, and reusability is destiny.

Constellation capitalism

The night sky once spoke of mystery; now it speaks of balance sheets. Thousands of satellites trace invisible grids above our heads, each link part of a larger network built not for romance, but for revenue. Investors who would once have poured money into oil rigs or shipping fleets now scrutinise orbital deployment schedules. Private capital has discovered something extraordinary: space services can scale like software, but they wield the leverage of infrastructure.

This is the quiet revolution behind constellation capitalism. It is not about selling spacecraft; it is about selling continuous service from orbit. Earth observation companies charge for insights, not images. Broadband constellations sell connectivity by the gigabyte, not satellites by the unit. And because these services operate globally, they nestle into markets once considered unreachable. A rancher in Argentina, a fisher off Indonesia, a humanitarian convoy crossing the Sahara—each becomes a customer of the sky.

The most powerful business model is subscription. A constellation that images the Earth daily offers a living record of agriculture, construction, border changes, and military movement. Clients sign multi-year deals because value compounds: one picture means little, a thousand pictures mean pattern. Hedge funds watch crop cycles in real time. Insurance firms evaluate flood risk with centimetre precision. National weather agencies refine seasonal forecasts. The satellites themselves are not the asset; the time-series is.

But subscriptions impose pressure. If a constellation loses satellites and cadence slips, the product degrades. Share prices wobble. Contracts come under review. Competitors whisper. Reliability becomes existential. That is why constellation operators now treat replenishment capacity the way airlines treat maintenance hangars: as lifelines. Launch cadence, ground segments, and manufacturing pipelines are tied directly to quarterly earnings calls. The stock market does not wait for solar storms to pass.

Broadband constellations operate on even thinner margins. To challenge terrestrial telecoms, they must offer low latency, global coverage, and hardware that is cheap enough for households. Every satellite adds capacity; every failure adds congestion. Antennas on ground stations must steer rapidly and hand off signals with military precision. A constellation with thousands of nodes is no longer a network but an economy—energy consumption, routing algorithms, orbital mechanics, customer churn. These firms compete with fibre-optic consortia that have spent decades burying glass beneath oceans. To survive, they need millions of users.

And here lies an uncomfortable truth: these networks influence geopolitics even when they claim neutrality. A company may promise universal broadband, but must still comply with national regulations. Some governments demand data routing through domestic ground stations. Others demand content filtering. A few insist on the ability to throttle service during unrest. Private operators become reluctant diplomats, weighing shareholder value against sovereign requests.

During crises, the leverage becomes visible. When a constellation has only so much bandwidth over a region, someone chooses who receives priority. Commercial airlines? Remote hospitals? Government ministries? A military coalition? The terms of service, written quietly in peacetime, become instruments of strategy in conflict. A country might find its drones blind or its field units silent because an operator has restricted coverage. It may not be an act of war—merely a contractual constraint enforced by lawyers.

This raises a philosophical problem: what happens when infrastructure essential to national security is owned by private boards answerable to markets? States can procure satellite services, but cannot always compel them. Some attempt to legislate control in emergencies, but global companies answer to multiple jurisdictions. Others buy equity stakes or form joint ventures to ensure influence. A few build domestic alternatives, but struggle to match the scale and innovation of global competitors.

Yet constellation capitalism offers benefits that governments alone could not achieve. Commercial Earth observation democratises intelligence. Images that once flowed only to classified analysts now appear on open platforms, allowing journalists, NGOs, and university labs to track deforestation, illegal fishing, or the movement of armour columns. During conflicts, civilians have used commercial imagery to verify war crimes, map damage, or plan evacuations. The gaze from orbit has widened—not just top-down, but bottom-up.

There is also the matter of price elasticity. When customers include farmers, truck companies, offshore operators, and small municipalities, constellations become politically resilient. Politicians may object to dependence on private networks, but voters rely on them. And when consumers experience global broadband as a norm, legislators think twice before imposing restrictions that would cut off rural areas. The market becomes its own lobby.

Still, not all business models succeed. Some operators bet on raw image sales and discover that commoditisation erodes profits. Others price too aggressively and drown in launch costs. A few build too many satellites before demand materialises. The irony of space services is that global coverage does not guarantee global customers. Companies must understand weather patterns, maritime routes, customs regulations, cyber risk, and local purchasing power. Orbit offers a perfect vantage point, but the Earth remains messy.

The strategic value of constellations lies not only in what they see or connect, but in the options they give. A satellite network can route traffic away from jammed fibre lines in natural disasters. It can restore connectivity after earthquakes, hurricanes, or sabotage. It can close blind spots over oceans or deserts. Militaries prize that resilience. So do multinational corporations. A constellation that keeps factories, ports, and hospitals online during crisis is more than a telecom system—it is continuity of civilisation.

And that continuity has price tags. Nations bidding for priority services may offer spectrum rights, tax incentives, or launch partnerships. Public procurement shapes private strategy. Companies, in turn, weigh which clients they can afford to offend. Some have declined service in contested territories, citing regulation; others have quietly configured geofences. The boundary between commercial policy and foreign policy grows thinner each year.

Yet beneath the spreadsheets lies something more subtle. Constellations are not just businesses; they are trust systems. A satellite operator asking governments to adopt its broadband is asking them to trust its encryption, uptime, and neutrality. An Earth observation firm selling imagery is asking markets to trust its calibration and cloud processing. In space, reputations orbit alongside hardware. A single outage on a single day can echo across years.

There is a final twist. Because satellites generate data across borders, export controls and national security laws lurk constantly in the background. Should a commercial network provide imagery of deployed armour? Should it supply bandwidth to both sides of a conflict? Should it reveal maritime patterns that could be exploited by smugglers? Companies that once saw themselves as infrastructure quietly develop geopolitical risk teams.

Constellation capitalism endures because the incentives are ferocious. If a network scales, it becomes too valuable to lose. If it fails to scale, it collapses under its own capital burden. There is no gentle middle. This creates a Darwinian landscape of orbital enterprises, some backed by hedge funds, others by sovereign wealth, all racing to launch faster, analyse quicker, and sell smarter than their rivals.

The tension is unresolved. Private constellations strengthen national capabilities while also creating new dependencies. They democratise intelligence while also giving corporations unprecedented geopolitical leverage. They provide resilience while generating new forms of risk. There is nothing neutral about these networks. Their power is economic, strategic, and deeply human. They serve markets, but define futures.

And so the sky that once belonged to states now hosts a market—volatile, ambitious, and increasingly indispensable. The most valuable real estate is not land or sea, but orbital shells. Those who occupy them will shape communications, surveillance, logistics, and diplomacy. Capital has migrated upward. The question that remains is whether politics will follow, or whether governments will discover, too late, that sovereignty today is measured not only in territory, but in access to constellations that never land.

Procurement rewired

For decades, when a defence ministry wanted satellite capability, it did the obvious thing: it ordered a satellite. Costs were astronomical, schedules glacial, and the result was a bespoke national asset launched every decade or so, guarded by security clearances and procurement committees. Today, militaries still need eyes, ears, and timing in orbit. What has changed is everything around it. Instead of owning hardware, they increasingly buy access, bandwidth, imagery, and analytics from commercial constellations that refresh themselves annually. The paradox is stark: the most secretive institutions on Earth now rely on services advertised on civilian websites.

A telling moment came when a European defence agency renewed its remote sensing contract not by commissioning a new satellite, but by subscribing to a commercial imaging platform. The procurement officer explained, diplomatically, that it made no financial sense to purchase a single, billion-euro asset when a private constellation could offer daily coverage at a fraction of the cost. Moreover, the constellation was already expanding, launching new sensors every quarter. The agency realised that ownership was less valuable than guaranteed access and service-level agreements. Hardware became someone else's headache. Governments rented the sky.

This is procurement rewired: militaries shifting from capital expenditure to operating expenditure, buying services instead of objects. A ministry does not need to care which satellite captures its imagery, only that the feed arrives, on time, at the promised resolution. If a solar storm knocks out one spacecraft, the constellation compensates. If a launch failure delays a replacement, another node fills the gap. Risk, once borne entirely by governments, is now distributed across global companies, insurers, and financiers.

The implications are profound. Procurement cycles that once took ten years now take months. Instead of designing a classified satellite bus, an agency might run a competitive tender for analytic dashboards, automated change detection, or encrypted tasking priority. The value migrates from metal to software, from orbit to ground. Suddenly, small start-ups can compete with legacy aerospace giants, offering niche products backed by commercial satellites they do not own.

Sceptics worry about sovereignty: can a nation trust a foreign company to deliver critical surveillance during conflict? The question is fair. Contracts cannot be enforced in a shooting war. Yet this concern often overlooks a counterpoint: commercial constellations are now so large and diverse that no state can replicate them alone. A government-built reconnaissance satellite launched in 2009 is almost quaint compared with the synthetic aperture radar constellations that now refresh imagery every few hours. In effect, public agencies face a choice: own something inferior, or rent something superior.

The calculus deepens when we consider analytics. Raw pixels are not the prize; information is. An oil facility leaks, a convoy disperses, a port's shipping backlog doubles overnight—algorithms digest millions of images and flag anomalies at machine speed. Defence buyers want those alerts, not terabytes of unprocessed data. Procurement officers now judge vendors less on aperture size and more on user interface, latency, and integration with national command systems. The military strategist and the cloud architect become uneasy colleagues.

This shift rewrites power within the defence-industrial ecosystem. Legacy primes, once guaranteed contracts, must either build commercial offerings or partner with fast-moving data firms. Meanwhile, venture-backed constellations court ministries with service demos, not satellite models. A procurement meeting might involve demonstrations of dashboard filtering, maritime domain awareness, or agricultural monitoring repurposed for battlefield logistics. The same platform that estimates wheat yields in Kansas can track armoured divisions on a border. Dual use is not a side effect—it is a business model.

Yet this new arrangement carries strategic tension. If a company with global clientele receives competing tasking from rival governments, who gets priority? What if commercial customers crowd out military users during a major crisis? Some firms sidestep these dilemmas by offering tiered access—premium clients pay for guaranteed windows, higher refresh rates, or direct downlinks. Others allow militaries to pre-empt commercial orders in emergencies, a clause buried in complex service terms. The politics of procurement now lives in boilerplate.

There is also the matter of surveillance secrecy. When reconnaissance was a sovereign activity, only states knew what they saw. Now, commercial satellites capture and sell imagery of missile silos, naval deployments, and weapons factories. Defence ministries cannot stop journalists, academics, or NGOs from purchasing the same pictures. The monopoly has gone. This forces militaries to rethink deception. Camouflage and denial are harder when hundreds of private sensors pass overhead at dawn, noon, and dusk. Procurement departments quietly buy services that help them track what everyone else can see.

Budgets reflect the change. Instead of single procurement lines for "National Reconnaissance Satellite," spreadsheets now contain annual subscription costs, data licences, and cloud analytics fees. Legislators who once toured classified facilities now read performance reports measured in gigabytes and revisit rates. And because commercial firms compete for customers, prices fall—a rare sight in defence. But falling prices come with a warning: if margins collapse, companies may disappear. A state can nationalise a failing shipyard; nationalising a global constellation is harder.

Beyond imagery, navigation and communications follow the same pattern. Ministries pay for encrypted channels, precision timing overlays, or protected regional beams. A thousand infantry radios connect via commercial LEO satellites. Engineers in a dispersed logistics chain rely on cloud-based situational awareness delivered from orbit. Whole brigades depend on bandwidth that arrives as a monthly invoice. The battlefield is billed like a mobile phone plan.

Critics argue that overreliance on private vendors creates vulnerability. A hostile actor could pressure a company into limiting service. A bankruptcy court could interrupt critical supply. A cyber assault on the ground network could blind a region. These risks are real. But so is the resilience that comes from scale. A state-owned satellite can be disabled by a single missile. A constellation of thousands cannot. In practice, militaries blend approaches: retain a sovereign core for the most sensitive missions, and purchase commercial coverage for everything else.

What unsettles traditionalists most is the pace. When technology outruns doctrine, procurement officers make decisions before generals have written strategy. The procurement cycle becomes the engine of modernisation. Ministries that remain tethered to old acquisition models risk strategic irrelevance. Those willing to treat space as a utility, not a monument, gain agility.

The re-wiring continues quietly. A defence budget hides it as "data services". An operations centre integrates commercial alerts without fanfare. Field units receive imagery faster than their predecessors dreamed possible. Politicians, who once cut ribbons in front of rockets, now cut ribbons in front of nondescript buildings full of servers and analysts.

Still, a haunting question lingers: when war demands absolute control, will rented capability prove enough? Could a government demand priority access when a commercial operator serves fifty nations? Could a minister compel a constellation to maintain coverage if shareholders oppose risk exposure? The logic of the market and the logic of national defence are not natural allies.

And yet, procurement rewired is becoming irreversible. Space has grown too fast, data too valuable, innovation too expensive for governments alone. The modern military does not simply deploy satellites; it buys the services of an industry that evolves faster than bureaucracies can legislate. As commercial firms become strategic partners, the boundary between public mission and private enterprise blurs. Who commands the future: the state that pays, or the company that owns the orbit? The answer will define the next age of power in space, and for now, it remains unresolved.

Standards and interoperability

On a quiet Australian coast, an unremarkable cluster of white antenna domes receives data from a dozen different satellite operators—government, commercial, and academic—without changing hardware. The same ground station that serves an Earth observation start-up in Berlin might, an hour later, downlink encrypted weather data for a Pacific island state or beam commands to a military reconnaissance craft passing overhead. To the casual observer, it looks like nothing more than a remote communications compound. To the space industry, it is a quiet revolution: satellites operated by rival companies, even rival nations, using shared infrastructure because their systems finally speak a common language.

Once, that would have been unthinkable. For most of space history, every operator built a closed world: bespoke satellites, bespoke ground stations, bespoke command protocols. Nations guarded their signals with the same zeal they guarded nuclear secrets. A spacecraft from Country A could not easily talk to a ground antenna from Company B, let alone share a cloud pipeline. In the age of constellations—hundreds of satellites, constant refresh, real-time analytics—such rigidity became a liability. The demand for speed and scale forced a change. The space industry discovered what the internet learned long ago: interoperability is power.

At the heart of this shift are open standards. Common data formats allow imagery, radar returns, and telemetry to flow straight into cloud processing tools, no matter who owns the satellite. Shared communication protocols mean a single ground station can schedule dozens of passes from different providers without reconfiguring hardware each time. In effect, a global network of shared antennae functions like roaming cell towers: when a satellite has something to send, any compatible ground station can catch it. For operators, this shrinks costs and increases resilience. If their own station goes down due to weather or attack, they can route data through a partner on the other side of the planet.

The commercial logic is irresistible. Why spend millions building a proprietary antenna network when a global array exists, pay-per-use, with redundant locations and round-the-clock staffing? Start-ups lean on these networks because it lets them launch satellites first and build infrastructure later—or never. Established players join because they cannot afford to fall behind. Even defence agencies, once allergic to sharing ground infrastructure, now accept that interoperability does not automatically mean vulnerability. Encryption, access control, and network isolation can protect sensitive traffic while still using shared steel and concrete.

Interoperability extends beyond hardware. Cloud integration has become the nervous system of modern space operations. Where images once arrived on secret tapes and were passed between secure facilities, today they flow into encrypted cloud buckets, triggering automated analytics, alerts, and user dashboards. Militaries subscribe to interfaces, not satellites. Logisticians download change-detection maps on rugged tablets. Naval officers view SAR-derived ship positions through commercial APIs. The orbit-to-cloud pipeline compresses time: from detection to decision, minutes instead of days.

There is a philosophical shift here. Instead of thinking of space systems as isolated national artefacts, operators treat them as nodes in a wider ecosystem. A radar satellite in one constellation might use a communications relay from another. A navigation system could adopt timing signals from a commercial provider if its sovereign one is jammed. Sensors from different firms feed into common analytic platforms for wildfire monitoring, maritime awareness, or disaster relief. Interoperability becomes not merely a technical convenience, but a strategic asset. It creates redundancy, flexibility, and a form of diplomatic glue: states that rely on shared infrastructure have incentives not to sabotage it.

Still, the transition is uneven. Some large incumbents cling to proprietary systems, fearing that open standards erode their competitive moat. Others hide behind "national security" to justify closed interfaces, even when external providers could offer more resilient or cheaper services. The tension is familiar: control versus collaboration, certainty versus adaptability. But the trend favours openness. Closed systems isolate their users. Open ones multiply their possibilities.

An instructive example lies in rideshare launch campaigns. When dozens of small satellites hitch a ride on a commercial rocket, they often come from different countries, research centres, or firms. Many lack their own ground infrastructure. Shared networks let them operate from day one, without waiting months to build antennas or hire radio engineers. The moment a satellite deploys, its data can travel through a global mesh of stations run by companies based everywhere from Alaska to Kenya. Scaling space becomes a matter of software and billing, not geopolitics.

Governments benefit in subtle ways. If a military intelligence satellite can downlink through multiple commercial gateways worldwide, adversaries cannot predict where its secrets are received. The diffusion complicates interception and targeting. In peacetime, it also saves money; fewer dedicated bases to build and maintain. Yet policymakers must wrestle with uncomfortable questions. If a shared ground station hosts both friendly and adversarial customers, who controls access during a crisis? Could a government compel a facility to deny service? Would that escalation ripple through the commercial ecosystem, provoking retaliation or countermeasure?

Cloud integration raises similar dilemmas. The same cloud provider that handles agricultural imagery might process classified reconnaissance. Data sovereignty, export controls, and encryption standards suddenly matter as much as rocket thrust or sensor resolution. Defence ministries scrutinise service agreements with intensity once reserved for missile treaties. Interoperability, while empowering, obliges trust. And trust is not free.

Interoperability also reshapes competition. When operators plug into shared infrastructure, differentiation shifts to software, analytics, and customer experience. The antenna becomes a commodity; the insight becomes the product. Companies race to build platforms that fuse data streams—optical, radar, signals intelligence—and deliver meaning. The most powerful firms are those whose systems play well with others. Lock-in is no longer achieved by proprietary bolts, but by the convenience of integration.

For all its promise, true openness remains aspirational. Standards bodies work slowly. Proprietary formats linger. Rival states hesitate to adopt protocols created abroad. And cybersecurity stakes grow higher: if a shared ground station is compromised, dozens of constellations could be affected. Resilience requires not just interoperability, but rigorous compartmentalisation and auditability. The architecture resembles a modern airport: shared runways and terminals, but secure gates and separate luggage systems for each airline.

Even so, the direction is clear. As constellations proliferate, launching weekly, then daily, the industry cannot afford bespoke silos. It needs scaffolding that treats space as infrastructure, not theatre. Interoperability brings efficiency, resilience, and a certain morality of practicality: why rebuild an antenna in Japan if a compatible one in Malaysia has spare capacity? Why design a unique command protocol if a secure, open one already exists and reduces engineering risk?

The deepest consequence may be invisible. When satellites, ground stations, and cloud systems interoperate, space becomes normal. No longer the domain of a few superpowers, but a utility woven into global networks of trade, emergency response, and scientific curiosity. Rockets may still draw the headlines, but the quiet work of standardisation—file formats, APIs, scheduling protocols—determines how well the world can use what orbit provides.

Yet a question lingers beneath the progress. Interoperability promises resilience, but also entanglement. When dozens of actors depend on shared infrastructure, who owns the responsibility for keeping it safe? Who sets the rules if standards become strategic chokepoints? If openness builds peace, can it also become a weapon? Space, once divided by rigid walls, is weaving itself together. Whether that fabric becomes a safety net or a new form of leverage will depend not just on engineering, but on politics—and those decisions remain very much unfinished.

Statecraft via service terms

At first glance, a satellite communications provider looks nothing like a diplomatic power. It sells bandwidth, not alliances; routers, not treaties. Yet in the middle of a modern conflict, the most important weapon may be its *terms of service*. The quiet lines in a commercial contract—acceptable-use clauses, geographic restrictions, throttling policies—now shape military operations as surely as terrain or weather. Armies plan advances based on where their satellite links will function. Civilians flee or stay connected depending on whether ground terminals are authorised. A clause drafted by corporate lawyers in a glass office block can decide whether a drone flies, a commander receives orders, or a town remains online.

This is the paradox of privatised space infrastructure. As governments outsourced connectivity to commercial constellations, they also outsourced a slice of political leverage. The ability to switch a region "on" or "off", to grant high-bandwidth access or limit traffic to text-only channels, became a strategic instrument. Companies that never sought geopolitical relevance found it forced upon them. Their commercial choices—who gets priority service, who is geo-blocked, who receives updates—now ripple across battlefields and borderlands.

Geofencing is the most visible manifestation. Satellite links rely on software-defined coverage maps. A firm can exclude a particular region with a database update. In peacetime, geofencing is mundane—protecting compliance with export controls or contractual obligations. But in conflict, geographic boundaries become political statements. Restoring full service to a besieged city can enable relief workers, journalists, and humanitarian convoys. Restricting service in a contested zone can disable drones, jam command links, or prevent propaganda broadcasts. The choice is not purely technical; it is inherently political, even if phrased in the neutral language of "operational constraints".

The commercial providers know this. Their legal teams negotiate with defence ministries, humanitarian organisations, and regulators. Their boards weigh moral hazard against shareholder risk. Turning off service to a combatant may appear principled, but it could expose the company to retaliation, cyber attack, or regulatory punishment. Turning service on may save lives or help an ally, but it may also blunt neutrality, drawing the firm into a conflict it cannot control. When a constellation becomes part of the kill chain—relaying targeting data, guiding munitions, tracking convoys—its operator inherits ethical responsibility for the consequences.

Some companies attempt to write neutrality into their policies. They add clauses forbidding military use or prohibiting integration with weapons systems. But enforcement is tricky. A commercial broadband link used by schoolchildren can also upload reconnaissance imagery. A cloud server designed for agricultural analytics can serve battlefield maps. Dual-use is not a theoretical nuisance; it is the nature of space data. Attempts to forbid it often collapse into ambiguity. And when governments are customers, contract clauses have a way of evaporating under pressure.

The rise of subscription-based imagery illustrates the complexity. Defence agencies no longer need to own satellites to obtain high-resolution pictures of a target. They rent access from commercial constellations, paying for daily coverage, tasking priority, or rush orders. In theory, this is efficient. In practice, it means a private firm controls the tap. During a crisis, who gets first access: the military client, the humanitarian agency, or the paying commercial customer? If capacity is saturated, does the provider ration bandwidth according to contracts, morality, or political pressure? No clause can neatly resolve these dilemmas.

There is also the uncomfortable question of selective transparency. Open-source analysts have used commercial imagery to expose atrocities, debunk propaganda, and track hidden deployments. This has strengthened journalism and civil society, but it has also alarmed governments. Some now lobby providers to restrict access during "sensitive periods", to delay releases, or to blur certain sites under national security exemptions. A company that refuses may face sanctions or loss of licences; a company that complies may be accused of complicity in crimes. Statecraft via service terms cuts both ways.

Meanwhile, competing governments court satellite firms like patrons once courted mercenaries. They offer launch contracts, spectrum allocation, regulatory favours, or tax breaks—if the company agrees to prioritise their forces or deny service to adversaries. In this environment, neutrality becomes a commercial risk. A constellation might lose half its market if it offends a major power. And if two rival states each demand exclusive access, the provider is trapped between competing sovereignties. The illusion that space networks are apolitical dissolves quickly under real-world pressure.

Export controls complicate the picture further. Some jurisdictions require companies to obtain licences before enabling service in certain countries. Others prohibit circumvention tools or impose data residency rules. Firms must navigate a maze of compliance regimes that do not always align with humanitarian imperatives. A starving region may remain cut off not because engineers lack capability, but because lawyers fear prosecution. In these cases, the architecture of global internet governance—bureaucratic forms, licensing agencies, national laws—decides who connects to orbit and who remains in silence.

The moral dimension is unavoidable. Connectivity can be life support. It enables hospitals to coordinate supplies, refugees to contact families, and researchers to monitor outbreaks. Cutting service is not merely a commercial decision; it can be a form of collective punishment. Yet unfiltered service can also allow belligerents to coordinate violence. The same command link that guides a humanitarian drone can guide an armed one. Corporations find themselves making triage decisions with geopolitical consequences—decisions for which they neither sought nor possess democratic legitimacy.

Governments, too, face dilemmas. If commercial firms now hold strategic power, should states regulate them more aggressively? Should they mandate neutrality, require transparency in geofencing decisions, or compel provision of service during humanitarian crises? But heavy-handed regulation risks driving firms offshore, slowing innovation, or pushing them to restrict services pre-emptively to avoid liability. Too little oversight, and companies become unaccountable arbiters of digital territory.

There are precedents outside space: undersea cable firms deciding whose data transits; cloud providers suspending accounts under sanctions law; social media platforms geoblocking content at government request. But satellites add a new dimension. They bypass local infrastructure entirely. A government cannot simply shut down an orbital link the way it can shut down a terrestrial internet exchange. Thus, the state's leverage shifts. Instead of wires and routers, it negotiates contracts and influence. Instead of soldiers seizing a telecom exchange, diplomats pressure a boardroom.

Some observers argue for explicit treaties governing commercial space services in conflict, akin to Red Cross protections for medical personnel. Others suggest escrow systems: if a provider withdraws service, a neutral party can switch on minimal humanitarian bandwidth. Still others propose cryptographic guarantees—smart contracts that enforce access rules independently of human decision. These ideas reflect a broader truth: space services have become part of critical international infrastructure, and leaving them to ad hoc corporate discretion is untenable.

Yet any rules would face the same problem as the services themselves. Politics leaks through every gap. A treaty may bind signatories, but non-signatories could weaponise flexibility. A neutral escrow may be hacked, jammed, or ignored. Smart contracts cannot adjudicate emergencies. And the actors with the most power—the firms with the largest constellations—may prefer the leverage that ambiguity affords.

Beneath the technicalities lies a human reality. Somewhere on the edge of a conflict zone, a medic refreshes a satellite-enabled map to locate the nearest safe corridor. In another corner of the same region, a drone pilot tries and fails to receive coordinates because coverage has been restricted. Both outcomes trace back to a quiet board decision or a line of automated policy code. When orbit becomes part of the social fabric of war and relief alike, control of service terms becomes control of fate.

That leaves an uncomfortable question hanging. If the future of connectivity is orbital, and if orbit is increasingly privatised, who gets to decide where the sky works and where it fails? The answer will not come from engineers alone. It will come from negotiators, lawmakers, and corporate strategists—people whose decisions will be felt by those with no voice in the discussion. The laws of physics are fixed; the laws of service are not. Whether they evolve toward fairness or power will shape conflicts long before the first shot is fired.

Chapter 5

How to Kill a Satellite

The first orbital kill did not resemble a battle. No explosions in vacuum, no laser-beam theatrics. A missile launched from Earth ascended quietly, the atmosphere thinning, guidance systems humming. Far above, a defunct weather satellite traced its predictable path. Moments later, a collision: one cold body striking another at more than twenty times the speed of sound. To observers below, nothing changed. Yet the skies had been altered. The shattered satellite fragmented into thousands of shards, each a tiny blade in permanent freefall. Some would remain in orbit for decades. The target was gone; the consequences lingered for generations.

The world barely noticed. Governments issued statements, diplomats murmured concern, analysts published cautious notes. But in physics, silence is louder than debate. Every scrap of debris added friction to the future: forcing manoeuvres, threatening space stations, raising insurance costs. A single strike had rewritten orbital risk calculus. And it demonstrated something far more unsettling: satellites are easier to destroy than protect, and the first casualty may not be a satellite at all, but the stability of space itself.

This is the unsettling truth of modern statecraft: the infrastructure that underpins navigation, communications, weather forecasting, banking, surveillance, and scientific discovery floats beyond borders, yet remains wide open. Nations rely on these assets for daily life—civilian and military alike. And although space is often described as a "sanctuary", it has become an exposed flank. The question is no longer whether a satellite can be killed, but how many ways there are to do it, and what each method signals about intent.

Some threats look like warfare from a pulp novel. Direct-ascent missiles that lance into orbit. Co-orbital hunters that shadow another spacecraft until the moment of attack. Kinetic strikes that replace a rival's strategic eyes with clouds of shrapnel. These are the spectacular options: dramatic, destructive, and impossible to hide. They are also the crudest. Shattering a satellite is easy; living with the debris field that follows is not. Every kinetic intercept is a confession of recklessness, a reminder that space is a common domain and that one broken object can poison an entire orbit for decades. When a state chooses this path, it is broadcasting a particular message: deterrence is valued higher than stewardship.

Other methods are far quieter. A targeted radio signal can drown out an uplink, leaving a satellite deaf and blind. Spoofed navigation data can mislead ships, drones, or financial networks without anyone immediately noticing. A cyber intrusion can turn a satellite's own software against itself, corrupting data or altering orbits by a few crucial degrees. Directed-energy systems—lasers or microwave beams—can temporarily dazzle sensors, degrading intelligence collection without creating debris or lasting evidence. These non-kinetic strikes occupy an ambiguous space. They reveal capability without leaving fingerprints. They disable without destruction. And they tempt policymakers because they are reversible, deniable, and psychologically unsettling.

Space warfare also has a terrestrial face. Ground stations are quiet targets: antenna farms tucked in remote valleys, data centres that link orbit to the internet, service terminals scattered across continents. A satellite intact in orbit can be rendered useless if its command link is severed or hijacked. Sabotage might appear as a corrupted firmware update, a compromised maintenance contractor, a counterfeit component inserted during assembly. Great powers have long understood that satellites rely on sprawling supply chains. They no longer ask only how to kill a spacecraft; they ask how to compromise the ecosystem that keeps it alive.

If killing is easier than protecting, deception becomes the art of survival. Satellites can change frequencies, pivot their antennas, rotate their bodies to disrupt tracking radars, or slip into different orbital planes. Constellations can spread risk across hundreds of nodes, making it harder to blind a network with a single strike. Some can mimic debris, reducing their electromagnetic signature until they are indistinguishable from space junk. Others deploy inflatable shields, hardened electronics, or onboard autonomy that allows them to continue functioning even if ground control goes dark. In this game, countermeasures evolve as quickly as threats.

None of these tactics exist in a vacuum of intent. A jamming pulse that lasts minutes can be interpreted as a warning, a test of response times. A brief spoofing attack can signal displeasure between rivals without escalating to open conflict. Cyber intrusions, especially those discovered and publicised, become diplomatic messages: "We can reach your crown jewels." By contrast, a kinetic strike is a severing of norms—a threshold that implies future operations will be fought in a dirtier, more unpredictable sky. The method chosen matters as much as the result. In space, how you kill speaks more loudly than what you kill.

The uncomfortable reality is that all major powers now rehearse these options. Some test interceptors. Others upgrade electronic warfare suites designed to blind satellites without firing a shot. Defence planners build frameworks for attributing attacks that leave little evidence. Intelligence agencies track manoeuvring satellites with curiosity tinged by suspicion. And all sides grapple with the same strategic dilemma: too much escalation risks a catastrophe no one can control; too little deterrence invites probing and brinkmanship.

There is no clean doctrine for space conflict. The laws that govern the domain were drafted in an era of two superpowers and a handful of satellites, not a world of commercial constellations, cloud-integrated ground stations, and dual-use payloads launched every week. The chapter that follows explores the toolkit that states now wield: missiles and mimics, lasers and laptops, saboteurs and silent signatures. It shows how these weapons shape political signalling, how they threaten civilian systems, and why the most dangerous strike may not be the loudest, but the one that leaves nothing visible at all.

The skies above are crowded, valuable, and fragile. Killing a satellite is easy. Keeping the peace after one dies is the real challenge. The methods on the table today will not merely decide who can blind whom; they will decide whether space remains usable for everyone. That is why the question is not simply *how* to kill a satellite—it is *what happens next.*

Kinetic intercepts

On a clear night in 2007, amateur astronomers noticed something odd. A familiar Chinese weather satellite, long retired, vanished from their tracking logs. Minutes later, radar stations began to register hundreds of new objects—tiny shards flashing across the sky at extreme velocities. A single missile, launched from Earth, had smashed a spacecraft into a swarm of jagged fragments. To the world below, nothing felt different. But space had been altered. The number of trackable debris pieces leapt by thousands; many would remain in orbit for decades. One strike had doubled the long-term collision risk in a critical altitude band. A satellite was gone. A problem was born.

There is a brutal simplicity to smashing machines in orbit. Satellites travel at thousands of metres per second; relative speeds in a deliberate intercept can exceed a rifle bullet by hundreds of times. No warhead is needed. The kinetic energy alone turns metal into shrapnel. When a direct-ascent interceptor climbs through the atmosphere on a ballistic arc and meets a satellite at altitude, the hit produces an expanding cloud of fragments that spread along the original orbit like broken glass scattered across a highway. Only the highway ends. The fragments don't fall. They persist, each one capable of killing another spacecraft in a silent, invisible cascade.

For military planners, the appeal of kinetic weapons is self-evident. They are demonstrable: a government can show its population, its allies, and its rivals that it can reach into orbit and destroy. They are also psychologically potent. A kinetic kill makes a point that no diplomatic note can match. The problem—visible to engineers, insurers and astronauts alike—is that the act of destruction does not stay contained. The fragments do not recognise borders or targets. They orbit Earth every ninety minutes, sweeping across continents indiscriminately. A weapon meant for one satellite reshapes the risks borne by every operator in that orbital band.

Two broad families of kinetic intercept exist. The first, direct-ascent missiles, are fired from Earth. They act quickly, sometimes in minutes, racing through the atmosphere until they reach the target's altitude. The second, co-orbital systems, are satellites designed to stalk and collide with a victim already in space. A co-orbital interceptor might manoeuvre for days or weeks, shadowing a target until the moment of impact. Both approaches seek the same outcome: a hit that is precise enough to destroy without a warhead, yet messy enough to scatter debris across a wide field.

Direct-ascent tests are the easiest to recognise. A carrier rocket rises from a known site. The plume is visible on radar. Tracking sensors on Earth see the sudden disappearance of the target and the appearance of new fragments. There is little ambiguity. It is a loud, deliberate gesture—one that says: we can destroy what you depend on. Nations that have tested these systems often justify them as deterrent signals. Yet deterrence achieved through environmental risk comes with irony. By demonstrating ability, a state simultaneously undermines the long-term usability of the orbit it depends on.

Co-orbital systems are a subtler class of threat. They do not rely on the brute acceleration of a ground-launched missile. Instead, they take advantage of prolonged proximity. A small satellite might rendezvous with another object, matching its orbit until the two travel as a pair. In peace, proximity looks innocent. It can be used for repair, refuelling, or inspection. In conflict, proximity becomes coercion. The attacker needs only a tiny delta-v—a slight change in speed—to shift from escort to weapon. A collision in this context can be tailored precisely, creating fewer fragments or targeting delicate components such as solar arrays. Some co-orbital designs even contemplate robotic arms or grappling devices, capturing and dragging a satellite out of operational orbit rather than shattering it. But proximity has its own escalatory signal. When a foreign spacecraft shadows yours, following each manoeuvre, it communicates intent without a word: we are close enough to break you.

Both types of kinetic attack share a flaw that is too often overlooked: debris. Every interception, whether explosive or unarmed, creates fragments that spread out through space. Some pieces are large enough to track. Thousands are too small. A one-centimetre bolt, moving at orbital speed, delivers the kinetic energy of a hand grenade. A single strike can produce thousands of such shards. Once dispersed, they cannot be called off, negotiated with, or reversed. They continue to orbit until atmospheric drag slowly pulls them down—sometimes over months, sometimes over generations. A short political message becomes a long technical burden.

There is a deeper strategic paradox at the heart of kinetic intercepts. By proving capability, a state may render its own satellites less safe. A nation that fills orbit with fragments today may find its own constellations threatened tomorrow. In a domain where public and private assets share the same orbital lanes, the costs of bluster are socialised. A kinetic demonstration is not a scalpel; it is a fragmentation grenade tossed into a room no one can leave.

Defenders sometimes argue that intercepts can be "clean". If a satellite is hit at a lower altitude, atmospheric drag can sweep away debris in a reasonable time. If the target is small or struck near perigee, fragments might degrade more quickly. These are true in principle, yet less reassuring in practice. Not all fragments circulate at the same altitude. Some remain aloft far longer than expected. Others drift into key orbits used by weather satellites, scientific missions, or global positioning systems. Even a low-altitude strike creates a short-term hazard for crewed vehicles like space stations, which must perform avoidance manoeuvres to avert collision. A clean strike is a relative concept; space is a shared commons, and damage inflicted on part of it reverberates across all.

The human dimension is easy to miss. Operators and analysts on Earth watch debris maps like storm forecasters, modelling the trajectories of thousands of fragments. When two objects threaten to cross paths within a few hundred metres, engineers decide whether to burn precious fuel to manoeuvre. A single debris cloud can trigger hundreds of such decisions. Fuel expended on avoidance is fuel lost for operations, shortening mission lifetimes. Insurance policies adjust. Costs rise. Launch schedules shift. The consequences are mundane, bureaucratic, expensive—and a warning that space conflict rarely stays tidy.

For militaries, kinetic intercepts offer a blunt instrument. They remove satellites from the sky. But they also leave fingerprints. Attribution is trivial. A nation that performs a kinetic attack cannot hide. It can only justify. That is why such options are often seen as escalatory and politically costly. They advertise hostility, not ambiguity. The attacker must accept not only diplomatic consequences but also the risk that others will respond with their own intercepts. A domain contaminated with debris becomes a domain where everyone loses.

Yet the harsh arithmetic of war can make destructive options tempting. If a rival relies heavily on a handful of key satellites—large strategic assets in geostationary orbit, for instance—a kinetic strike could cripple early-warning systems or damage a national communications backbone. If leaders believe a decisive blow could tilt the balance of conflict, restraint becomes fragile. History shows that technologies built for symbolism often become tools for action.

To understand why kinetic intercepts persist despite their dangers, one must remember the logic of deterrence. Some states believe that demonstrating the ability to kill in orbit discourages aggression. The presence of such weapons is meant to foster caution, much like nuclear tests were once used to signal capability. But space is not the seabed or the desert. The medium does not heal. The debris from a single strike can survive longer than any political regime that authorised it. Deterrence purchased with orbital pollution is deterrence that mortgages the future.

There is also the defence of defence. Nations invest immense resources into satellite constellations that support troops, ships, aircraft, and command networks. If they feel vulnerable, they search for ways to respond in kind. Sat-killers become part of the strategic equation: a threat to prevent coercion. Yet as the number of satellites rises and commercial operators proliferate, the distinction between civilian and military targets grows thin.

A cloud of fragments does not respect neutrality or ownership. It does not differentiate between a spy satellite and one that maps wildfires or monitors crops. Collateral damage becomes universal.

Even so, the pursuit continues. States test missiles. Engineers refine tracking algorithms. War colleges write scenarios in which first strikes are silent bursts of shrapnel above the atmosphere. The world is uncomfortably close to a future where a conflict on Earth spills upward with devastating consequences. And the lesson is not simply that kinetic intercepts are crude. The deeper lesson is that strategy constrained by physics often leads to outcomes no treaty can undo.

There is a quieter trend emerging in response. Some nations have pledged not to test debris-creating anti-satellite weapons. Space agencies warn that even small debris fields can multiply disaster risk. Diplomats push for norms that shame reckless behaviour. Yet without legal compulsion or universal agreement, restraint remains voluntary. The fundamental capability persists, and so does the temptation.

The final irony is the simplest: in a world that depends on satellites for communication, forecasting, navigation, and surveillance, the easiest way to blind an adversary is also the most self-harmful. Kinetic intercepts offer certainty of destruction. They also guarantee uncertainty of aftermath. Every fragment becomes a reminder that in space, violence is never contained.

The question is not whether military planners understand these risks—they do. The question is whether, in the pressure of rivalry, caution will hold. What happens when a nation decides that the benefit of a kill outweighs the future of the orbit it ruins? And if that line is crossed once, who will trust that it will not be crossed again?

Non-kinetic disruption

A special forces team in a dusty forward base waits for a drone feed that never arrives. The aircraft is airborne, its camera working, its pilot ready—but the signal is swallowed by a wall of noise somewhere between Earth and orbit. On nobody's screen does an image flicker. There is no explosion, no obvious attack, no burning wreckage. Yet the effect is identical: blindness. The simplest of radio tricks—broadcasting a louder signal on the same frequency—has just denied an army the eyes it expected to have.

This is the unsettling power of non-kinetic disruption. Spacecraft are often imagined as hard, mechanical, metallic things, vulnerable only to something equally physical. In reality, satellites are as much information conduits as they are hardware. That makes them prey to subtler forms of attack: noise instead of shrapnel, bits instead of bullets. When the aim is to silence, mislead, or confuse rather than destroy, the most effective weapon may not touch the satellite at all.

Jamming is the bluntest instrument in this category, but even its crudity is deceptive. A satellite dish does not magically accept "its" signals and ignore others. It simply absorbs whatever radio energy lands in its aperture. Uplink jamming—the deliberate flooding of a satellite's receiver with overpowering noise—can choke communications across a theatre of war. Downlink jamming, directed at ground terminals, can leave soldiers with silent radios or emergency workers with frozen maps. In modern conflict, where information moves as urgently as ammunition, silence itself can kill.

Spoofing takes a different path. Instead of denying the signal, it replaces it. A spoofer mimics the real message, sending plausible but false data. The result can be dangerous in ways jamming is not. If a GPS receiver is jammed, it fails. If it is spoofed, it lies. Navigation receivers can be fooled into reporting positions kilometres from the truth. Ships can be nudged off course. Uncrewed systems can be misdirected or lured into traps. The unsettling part is that a spoofed system often believes everything is fine. The victim's instruments may show perfect health, even as they walk confidently into error.

Military GPS receivers defend themselves with encrypted signals and anti-jam antennas, but commercial devices lack such armour. As civilian infrastructure leans heavily on satellite timing—banks, stock exchanges, power grids—the prospect of spoofing has moved from espionage to potential sabotage. No debris is created. No missile is launched. Yet the effects could ripple through economies.

If spoofing is the art of lying, cyber compromise is the art of disguised control. A satellite, at heart, is a computer with engines and sensors attached. It receives commands, executes code, stores data. That makes it a target for hacking as much as a missile is a target for gunfire. If an adversary infiltrates a ground station, a software update pipeline, or a control interface, they can masquerade as a legitimate operator. The range of possible effects is unnerving: deleting imagery, locking antennas, altering orbits, shutting down power systems. The satellite need not be damaged to be lost. A hijacked spacecraft is a ghost ship—still intact, still outwardly present, but no longer under the owner's command.

The lesson is that the perimeter of a satellite is not drawn at the edge of its metal skin. It extends down earthbound networks, across cloud servers, through vendor supply chains, and into systems that manage encryption keys and command processes. A cyber intrusion against a satellite operator can take place thousands of kilometres away, in a quiet office, by someone whose only weapon is a laptop. Attribution becomes harder. So does retaliation.

Then there are directed-energy systems, which often seem like the most science-fictional of all. They are not. Lasers and high-power radio beams are already used for precision ranging, tracking, or imaging. Turn up the wattage and change the intent, and they become weapons. A laser that dazzles or saturates a satellite's optical sensor can blind an imager without touching its body. A microwave beam can overheat electronics or scramble memory cells. The destructive power can be dialled from reversible to permanent. In their mildest form, these attacks leave no wreckage, no fragments, no catastrophe—just a satellite that suddenly cannot see.

Directed-energy weapons highlight a distinction often overlooked: damaging can be more strategic than destroying. A blinded spy satellite may be as useless as a shattered one, but the method of attack leaves no debris, no international outrage, and perhaps no proof. Analysts may notice the satellite stops returning imagery, but the cause remains ambiguous. Was it a fault? A solar flare? A malfunction? Or a laser stationed on a remote mountaintop? Ambiguity becomes a shield for the attacker. Meanwhile, the defender must prepare for a threat they cannot definitively confirm.

The real-world consequences of non-kinetic attacks are not theoretical. In multiple conflicts, uplink jamming has silenced satellite phones used by journalists and aid workers. Commercial imagery providers have reported unexplained outages near active warzones. Ships in major maritime corridors have documented spoofed GPS coordinates that place them on land or far from their true positions. That such incidents rarely carry dramatic headlines is part of the point. They are most powerful when they are quiet.

These tools introduce an uncomfortable philosophical tension. Kinetic attacks are violent but clear. Non-kinetic attacks are quiet but corrosive. Silence becomes a battlefield, doubt an instrument. A non-kinetic strike offers deniability; states can disrupt without accepting public blame. It is easier to stay below the threshold of open conflict when the weapon is a radio signal rather than a missile plume. That is why intelligence agencies worry more about subtle interference than dramatic explosions. The greatest danger lies in the ability to coerce without triggering defence treaties or public outrage.

The commercial world has stumbled into the same vulnerabilities. Space-based broadband networks promise global coverage at low price. But any system that depends on clean radio frequencies inherits the risks of interference. Criminal groups have used jammers to thwart tracking devices on stolen cargo. Rogue actors have experimented with GPS confusion near ports and airports. The receivers at the heart of global timing systems—essential for high-frequency trading and synchronising financial records—would be dangerously exposed if spoofed at scale. A few false nanoseconds can corrupt a market.

Non-kinetic disruption also alters escalation dynamics. States may experiment with small, reversible actions to probe defences. A brief jamming episode, lasting minutes, might serve as a warning or a demonstration. A spoofed signal could lure an uncrewed vehicle harmlessly off course to prove vulnerability without causing casualties. In theory, this makes space competition safer by substituting reversible pain for irreversible harm. In practice, ambiguity breeds paranoia. If a satellite goes dark for two hours due to a cyber glitch, no one can be entirely sure it was a glitch. Doubt itself becomes a weapon.

Yet to treat non-kinetic disruption purely through a military lens is to miss its civilian impact. The same tools that can blind a reconnaissance satellite can also cripple emergency communications during a natural disaster. The same spoofing tactics that mislead a naval vessel can send a commercial airliner's navigation reading astray. The same cyber intrusion that shuts down a military drone link can compromise a weather satellite distributing storm warnings. Space is a dual-use infrastructure. Every non-kinetic weapon pointed upwards inevitably points downwards.

There is also an ethical unease. These attacks rely on the fragility of trust—trust that data is honest, that links are open, that sensors are truthful. When deception and interference become military norms, civilian systems suffer collateral damage even without being targeted. Democracies depend on open skies and open information. Manipulation of space-based signals eats away at that foundation quietly, invisibly. Some militaries like digital harassment precisely because the public rarely notices.

The countermeasures are elaborate but imperfect. Anti-jam antennas reject hostile signals coming from the wrong angle. Receivers compare multiple signal sources to reject inconsistencies. Satellites use frequency hopping, spread-spectrum modulation, and encryption to resist spoofing. Ground networks deploy hardened firewalls and zero-trust architectures to keep intruders out. Directed-energy attacks require line of sight and precise pointing, allowing defenders to monitor tell-tale beams.

But defence is always slower than innovation. Jammers get smarter, adjusting power and waveform to blend with normal traffic. Spoofers craft highly realistic signals that fool even professional-grade receivers. Cyber attackers exploit the weakest point in sprawling software supply chains: an unpatched library, a forgotten credential, a subcontractor's compromised server. Directed-energy systems grow more portable and more clandestine. Vulnerability is not static; it is a moving contest between ingenuity and restraint.

If kinetic attacks create debris that lasts decades, non-kinetic disruption creates habits and precedents. Once states normalise jamming during crises, it becomes harder to object when rivals do the same. Once cyber intrusion becomes routine, trust evaporates. And once civilians discover they cannot rely on satellite navigation or communications in a pinch, confidence in the entire space ecosystem erodes. The damage can be psychological as much as technical.

The uncomfortable truth is that non-kinetic disruption is attractive precisely because it is quiet. There are no tumbling fragments, no ruined orbits, no diplomatic spectacles. It allows states to flex power while keeping their fingerprints smudged. It is the kind of weapon that fits a world where conflict increasingly hides behind ambiguity.

But a question hangs over the future: if every nation develops the ability to blind, spoof, hack, and dazzle, what becomes of the space systems on which humanity now depends? When silence is as dangerous as shrapnel, and lies are as potent as lasers, what prevents a slow slide into permanent mistrust? The first shot in a space conflict may never be heard—and the last may leave no crater at all.

Insiders and supply chains

A satellite can be guarded by encryption, shielded against radiation, and watched by air defence radars, yet fall victim to a tampered USB stick in a contractor's office. The paradox is uncomfortable: the most advanced machines ever launched by humankind are often undone not by missiles or lasers, but by human error, compromised code, and quietly poisoned supply chains. A spacecraft in orbit may be secure; the company laptop that uploads its firmware may not be.

The space industry learned this lesson early. In the 1980s, intelligence services discovered that sabotaging Soviet procurement pipelines produced far greater disruption than traditional espionage. Corrupted microchips, adulterated industrial software, and subtly flawed turbine controls caused malfunctions that looked like bad luck rather than sabotage. The principle has only grown sharper. Modern satellites are built from hundreds of thousands of components, sourced from dozens of firms, across multiple jurisdictions. No military hardening can eliminate a flaw buried in a subcontractor's code or a compromised test instrument used during assembly.

At the heart of the problem lies a misconception: that a satellite's perimeter exists at the edge of its metal body. In reality, the security envelope reaches into factories, ground stations, cloud servers, maintenance laptops, and even the contractors cleaning antenna dishes. Any breach in that chain—accidental or malicious—can cascade into orbit.

Ground stations are an especially fragile point. They are the control rooms of the space age: small clusters of racks and consoles that speak the language of spacecraft. Many are tucked in remote regions for clear skies and radio silence. Remote also means low profile: modest fences, a handful of staff, sometimes a single network administrator. These sites run software that issues commands, updates operational schedules, and pushes patches to satellites thousands of kilometres away. If an attacker compromises a ground station, they do not need to hack a spacecraft directly. They simply impersonate the operator.

In 2022, a European satellite network experienced a destructive intrusion the moment Russian armour crossed into Ukraine. Ground terminals used by civilians and militaries alike were knocked offline. The satellite itself did not explode, jam, or collide; its users were simply cut loose from the network. The compromise took place in terrestrial infrastructure—routers and firmware—managed far from orbit. It was a grim preview of how supply chain vulnerabilities can become strategic tools.

As the commercial space market has expanded, the number of actors touching a satellite's life cycle has multiplied. Hardware vendors, software developers, launch brokers, antenna providers, data processors—all form a complex ecosystem. Each node presents a possible breach. A malicious firmware update in a vendor's system could implant dormant code across a fleet of ground terminals. A disgruntled employee could steal cryptographic keys. A lax vendor might store sensitive logs on an unsecured cloud bucket. Satellites do not live in space alone; they are tethered to Earth through these invisible threads, and those threads can be severed or rewoven.

The greatest threat often comes from within. Insiders—engineers, contractors, administrators—are uniquely positioned to bypass security controls. Their logins are real. Their badges open doors. Their actions appear routine. A single technician with quiet access to a power control system could issue a shutdown command that looks like operator error. A systems engineer with access to flight software could upload a subtle logic change that disables a satellite weeks later, when the author has left the company and the trail has gone cold.

This is not a hypothetical worry. Critical infrastructure from oil pipelines to water plants has been crippled by insiders and supply chain failure. Space systems are simply the next frontier. A rogue employee does not need deep technical knowledge to cause damage. Misconfiguring a firewall or deleting a key signing certificate can orphan a satellite as surely as a collision can.

Even benign negligence carries risk. Many satellite operators rely on legacy control systems designed decades ago, long before cyber warfare became central to statecraft. These systems communicate with spacecraft using protocols that assume trust. If an attacker gains access to an internal network—through a phishing email, an infected contractor laptop, or a misconfigured VPN—they can sit inside the trusted zone. From there, issuing commands to a spacecraft may be as trivial as filling out a control form. There is no explosion, no breach alert, only a satellite quietly drifting off-script.

Commercialisation has magnified exposure. Start-ups race to launch constellations on tight budgets, leaning heavily on off-the-shelf components and outsourced software. Supply chain audits are expensive. Security testing slows schedules. Venture capital rewards speed. In this environment, cutting corners is not malice; it is survival. But the vulnerabilities do not vanish merely because the spacecraft is civilian. A breached commercial imager can be used to deny governments critical data during crises. A compromised communications satellite can become a relay for hostile espionage. The line between commercial and military value has blurred.

Cloud integration introduces an additional attack surface. Satellite operators now store command histories, cryptographic keys, telemetry archives, and operational plans on cloud platforms. This brings convenience and scalability, but also dependency. A misconfigured bucket or an overlooked API token can expose sensitive data. In a world where intrusion often begins with credential theft, the idea that a stolen laptop from a subcontractor could serve as a ladder into an orbital network is not far-fetched. Defence agencies have begun to treat cloud credentials as national security assets.

The physics of space offer no protection against human behaviour. A satellite is only as trustworthy as the chain of people and systems that feed it instructions. A compromised firmware package can send a power subsystem into an unrecoverable state. A corrupted timing file can break navigation. A falsified orbital ephemeris can trigger false manoeuvres, draining fuel or throwing a satellite into a hazardous region. The spacecraft itself appears healthy on telemetry—voltage normal, temperature nominal—until it is too late.

The strategic ramifications are profound. States no longer need to risk debris-generating interceptions when they can sabotage a supplier. Tampering with a single component batch can infect dozens of satellites across multiple customers. The effect is slow, creeping, plausibly accidental. When failure comes, it looks like bad engineering, not an attack. Arms control frameworks struggle to address sabotage without fingerprints.

There is also a democratic discomfort here. Civilian satellites support everything from GPS-enabled tractors to disaster responders. Yet the companies that build, operate, and maintain them often rely on global supply chains. Components may pass through factories in countries with competing interests. Software may be written by contractors who also work for rival clients. Legal oversight lags far behind this global complexity. A nation may not even know that its satellite depends on a subcontractor halfway across the world—until something goes wrong.

Defenders have begun to adapt. Zero-trust architectures assume no system or user is inherently reliable. Sensitive commands require multiple signatures. Flight software is containerised and verified. Operators segment their networks, isolating ground stations from corporate IT. Firmware is signed and attested. Some organisations build shadow fleets of test terminals, watching for anomalies in real time. Yet even these measures struggle with the weakest link: humans.

Consider a simple scenario. A field-deployed terminal used by peacekeepers receives a routine firmware update from a vendor. The update appears legitimate, cryptographically signed, and automatically installed. Days later, a latent feature activates. It begins exfiltrating decrypted traffic to an unknown server. No satellite is touched. No ground station is hacked. The vulnerability enters through a trusted supplier and spreads quietly through the fleet. Detecting this intrusion requires forensic analysis that most operators lack the resources to perform. The compromise becomes a silent occupation of the network.

The philosophical tension is stark. Space has always been a domain of engineering triumph—precision, logic, redundancy. Supply chain and insider threats feel messy, unglamorous, and human. Yet they may be the decisive front in space security. A nation can spend billions on anti-satellite weapons and still lose capability through a corrupted driver at a subcontractor's workshop. Power in space now depends not only on rockets and solar arrays, but on procurement audits, background checks, and patch hygiene.

And there is a darker possibility. As states recognise that sabotage is effective and hard to attribute, they may invest more heavily in it. Quiet interference encourages escalation without visibility. Hundreds of satellites could fail over a decade, each loss plausibly explained as fatigue, radiation, or manufacturing defect. No debris to analyse, no launch plume to observe. A war that no one can prove has begun.

In that light, the question becomes unsettling: what does deterrence look like when the battlefield is a supply chain? When the most potent weapon is a line of code hidden in a vendor's software library, how can any state be sure its satellites are truly its own? The fortress in orbit may be impregnable. The back door may be a bored technician, a compromised router, or an update server quietly repurposed by an adversary. Space power once depended on rockets and radar. Increasingly, it depends on trust—and trust, once lost, leaves no crater but may be harder to rebuild.

Masking and manoeuvre

A satellite on a public tracking website looks immutable: an object on rails, circling Earth with clockwork predictability. Yet in conflict, predictability is a liability. The very physics that make orbital flight possible also make surveillance effortless. If an adversary knows where a satellite will be next Tuesday at 14:12 UTC, they can plan when to jam it, dazzle it with a laser, or target it with a co-orbital stalker. The paradox of modern space operations is sharp: the machines that must broadcast their existence to function are simultaneously trying to hide.

During the Cold War, this problem was considered unsolvable. Space was too transparent, too vast, and too well-observed. Optical telescopes could track anything larger than a grapefruit in low orbit. Radars could sweep for objects in darkness. Precision catalogues grew, and soon every serious space power knew the whereabouts of every major spacecraft. Secrecy seemed to belong to submarines, not satellites. The consensus was simple: you cannot hide in the sky.

Today, that certainty is fading. The new art is not invisibility but *deception*: making a satellite harder to identify, harder to predict, and harder to exploit. It is a shift from brute protection to strategic ambiguity—masking intent, obscuring capability, and presenting an adversary with a mosaic of false leads.

One of the oldest tools is frequency hopping: a technique borrowed from radio pioneers and wartime codebreakers. Instead of broadcasting on a single band, a satellite can skip rapidly across frequencies according to a cryptographic schedule. To a civilian, the signal looks like noise. To a military terminal with the right key, it is clear and reliable. When an adversary tries to jam the link, the satellite slips away to another slice of spectrum. A single jammer becomes useless; dozens might still fall short. The satellite has not moved physically, yet it has manoeuvred in the electromagnetic domain—the most important battlefield of space.

Manoeuvre in the literal sense is more dramatic. Contrary to popular imagery, satellites are not frozen in place. They carry propellant, thrusters, and increasingly, electric propulsion systems that sip xenon like a miser. A small burn can shift an orbit slightly higher, slightly faster, slightly more inclined. Over weeks, such changes can accumulate into a new trajectory. A spacecraft can take itself out of harm's way or shadow its adversary in turn. Or it can do something subtler: create uncertainty. If an attacking vehicle expects its target to be in a specific position, a few hundred metres of unexpected deviation can waste the engagement. Miss by centimetres on Earth and you have a near miss; miss by centimetres in orbit and you might as well be a kilometre away.

Some manoeuvres are barely perceptible. A defensive satellite might perform attitude slews—rotating itself to minimise its exposed surface to a laser dazzler or to hide optical sensors behind a sunshield. To the ground-based observer, the spacecraft is still there, but it becomes harder to blind, scorch, or illuminate. Other forms of hardening are built into the spacecraft body: reflective coatings, radiation-resistant detectors, shutters that can snap shut when a threat is detected. Spacecraft designers once considered such defences exotic; now they are entering the mainstream.

Yet manoeuvre is costly. Every burst of propellant eats into lifetime. Every adjustment complicates station-keeping. The trade-off is philosophical as much as technical: is it better to preserve fuel and remain predictable, or spend it and become a ghost in orbit? Militaries increasingly lean towards the latter. Fleets of small satellites—cheap, agile, replaceable—are designed with manoeuvre in mind. A single, precious spacecraft is a sitting target; a distributed network of dozens, each capable of evasive motion, becomes maddening to pin down.

Deception also extends to identity. Not all satellites declare themselves. Some transmit under misleading IDs. Some vary their beacons or reduce power to blend into the background noise of space. A small spacecraft might masquerade as space debris, its signature so weak that catalogue operators overlook it. Only when it fires its thrusters does it betray its nature. This is the orbital equivalent of a submarine running silent. Legally, such behaviour inhabits murky territory, but legality has rarely been the foremost concern in military affairs.

A more subtle approach is data camouflage. A reconnaissance satellite might alter its downlink pattern to obscure when it has collected imagery. If an adversary sees that every time the satellite passes overhead, a high-bandwidth transmission follows, they can infer when and where it is photographing. By inserting dummy traffic at random intervals, operators muddy the signal. The satellite's behaviour no longer maps cleanly to intelligence collection, denying the enemy the ability to time their concealment.

Some techniques aim not to hide but to overwhelm. By generating decoy signatures—auxiliary beacons, false telemetry packets, or simulated orbital tracks—defenders can force an attacker to chase phantoms. In terrestrial warfare, this is electronic countermeasures; in space, it becomes orbital disinformation. An adversary with uncertain targeting intelligence is one who starts to hesitate, delaying costly decisions or miscalculating engagement windows.

All of these methods exploit a fundamental truth: space conflict is slow, deliberate, and unforgiving. Engagement windows are brief. Geometry is constraining. If a target is not perfectly where it should be, the attack fails. If its signal is garbled just long enough, the jammer gains nothing. If its sensors are shielded for a few seconds, the laser loses its chance. In a domain defined by orbital mechanics and precision timing, small disruptions have outsize effects.

Of course, no defence is perfect. Fuel runs out. Thrusters degrade. Camouflage can be detected by more sensitive instruments. And every manoeuvre announces itself to the world. Even if an attacker cannot strike, they might learn more about a satellite's propulsion reserves than the operator would prefer. To manoeuvre is to reveal capacity. To hide is sometimes to signal fear.

There is also an ethical discomfort. When satellites begin hiding and deceiving, escalation shadows the horizon. Transparency has long been a stabilising force in space. If states distrust what they see—or cannot see—they may assume the worst. Manoeuvre becomes a language of signals: a defensive shift could be interpreted as preparation for attack; a deceptive transmission pattern could appear as offensive cyber activity. Ambiguity cuts both ways.

The future intensifies this tension. Autonomous satellites will soon evaluate threats and manoeuvre without waiting for human approval. Machine learning will filter sensor data, detect hostile approaches, and choose evasive actions. These systems will react faster than diplomats can talk. A robotic decision to jink away from a perceived collision could be misread as a hostile dodge. In a crowded orbit, misunderstandings are dangerous.

Yet doing nothing is riskier still. A satellite that sits still is a satellite that dies still. Masking and manoeuvre—whether electromagnetic, digital, or physical—form the playbook of survival. The craft that can flicker its frequencies, harden its sensors, adjust its orbit, or feign inactivity does not need to be invincible. It only needs to be uncertain enough to force its adversary into hesitation.

Space was once imagined as a realm of perfect clarity: physics, predictability, and the cold logic of orbits. But war, even in the heavens, is a contest of perception and misperception. The most powerful weapon may be doubt—the possibility that the target is not where it appears, not what it seems, or not vulnerable in the way an attacker expects. The satellites that endure will not merely be the strongest; they will be the least understood.

Escalation ladders

On a clear night, satellites glide across the sky without a sound, indifferent to the borders beneath them. They appear apolitical: silent, steady, removed from human quarrels. Yet these objects—so small against the dark—sit on the most delicate fault line in geopolitics. They are not simply tools; they are signalling devices. In space, how a state chooses to interfere with a satellite matters almost as much as whether it succeeds. The style of attack can be a message, a warning, a threat, or an opening gambit in a far larger game.

There is an unsettling irony here. On Earth, escalation is often loud: troops mobilise, ships sail, missiles arc across borders. In orbit, escalation begins with silence. A satellite stops answering. A navigation signal falters. A downlink degrades to static. At first, the line between malfunction and malice is hazy. In that ambiguity lies danger—and opportunity.

The lowest rung of the escalation ladder rests on ambiguity by design. Jamming a satellite's uplink, for instance, is technically crude and operationally reversible. It is the geopolitical equivalent of throwing sand in the gears: irritating, disruptive, but not catastrophic. If a state wants to warn an adversary without handing them a casus belli, this is how it begins. Radio interference can be dialled up or down, localised to a single theatre, and switched off instantly if diplomacy demands. It sends a message while preserving deniability. No debris, no explosion, no irrevocable loss—just silence.

Move one step higher and the sand becomes a stone. Spoofing a navigation signal does not merely degrade service; it lies. A falsely shifted GPS or Galileo reading can mislead a drone, divert a merchant ship, or scramble synchronisation between military units. The victim may suspect manipulation, but proving it publicly can be politically costly. For states that want leverage without headlines, spoofing is a powerful temptation. It is still reversible—turn the transmitter off and the world returns to normal—but the consequences of a navigational lie can be profound. The difference between a failed artillery strike and one that finds its target might rest on a few microseconds of timing.

Higher still sit cyber intrusions. A compromised ground station or satellite terminal blurs the border between the celestial and the terrestrial. It shows intent and capability without producing any visible damage. It can be tightly scoped—alter a single data stream—or opened into a wider campaign of espionage and sabotage. The attack may be discovered weeks later, but the signalling is clear to those meant to see it: *we can reach you, and we can return whenever we choose.* Cyber compromise sits awkwardly in international law—less than war, more than nuisance—and that grey zone is exactly why it is appealing.

Directed energy—lasers used to dazzle or blind a satellite's sensors—sits mid-ladder. The effect can be temporary or permanent. A momentary flash might be a warning shot; a burnt-out detector is a declaration of hostility. Importantly, no debris is created. To diplomats, that detail matters. To insurers, it matters more. A struck satellite can be quietly written off; a destroyed one, scattering thousands of fragments, becomes a global hazard. Lasers allow punishment without poisoning orbit.

Above this midpoint the stakes shift. Co-orbital stalking—parking a mysterious satellite near another spacecraft—may do nothing at all. It can loiter for weeks, merely *watching*. But its presence is a taunt. If it fires thrusters and closes in, the message sharpens: *we can touch you*. Whether it ultimately collides, captures, or simply shadows, the signal is unmistakable. A co-orbital approach is not an accident; it is choreography. Even if no damage occurs, a line has been crossed.

Then comes the sharp edge: kinetic attack. A direct-ascent interceptor launching from Earth to obliterate a target in orbit leaves no ambiguity. The flash of impact, the spray of fragments, the instantaneous death—this is the unmistakable language of force. But it speaks recklessly. It tells not only the target but every nation on Earth that the attacker is willing to contaminate a shared domain for decades. It is the ultimate punctuation mark of escalation: brutal, blunt, and strategically self-incriminating.

In theory, escalation ladders offer control. Each rung allows calibration: reversible measures at the bottom, catastrophic ones at the top. But satellites are unforgiving actors in this play. Detection is imperfect. Attribution is slow. A malfunction might be misread as an attack. A clumsy manoeuvre might appear as a hostile intercept. Misperception—long feared on Earth—becomes lethal in space because the room for correction is tiny. The domain rewards clarity but often delivers fog.

This strategic ambiguity cuts both ways. A state wishing to probe an adversary's defences can apply just enough pressure to learn how systems respond. A brief jamming episode during a crisis can reveal resilience—or panic. A cyber intrusion can test protocols. A laser flash can demonstrate reach. Each action broadcasts capability while allowing the aggressor to retreat before escalation crosses a political threshold. These are not random aggressions; they are calibrated experiments in deterrence.

Yet escalation ladders are not ladders at all. They are scaffolds bolted to the psychology of state leaders. What one country interprets as a warning, another may see as a provocation. The very feature that makes reversible attacks attractive—their deniability—can also make them dangerously unpredictable. If a satellite vital to early warning systems goes dark, no general sleeps easily. Even if the cause was a benign malfunction, suspicion amplifies risk.

The world's most responsible space powers understand that restraint is a currency. Reversible attacks may be tolerated; irreversible ones are invitations to escalation on Earth. But restraint is not permanent. If one state believes its constellation is under systematic non-kinetic assault, the temptation to leap several rungs at once grows. A cyber campaign could be answered with a kinetic strike. A spoofing incident could provoke retaliation against ground infrastructure. Escalation ladders can be climbed—slowly or in a single furious step.

For that reason, satellites are increasingly designed to *ride out* the lower rungs. Hardened receivers, encrypted navigation corrections, automated fault detection, and manoeuvre capability help keep crises from boiling over. If a satellite shrugs off a jamming attempt, the attacker gains nothing by pushing harder. If a spoofing signal is detected and countered through cross-constellation verification, the space for miscalculation shrinks. The ladder remains, but it is harder to climb.

Still, the highest rung remains the most dangerous. A kinetic attack in orbit is not only an act of war; it is a vandalism of the commons. The debris it creates does not recognise borders or politics. It crosses orbits, threatens neutrals, and multiplies risk for decades. The attacker signals strength, but also recklessness. Even allies will take note. That is why some of the most ambitious defence doctrines now define kinetic anti-satellite attacks as triggers for terrestrial retaliation. Destroy a satellite, and you may invite consequences on the ground.

This is the uniquely perilous logic of space: a domain where reversible acts speak loudly, and irreversible ones echo for generations. States will continue to probe, to jam, to blind, to hack—not because those actions break satellites, but because they shape psychology. A silent spacecraft becomes a strategic conversation, argued in signals and shadows.

And the question that haunts every strategist remains unanswered: when the next satellite goes dark, will the world wait for an explanation, or will someone climb the ladder at speed?

Chapter 6

Law Above the Line

The first image of Earth from space—cloud-white, ocean-blue, borderless—gave humanity a new vantage point. It suggested a shared planet, small and fragile, watched from a domain where no flag waved and no soldier stood. In the decades that followed, diplomats wrote that ideal into treaties: space would be peaceful, open to all, and owned by none. The imagination of the age was confident. If we could send men to the Moon, surely we could keep the heavens pure.

The world kept the photograph. The purity proved harder to defend.

Satellites became strategic assets. Orbits became crowded. Commercial launch firms replaced superpower monopolies. And today, the most contested military front has no trenches, no trenches at all—just orbits that cannot be seized but can certainly be denied. The laws built for a Cold War duet now strain under a twenty-first century chorus: dozens of states, thousands of satellites, and corporations whose budgets exceed those of many governments.

The paradox is stark. International law proclaims that no nation may claim territory in space, yet every operational satellite occupies a slot that no one else may use. The same documents celebrate peaceful use, while militaries quietly depend on constellations for targeting, early warning, and command-and-control. The language of idealism sits beside the reality of force projection. The text has not changed, but everything else has.

Treaties set broad principles, not detailed rules, and ambiguity has become a kind of unspoken policy tool. States prefer wide legal grey zones because they enable flexibility. If the law does not explicitly forbid rehearsing an anti-satellite intercept, perhaps it is legal enough. If a commercial constellation provides encrypted communications to troops on the ground, does that make the firm a combatant? The answers are not written; they are inferred. In space, inference is as dangerous as intent.

Liability reveals the depth of the problem. On paper, a launching state is responsible for any damage its objects cause. Simple enough—until one asks who is to blame when attribution itself is uncertain. A satellite might malfunction. A ground station might receive forged commands. A collision might result from a manoeuvre based on falsified tracking data. Proving fault in a vacuum of evidence is harder than firing a missile. Diplomats know this. Strategists exploit it.

And while governments wrestle with doctrine, commercial actors now sit on the front line. They provide the eyes, ears, and infrastructure modern militaries cannot operate without. Yet private firms are not signatories to the treaties that govern the domain they serve. Their levers of compliance come from export controls, licensing regimes, and insurance markets. A company can legally operate a constellation that quietly reshapes warfare, so long as the correct paperwork is filed. Policy has never relied so heavily on paperwork.

The rise of commercial intelligence has made space law feel oddly inverted. Open-source analysts—students, journalists, small start-ups—use commercial imagery to track troop movements, naval deployments, and missile tests. They publish what governments once guarded. Small organisations now shape global narratives. The law was not written with them in mind, yet they are altering how attribution, escalation, and diplomacy unfold in real time.

In response, the most serious conversations in space governance have shifted away from treaty drafts and toward norms of behaviour: no-debris testing, responsible proximity operations, and transparency before manoeuvres. These rules are not signed in marble tablets. They survive because states benefit from them—or because insurers demand them. A constellation equipped with collision-avoidance thrusters is cheaper to insure. A satellite that can broadcast its intentions lowers risks for everyone sharing its orbit. Commerce is quietly becoming custodian of stability.

And so an odd, quiet truth has emerged: the laws of space may increasingly be written by underwriters. Premiums reward caution and punish recklessness. They turn debris mitigation from a moral appeal into a balance-sheet calculation. When sabotage, cyber compromise, or negligent disposal threatens payouts worth hundreds of millions, insurers demand better standards than any treaty negotiator could ever enforce.

This chapter examines the strange, evolving architecture of governance above the atmosphere: treaties that promise peace but contain loopholes large enough to navigate fleets through; liability regimes that falter in the fog of attribution; companies that find themselves dragged into geopolitical conflict through service contracts; norms that matter more than the number of signatures beneath them; and insurance markets that may ultimately do more to protect orbit than any declaration of ideals.

The laws of space are not celestial commandments. They are fragile, provisional, and profoundly human—shaped by ambition, fear, profit, and pride. They have kept conflict at bay so far, but the pressures are rising. Thousands of new satellites launch each year. Militaries rehearse attacks. Commercial networks become instruments of power.

If the next dispute is fought not with missiles but with terms of service, licence revocations, or the quiet withdrawal of coverage, will anyone notice when the law bends—or when it breaks?

Treaties and gaps

The most famous legal promise about space was drafted with the optimism of a new age: the heavens belonged to everyone and to no one, a shared frontier free from conquest. The declaration sounded definitive—no state could seize celestial territory, no orbit could be claimed as sovereign ground. Yet, as satellites multiplied and military dependency grew, the same legal framework was quietly stretched, interpreted, and outmanoeuvred. Space was to be peaceful, but peace turned out to be a negotiable concept.

Consider the paradox etched into daily operations. States cannot own space, but they reserve orbital slots for themselves through international coordination, securing positions that no rival may occupy. The paperwork grants exclusivity without calling it ownership. A nation may not plant a flag on a lunar plain, but it can operate constellations that shape global communications, weapons guidance, and intelligence flows. The difference between control and sovereignty is largely semantic—and powerful states are fluent in semantics.

The earliest agreements assumed that the greatest threat in space was colonialism: land grabs, territorial claims, annexation of moons or asteroids. They did not anticipate that the real struggle would be functional rather than territorial: who controls the infrastructure, who defines the rules of access, and who decides what counts as peaceful when every satellite carries dual-use potential. The treaties condemn weapons in space, yet they remain silent on satellites that provide targeting coordinates, or radars that warn of missile launches, or robotic craft able to approach foreign satellites under the banner of "inspection".

Military realities developed faster than legal vocabulary. Peaceful purpose, once a moral line, has become a rhetorical shield. If a satellite relays encrypted command signals to troops, is it a civilian asset used for military support—or a military asset posing as civilian? Governments rarely answer such questions. They prefer ambiguity, because ambiguity buys freedom.

Even the most revered principle—non-appropriation of celestial bodies—contains an invisible footnote. If space cannot be owned, how can states reserve exclusive communication frequencies, orbital inclinations, and geostationary positions? The answer lies in regulatory mechanisms that behave like property rights while denying that they are property. The silence of a treaty becomes a loophole; a loophole becomes policy.

This legal grey zone scales effortlessly to geopolitics. When a satellite is nudged into a new orbit, perhaps to inspect a neighbour, the manoeuvre can be framed as routine, scientific, even cooperative. But every operator knows the uncomfortable truth: proximity can be reconnaissance, rehearsal, or warning. If the law does not forbid it, states judge legality by precedent and by power. Space becomes governed not by prohibitions, but by tolerance thresholds.

The challenge deepens when actors proliferate. The original treaties imagined a world of superpowers. The modern orbital economy is a crowd. Private companies design, launch, and operate constellations that rival national inventories. Universities build microsatellites. Start-ups provide imagery more frequently than governments ever managed. Treaties that speak in terms of "states" now struggle with players who are not states at all.

Commercial operators stand at an awkward intersection. A firm may lease bandwidth to a defence ministry while being headquartered in a neutral country. A constellation might downlink weather data for farmers and high-resolution imagery for intelligence agencies. Export controls try to police ethics with licensing forms and compliance manuals. But the distinction between civilian and military utility is not technical; it is contextual. A sensor that spots wildfires can just as easily track tank columns. In space, dual-use is not the exception—it is the default.

The result is a regime of words that mean less than they appear to. Peaceful intent is subjective. Ownership is disguised under coordination.

Transparency is voluntary. And gaps—those empty spaces between definitions—become strategic breathing room.

States exploit those gaps knowingly. Some test anti-satellite weapons but insist they are merely validating interceptor reliability. Some deploy manoeuvrable craft that can dock, capture, or push another satellite, while claiming benign utility: debris removal, satellite servicing, orbital tutoring. Every new capability offers a civilian description and a military shadow. The law recognises only the description.

Yet the absence of strict rules is not random incompetence; it is partly design. Ambiguity enables states to act without openly violating commitments, to escalate without crossing declared red lines, and to signal power without admitting intent. A brittle treaty invites defection. A flexible one invites interpretation. Great powers prefer interpretation.

And so the gaps widen. A weapon in orbit is prohibited, but a weapon launched from the ground to strike an object in orbit is not explicitly named. A satellite cannot carry nuclear arms, but can it carry lasers that dazzle sensors, or cyber tools embedded in firmware? If a state destroys its own satellite with a missile, is that an internal matter—or an unacceptable creation of debris that threatens others? The text offers no firm position. Diplomats disagree politely. Militaries prepare regardless.

Even violation is hard to prove. When a satellite fails, operators must ask: was it aging hardware, accidental collision, spoofed commands, or a kinetic strike disguised as malfunction? Without evidence, there is no claim. Without a claim, there is no accountability. The law functions most effectively when nothing serious happens—an uncomfortable reality in an environment where serious events are becoming more likely.

Despite all this, the treaties still hold power. They define aspirations. They discourage the most dramatic provocations. They provide diplomatic vocabulary when tempers rise. But they are increasingly metaphors rather than mechanisms—statements of hope rather than systems of control. As actors multiply, orbits congest, and constellations become instruments of military strategy, principles alone cannot keep peace.

The irony is striking. We built laws to stop anyone owning space, but we never built laws to stop anyone dominating it. We declared space peaceful but did not define peace in a world of surveillance satellites and missile warning radars. We wrote treaties for a universe of nations, only to discover a universe of stakeholders.

What emerges is a legal architecture that looks solid from a distance but dissolves on contact with reality. It is not broken, yet it is insufficient. It is not obsolete, yet it is outpaced. If peace in orbit ever fails, it will be because everyone followed the rules as written—and interpreted them as they wished.

The gap between principle and practice is widening every year. One question now shadows every negotiation: is it better to rewrite the rules, or to cling to ambiguity because clarity would expose how fragile stability truly is?

Liability and attribution

When a satellite dies unexpectedly, the obituary is rarely straightforward. Operators pore over telemetry logs, radar tracks, and cryptic error flags, trying to decipher a cause. Was it a micrometeoroid? Ageing batteries? A careless orbital manoeuvre by a neighbour? Or something darker—a malicious signal, a quiet cyber intrusion, a spoofed command crafted to look legitimate? In space, everything leaves fingerprints, yet almost nothing leaves certainty. This is the central discomfort of orbital law: states are responsible for their satellites, but proof of fault is maddeningly hard to obtain.

The legal principle sounds simple enough. If a spacecraft owned by Country A damages one operated by Country B, Country A must compensate. The idea mirrors maritime and aviation norms, where liability sits with the flag on the hull or the registration painted on the fuselage. Space adapted the rule with admirable confidence. But ships and aircraft crash in environments full of witnesses, sensors, divers, and debris fields that can be retrieved and examined. Satellites collide in silence, hundreds of kilometres overhead, without a single human observer. Evidence arrives as radar reflections and orbital calculations, ambiguous telemetry, or the eerie cessation of a radio signal.

Imagine two satellites passing within a few kilometres of each other. An hour later, one suffers catastrophic failure. The surviving operator might deny any involvement, perhaps insisting its satellite merely drifted due to solar pressure or station-keeping thrusters. No wreckage can be collected. No cockpit voice recorder can be pulled from the seabed. The truth is mathematical inference and educated guesswork. Legal systems, however, are not built on guesswork.

Attribution becomes even stranger when interference is invisible. A kinetic strike produces debris flares and trackable fragments. Jamming, by contrast, can be turned on and off like a light. Spoofed commands can be routed through compromised terminals in other countries. Cyber tools can burrow into ground stations—far from the battlefield—leaving only signatures indistinguishable from corrupted memory or operator error. The more sophisticated the attack, the more it resembles an accident.

This uncertainty is not just an engineering problem. It is political leverage. If responsibility is unclear, culpability is negotiable. A state can quietly impede an adversary's satellite and deny everything, knowing that no tribunal can compel proof. Even if the victim is confident, it may hesitate to accuse, wary of escalating a conflict on the basis of circumstantial intelligence. In this grey zone, liability becomes a diplomatic bargaining chip rather than a legal endpoint.

Some governments respond by cataloguing every scrap of orbital behaviour. They track manoeuvres, intercept telemetry leaks, and fuse commercial observations with classified material. These intelligence dossiers allow them to assert, in private or public, that an adversary caused harm. Yet even perfect tracking cannot solve all puzzles. Consider coordinated interference: jammers aboard ships in international waters, relay stations in third countries, or spoofed packets routed through civilian ground networks. The trail bends through jurisdictions, allies, and unsuspecting intermediaries. Everyone is responsible; no one is responsible.

This difficulty matters because responsibility underpins deterrence. When states know they will be blamed—and billed—for damages, they tread carefully. When blame is murky, restraint weakens. It is easy to sabotage a satellite's uplink and pretend ignorance. It is harder to hide a missile launch that showers orbit with debris. Predictably, the most aggressive behaviour emerges not in the dramatic acts that everyone can see, but in the reversible disruptions no one can conclusively prove.

Liability also acts as financial ballast for space. Insurers study every collision, anomaly, and near miss. They adjust premiums based on perceived risks, nudging operators towards safer designs, onboard manoeuvring fuel, and collision avoidance software. Yet insurance contracts rely on something the orbital environment struggles to deliver: a clear understanding of causality. If a satellite fails but the reason cannot be determined, insurers may balk. Operators dispute. Lawyers argue about probability. Sometimes a settlement is reached without ever agreeing on what happened.

The emergence of private constellations compounds the puzzle. When a state owns and operates its satellites, responsibility is clear. When a private firm sells services to multiple nations, each with different regulations and national allegiances, responsibility splits across contracts and jurisdictions. A malfunctioning constellation operated by a company headquartered in Country A, licensed in Country B, launched from Country C, and providing data to Country D creates a web of accountability so tangled that liability almost dissolves. If something goes wrong, all four states may point in different directions.

The same fragmentation undermines attribution. A malicious command might originate from a hacked terminal in a neutral country, routed through commercial networks before reaching a ground station in yet another state. The owner of the ground station can plead ignorance. The neutral country can insist it knew nothing. The operator can claim the command was valid because the encryption keys matched. Every party can be technically correct, yet the attack still succeeds.

This is the uncomfortable reality: the space environment assumes that states can control what their satellites do. In practice, states struggle to control who accesses their ground stations, who packages their software, and who writes their firmware updates. A remote maintenance technician can inject a vulnerability without ever touching a satellite. A compromised subcontractor can install back doors in navigation software. In such cases, assigning blame becomes a philosophical exercise. Who is liable—the state, the company, the contractor, or the intruder who may never be found?

Attempts to improve attribution exist. Some nations deploy high-resolution space surveillance networks. Others propose mandatory beacon signals, transparency exchanges, or shared tracking portals. But states are reluctant to reveal capabilities that could limit freedom of manoeuvre. The very tools that would help prove responsibility—precise tracking, real-time telemetry-sharing, public logs of orbital manoeuvres—also expose intentions, operating patterns, and vulnerabilities.

Liability becomes a mirror for broader politics. Powerful spacefaring nations prefer ambiguity because it protects their room for covert action. Smaller nations prefer clarity because it protects them from intimidation. Commercial operators want predictable rules to secure investment, but not rules so strict they restrict business models. Everyone agrees in principle; almost no one agrees in detail.

Some propose no-debris pledges, binding operators to responsible behaviour. Others argue for a neutral investigative body that analyses orbital incidents and issues authoritative assessments. Yet even these solutions falter at the edge of national security. States will not allow foreign inspectors to examine encrypted telemetry or classified spacecraft architecture. They will not permit independent investigators to access sensitive radar tracks that could reveal surveillance range or sensor fidelity. Trust is scarce, and technical transparency threatens military advantage.

All the while, the stakes climb. More satellites mean more collisions. More dual-use missions mean more suspicion. More commercial actors mean more hands touching the machinery. And more geopolitical friction means more incentive to strike quietly.

Space law assumed a world where bad actors would be visible. It did not anticipate a world where disabling a satellite could look like component fatigue, harmless spoofing, or a software glitch. Nor did it imagine that responsibility would be so dispersed that liability itself could evaporate.

The most troubling question lingers at the edge of strategy: what happens when a major power decides that ambiguity is not a flaw, but a weapon? When disruption is deniable, retaliation must be cautious. When causality is uncertain, escalation slows. Deniability becomes deterrence. In the shadows of attribution, a new form of stability emerges—shaky, opportunistic, and dangerous.

Commercial actors in public fights

A satellite company once insisted it was neutral. Its job, executives said, was to beam data and bandwidth, nothing more. Then came a conflict half a world away. Governments leaned on the firm to prioritise military customers. Rival states demanded it restrict access. Civilian users complained of outages as capacity was repurposed for armed forces. Neutrality, it turned out, was a marketing slogan. In war, commercial space firms do not stand outside the battlefield; they become part of it.

This shift is not abstract. Constellations that serve farmers, freight managers, and remote villages can also provide targeting data, encrypted messaging, and resilient internet to troops under fire. A company handing over high-resolution imagery to a humanitarian mission may one week be assisting disaster relief, and the next be supporting precision strikes. Civil and military customers are now entangled within the same infrastructure. The boundary between public good and strategic asset has faded.

In theory, firms can choose whom they serve. In practice, national laws dictate the terms. Export control regimes decide which states may buy high-quality images or advanced satellite terminals. A company that disobeys risks sanctions, licence revocation, or even criminal charges. If a government orders prioritisation for national security, compliance is rarely optional. The marketplace yields to the state.

The logic extends beyond images. Broadband constellations can uplift or frustrate a war effort simply by deciding who has bandwidth. A region can be given high-capacity links, throttled to a crawl, or cut off entirely. These decisions are written into service agreements, terms of use, and technical geofencing policies. They are business choices with geopolitical consequences.

Commercial remote-sensing companies sit at an even sharper edge. Their imaging satellites can locate armour columns, naval groups, or airbases. Their ground stations can be tasked by governments in minutes. When they provide archive data, analysts can reconstruct months of troop movements. For intelligence agencies, commercial imagery is not a supplement; it is a pillar. For targeters, it is actionable. For adversaries, it is a threat.

That raises a profound question: when does a company become a participant in war? Some states argue that supplying imagery to a combatant makes the firm a legitimate target. Others insist that private companies are protected as civilian objects. Yet the services they provide—command links, navigation timing, reconnaissance—are indistinguishable from those supplied by national militaries. The law has opinions. Reality has gravity.

This tension plays out in strategy rooms. Defence ministries know commercial support is vital in a crisis. They sign contingency contracts to guarantee access. They quietly pressure firms to maintain service in contested regions. Some companies agree immediately—out of patriotism, fear, or pragmatic alignment with their host nation. Others resist, wary of losing customers in rival states or being dragged into geopolitical feuds.

Even data sharing has diplomatic weight. When a firm gives high-resolution imagery to one government, others wonder why they were excluded. A company that publishes maritime tracking of foreign submarines may win praise from one capital and condemnation from another. Seemingly technical decisions—what resolution to release, how often to refresh data, whether to blur sensitive facilities—become gestures of allegiance or provocation.

Money complicates everything. Commercial space firms rely on investment, contracts, and market access. A state can reward compliance with subsidies or launch deals. Non-compliance can be punished by blocking access to ground stations, withholding licences, or banning terminals. Few companies can stand against a sovereign with regulatory and financial leverage. The notion of corporate autonomy shrinks under political pressure.

Moreover, space firms increasingly depend on global supply chains. They purchase antennas from one country, optical sensors from another, encryption chips from a third. Any node in that chain can be used as a choke point. Governments know this. Export controls may stop a rival buying high-performance sensors. Sanctions can freeze a firm's access to cloud infrastructure. When militaries depend on commercial satellites, geopolitics enters the bill of materials.

Firms also face scrutiny from the public. If a constellation keeps the internet alive for civilians in a war zone, the company may be cheered. If it cuts coverage after state pressure, it may be accused of aiding aggression. Shareholders care about both brand reputation and regulatory goodwill. Boards must navigate ethics, law, and markets—three forces rarely aligned.

As the private sector grows, so does its bargaining power. Some firms have enough satellites, bandwidth, and customer base to push back against governments. They can negotiate terms or delay decisions, knowing states need them. This is a new kind of power: geopolitical leverage held not by nations but by network operators, imagery providers, and launch companies.

But power invites scrutiny. Intelligence agencies now monitor not just foreign militaries but private constellations that could tilt a conflict. Rivals may seek to hack or jam a commercial network to blind an adversary's forces. The battlefield has gone corporate.

The legal frameworks lag behind. International law was written for states, not firms. It assigns responsibilities to flag nations, not shareholders. When commercial actors are asked to restrict data, prioritise bandwidth, or shut down terminals in a region, there are few global guardrails. Instead, decisions are shaped by licences, export rules, and informal agreements between governments and boards.

This creates a quiet asymmetric advantage. Nations with powerful space companies can exert influence abroad without firing a shot. They can deny imagery to an adversary, throttle internet to a militia, or surge capacity to an ally. Those without strong domestic providers must plead, pay, or pressure foreign firms for access. Power shifts from launch pads to contract clauses.

The most unsettling part is that these choices are made behind login pages and boardroom doors. Terms of service can be updated overnight. A firmware patch can turn a terminal off in one country and on in another. No parliament debates it. No treaty governs it. Yet thousands of people on the ground may feel the result.

Commercial firms now occupy a strange dual identity: private companies with public consequences. They claim neutrality, yet their services decide who sees, who communicates, who navigates, and who fights blind. They sell bandwidth and gigabytes, but in the field those become lifelines.

And the world has barely begun to contend with the implications. What happens when a company refuses a government request during a conflict? What if it complies with one and alienates another? What if a state insists on backdoors to enforce export controls, and a rival state retaliates? The private sector could become a proxy battleground long before weapons are fired.

The more satellites fill the sky, the more this tension tightens. Commercial space is no longer an observer of geopolitics. It is one of its primary agents. The architecture of orbit is being written in contracts as much as in treaties, and those contracts are written faster. The question is no longer whether firms will shape conflicts, but how—and at whose command.

Norms over numbers

When two satellites drift towards each other in low Earth orbit, there is no police patrol to intervene, no orbiting judge to issue orders. There is only physics, probability, and the willingness of operators to act responsibly. Sometimes a brief e-mail is enough to avert disaster: an operator warns another of a predicted conjunction, manoeuvres are agreed, crisis fades. Other times, silence. No response. No intent to move. In the void above, courtesy becomes a form of collective self-preservation.

The most telling thing about space safety today is what is not written down. Treaties describe broad principles of peaceful use, but they do not dictate how close a spacecraft should approach another. They prohibit harmful interference, yet leave room for tests that spray debris across the orbital neighbourhood. And while regulators count satellites, filing requirements and licensing burdens do not answer the deeper question: how should actors behave?

Technical capacity allows mischief. A satellite can manoeuvre within a few kilometres of a rival's asset without colliding, but the message is unmistakable. Operators interpret proximity as surveillance, intimidation, or rehearsal for more aggressive acts. Without norms, every shadowing manoeuvre becomes a political statement.

The emerging answer is behavioural rules—restraints that bind because breaking them imposes reputational and strategic damage. A state that destroys a satellite in orbit and leaves thousands of fragments is publicly shamed, not for violating a perfect treaty clause, but for poisoning the commons. The punishment is diplomatic cost and long-term self-harm, as its own future spacecraft must now sail through the debris field it created.

No-debris testing has become the litmus test of responsibility. Militaries seek to demonstrate capability, but global pressure pushes them to do so without scattering shrapnel across orbital lanes. If they must disable a satellite, they are nudged towards non-destructive methods: cyber compromise, jamming, spoofing. Kinetic explosions invite weeks of condemnation and years of tracking fragments. States have started signalling their restraint, publishing statements that they will not conduct debris-generating tests. Their credibility rests not on the perfection of their words, but on the consistency of their actions.

Proximity operations demand even finer judgement. A spy satellite edging near a communications relay can be explained as research, calibration, or harmless curiosity. Yet when the approach is close and repeated, intent speaks louder than language. Norms begin to form through practice: operators notify each other before rendezvous, keep a respectful buffer, and limit manoeuvres that could be mistaken for a co-orbital attack. These are unwritten rules, but they help prevent a nervous ground controller misreading a docking rehearsal as the start of a disabling strike.

Transparency serves as the scaffolding of good behaviour. When a constellation publishes its ephemeris, announces manoeuvres, or alerts neighbours of a close pass, it lowers suspicion. When it hides movements, the opposite occurs. Silence can be interpreted as deception. In space, uncertainty is a weapon. Norms try to blunt its edge.

Commercial actors have discovered that transparency protects balance sheets. Insurers prefer operators who share orbital data and install collision-avoidance autonomy. Markets reward companies that avoid risky practices.

Investors would rather back a constellation praised for responsible conduct than one blacklisted by regulators or threatened with litigation after a near-miss. In this way, norms become economic gravity, pulling firms towards safer habits.

Even adversaries rely on common standards. Rival states exchange conjunction data to avoid accidental collisions that could trigger diplomatic crises. Space command centres sometimes coordinate with competitors to minimise the likelihood of dangerous manoeuvres. It is a quiet acknowledgement that mutual vulnerability breeds cooperation. If a foreign satellite tumbles into yours because nobody picked up the phone, both sides lose.

But norms are fragile. A state under pressure may choose demonstration over restraint, detonating a target to make a point. A covert actor may shadow a satellite, hoping to map its capabilities before slipping away. When norms crack, escalation beckons. A supposedly harmless test can be interpreted as hostile rehearsal. Trust evaporates, and future manoeuvres are read through a darker lens.

Some analysts argue that norms are too soft—that without binding treaties, irresponsible actors will exploit loopholes. Others counter that rigid rules risk freezing innovation and ignoring the fluid realities of orbital life. Behavioural norms occupy the middle ground: flexible enough to adapt to new technology, firm enough to create predictable expectations.

This debate touches a deeper truth. Space is not governed by statute alone; it is governed by reputation. A state that repeatedly violates expectations—fails to notify, conducts reckless approaches, or litters the heavens with fragments—may find future partnerships drying up. Its commercial firms could lose contracts, its launch providers could face restrictions, its satellites could be shadowed in response. The costs are cumulative.

For newer spacefaring nations, norms are a path to legitimacy. They publish debris mitigation plans, adopt open data sharing, and participate in crisis coordination. By behaving well, they earn trust and access to shared infrastructure. Good neighbours are welcome in crowded orbits.

The most intriguing development is the rise of consensus statements. Coalitions of states and private firms are beginning to articulate shared expectations: no destructive testing, timely notifications before close approaches, transparency in ephemeris, rapid deorbiting of defunct spacecraft. These are not laws, but social contracts. If enough actors sign on, violators become outliers.

Yet every rule invites the question: who enforces it? There is no orbital tribunal, no sheriff. Enforcement comes from naming and shaming, from diplomatic demarches, from sanctions that restrict market access or technology transfer. Sometimes the punishment is physics itself: debris does not discriminate between flags.

Behaviour-based rules offer one final advantage: they highlight intent. A manoeuvre accompanied by notification looks like calibration. A silent approach looks like a threat. States that prize stability prefer the former. States seeking ambiguity may choose the latter. Norms illuminate choices that were once murky.

Still, space is young, and its culture of restraint remains experimental. A single reckless test can undo years of careful diplomacy. A stealthy spacecraft can humiliate a rival by approaching unnoticed. Operators must decide whether secrecy is worth the strategic cost.

Norms over numbers speaks to a mindset shift. Counting satellites or licensing launches will not make orbit safer. What matters is how actors behave: whether they warn, whether they coordinate, whether they avoid turning the sky into a scrapyard of their own making. The rules will not be signed in marble. They will be etched into practice, reaction, and precedent.

And the real test has yet to come. When tensions rise, when a state feels cornered, will restraint hold? Or will the temptation to send a message override the unwritten agreements that keep orbits navigable? The answer will determine whether the spacefaring world learns to share the sky—or risks losing it.

Insurance and pricing risk

It is a strange sort of underwriter who must price the dangers of orbit. Lloyd's of London can count shipwrecks and model storms; car insurers can quantify collisions on a motorway. But a brokerage tasked with insuring a satellite must reckon with debris the size of paint flecks travelling faster than rifle rounds, unpredictable solar weather, and neighbours who may be polite today and reckless tomorrow. Space insurance sounds like science fiction, yet it has quietly become a hidden regulator—shaping how missions are designed, launched, and retired.

The paradox is simple enough: insurers do not launch rockets, yet they influence which rockets fly. They do not write space law, yet they punish spacecraft that ignore good practice. When premiums rise, business models buckle. When insurers reward safer behaviour, fleets evolve.

Spacefaring nations have discovered that the most persuasive nudge towards responsibility may not be an international treaty or a diplomatic reprimand, but a stern letter from an insurer reviewing loss probabilities.

Underwriters ask unwelcome questions. Has the satellite got propulsion for collision avoidance? Are its thrusters reliable? How long before it deorbits? What tracking data will the operator share? Insurance is a mirror reflecting the consequences of design decisions. A spacecraft built cheap and launched dirty will find its premium swollen; one built with fault tolerance and autonomy may receive a discount. Through these quiet incentives, insurers push space actors to adopt mature habits well before regulators intervene.

Consider collision-avoidance capability. A decade ago, it was a luxury. Now it is nearly mandatory for anything launched into busy orbital shells. Propellant adds cost and weight, but insurers have begun offering lower premiums for satellites capable of manoeuvring around debris and coordinating with traffic alerts. The business logic is ruthless: collisions produce claims, and claims eat profit. Safer spacecraft reduce the likelihood of catastrophic loss, and so insurers price accordingly. The invisible hand of the market becomes a stabilising force in the digital sky.

The same logic applies to deorbiting plans. Once, a failed satellite could simply be left to drift, a long-term hazard. Now, uncontrolled hulks threaten dense constellations and raise insurance claims for nearby operators. Underwriters reward missions that guarantee clean retirement, whether through drag sails, propulsion reserves, or low perigees that hasten atmospheric burn-up. A constellation that promises to remove its dead satellites quickly can secure better rates and easier financing. Investors like predictability, and nothing ruins predictability quite like a billion-pound collision.

Launch risk is another battleground. Rockets fail. Payload fairings jam. Second stages misfire. Insurers study failure logs with forensic obsession. A launcher with a string of perfect flights might win lower premiums, but one catastrophic failure can stain its pricing for years. Some insurers insist on independent audits of manufacturing quality; others demand design redundancy. The effect is subtle but profound: launch providers internalise the cost of risk. If they want to keep premiums competitive, they must demonstrate reliability not through marketing presentations but through engineering choices.

Even orbital neighbourhood matters. An operator deploying satellites in a crowded shell faces higher premiums than one flying in a quieter band. The risk is statistical: more objects mean more potential conjunctions. By making congestion expensive, insurers create an incentive to spread deployments or invest in better tracking. It is a rare example of a market tool nudging collective behaviour in the right direction.

There is a deeper philosophical question beneath the spreadsheets. When insurance dictates design, who really governs space? A private syndicate in London or New York can punish a state-backed operator more effectively than a distant treaty body. If a country launches a reckless anti-satellite test and showers orbit with debris, insurers react instantly: premiums rise across the board, launch contracts are renegotiated, capital becomes cautious. The debris creator may face no formal sanctions, but its partners pay the bill. Space becomes pricier for everyone. The market remembers what diplomacy forgets.

Of course, insurance is imperfect. Underwriters rely on data, and orbital data is messy. Space is vast, tracking is inconsistent, and attribution of failure is often contested. Did that satellite die because of a hardware fault or an untracked fragment? Did a manoeuvre fail due to poor design or an unexpected solar flare? Insurers sometimes face claims built on probabilities rather than certainties. They respond by demanding transparency, telemetry sharing, and incident reporting. Secrecy becomes expensive; openness becomes profitable.

This creates tension with military missions, where secrecy is currency. A government launching classified payloads may accept higher premiums rather than reveal sensitive telemetry. Commercial constellations, by contrast, often embrace openness to save costs and reassure investors. The result is a split culture: opaque defence satellites in high-risk insurance brackets, transparent commercial fleets enjoying cheaper rates. In space as on Earth, secrecy has a price.

There is also a moral tension. Insurance spreads risk, but in space, risk is shared with innocents. A collision in low orbit does not just destroy one satellite; it endangers others for years. Should insurers compensate the victims of debris? Should premiums reflect the collective harm caused by irresponsible actors? Some in the industry argue for differential pricing that punishes reckless missions not just in cost but in coverage exclusions. Others worry that too much punishment could drive operators to self-insure, evading the market's disciplining effect entirely.

Yet despite imperfections, insurance has become a quiet architect of restraint. Launch providers invest in quality control because a single failure can raise premiums across their customer base. Operators add propulsion and redundancy not just for engineering pride, but because risk pricing demands it. Start-ups designing constellations learn early that venture capital prefers insurable missions. An uninsurable satellite is a business model without a parachute.

The most intriguing shift is the arrival of usage-based insurance. Instead of static premiums, operators are offered dynamic pricing tied to behaviour: share high-quality orbital data, avoid congested lanes, perform timely manoeuvres, and premiums fall. Ignore alerts, allow spacecraft to drift, and the bill rises. This is actuarial carrots and sticks applied to orbital traffic. It rewards good citizens and pressures laggards without a single regulation being passed.

Will insurance become the de facto regulator of space? Perhaps not. But it already functions as a steadying force at a time when governance lags technology. Where treaties are vague and supervision weak, insurers bring pragmatic arithmetic. They make the intangible risks of orbit painfully concrete. A careless operator pays more. A careful one pays less. No grand speeches, no diplomatic wrangling—just invoices.

But the next decade will test this quiet system. What happens when mega-constellations multiply faster than actuarial models can adapt? How will underwriters price risks of thousands of manoeuvring spacecraft using autonomous collision avoidance? And can insurers keep pace if geopolitical tensions drive more covert operations that avoid telemetry sharing altogether?

There is a final irony. Insurance is supposed to make loss bearable. Yet in space, its true value may be the opposite: making loss too expensive to tolerate. If that cost deters destructive tests, encourages responsible design, and pushes operators to clean up after themselves, then the underwriters of the 21st century may become unlikely stewards of the orbital commons.

The question remains: will the cold logic of premiums succeed where diplomacy hesitated? Or will the market's grip slip as the skies grow crowded and the risks compound, leaving responsibility once again a matter of trust and goodwill?

Chapter 7

Commanding from Orbit

The first time a battalion commander in a desert tent received satellite imagery less than five minutes after asking for it, the room fell silent. The maps were not grainy prints flown in by courier, nor low-resolution sketches passed through layers of bureaucracy. They were crisp, tagged, and timestamped, showing tyre tracks that did not exist a quarter of an hour before. A few clicks later, an artillery battery was retasked, and a convoy took a different road. No rockets were launched from space, no laser beams descended from the heavens. Yet orbit had just rewritten how a battlefield was run.

For most of history, commanders fought with what they could see or what scouts could survive to tell them. Orbit broke that rule. Satellites became witnesses who never sleep, cartographers who redraw maps every morning, and messengers who carry orders across oceans faster than any aircraft can fly. The paradox is that this enormous distance—hundreds of kilometres above the Earth—now feels closer than the next valley. Orbit has become a command post.

But commanding from orbit is not as simple as sending data down and orders up. Militaries have learned that satellites must be organised like fleets, that ground stations must survive attack, and that control signals must endure jamming, cyber intrusion, and deceit. Command and control from space is not merely a technical puzzle; it is a philosophical shift. Authority, decision-making, and situational awareness no longer reside solely on the ground. They circulate continuously between humans, algorithms, and machines in orbit.

Much of this transformation begins with structure. When countries first placed military payloads in space, they treated them as specialised outposts reporting back to air forces or intelligence agencies. Now, the most advanced militaries maintain dedicated space commands, staffed with officers fluent in orbital mechanics, electromagnetic propagation, and mission planning. They sit alongside air, sea, land, and cyber leaders, tasked with integrating orbital effects into everything from humanitarian relief to nuclear deterrence. In joint operations centres, targeting cells fuse space-derived intelligence with drone feeds and radar tracks, collapsing the time between detection and decision.

Space order of battle is no longer abstract. It is visible in the way ground generals request satellite cues the way they once requested artillery. It is visible in how naval commanders expect secure satellite links for ships at sea, and in how fighter pilots download targeting updates through protected satellite channels mid-flight. Orbit is not a supporting theatre; it is part of the combat system itself.

Yet beneath this sophistication lies fragility. Command and control in space depends on an unbroken thread of communications between satellites and ground nodes. That thread can be cut. Jamming can drown uplinks in noise. Spoofing can send false commands. Cyber intrusions can claw their way into mission systems. The response has been a burst of ingenuity: satellites now cross-link with each other so that control can hop between them, bypassing compromised ground pathways. Some constellations route commands through multiple beams, frequencies, or encryption schemes, turning interference into mere inconvenience. Ground stations disperse across continents; mobile terminals hide in trucks or aircraft, ready to restore links after a single strike.

These measures hint at a new philosophy: resilience at the edge. Militaries have discovered that a centralised network is a brittle network. So they scatter nodes, harden antennas, and teach field units to operate fly-away terminals that can set up control in a clearing or on a rooftop. A satellite constellation does not go dark just because one bunker loses power. Control can be rebuilt from fragments.

This resilience is vital because targeting cycles have changed. In the past, gathering imagery, interpreting it, and planning a mission could take days. Now, a commercial synthetic aperture radar satellite can be tasked, imaged, and downlinked within hours—or minutes if priority is assigned. Data is piped directly into fusion cells that combine it with signals intelligence, optical imagery, and drone video. The loop tightens. The shooter—whether a missile battery, aircraft, or special forces team—receives actionable coordinates guided by sensors orbiting hundreds of kilometres overhead. The commander does not wait for the weather to clear or scouts to report back. Space provides options almost in real time.

Commercial companies are now embedded in this chain. Their satellites are bought like subscriptions, queued with priority flags, and tasked for time-sensitive targets. Some governments have learned that the fastest way to understand a battlefield is not to wait for a military satellite to pass overhead, but to pay for a commercial slot and have it in twenty minutes. It is outsourcing, but strategic. The speed of orbit becomes a competitive advantage.

Still, command from orbit is only as good as the people trained to wield it. Militaries now run space wargames that test how to fight without GPS, how to re-route communications when a satellite is blinded, and how to operate when timing signals are corrupted. Red-team hackers practise breaking into satellite control software; blue teams learn to recover, defend, and deceive. Pilots train with simulated blackout zones. Naval crews drill manual navigation. A modern commander must assume that one day space will be contested, and command will depend on invention under pressure.

Doctrine, once written for map tables and radio nets, now includes orbital playbooks. When a sensor spots a missile battery, who is allowed to retask the satellite? When an adversary jams a command link, who authorises cross-linking or manoeuvre? When commercial imagery reveals troop movements to the whole world, how does a commander adapt? Every answer involves space.

The stakes are larger than a single battle. Commanding from orbit offers a form of global presence without global bases. A nation with satellites and resilient control links can monitor borders, coordinate allies, and project influence over oceans and deserts without ever placing a soldier abroad. But this power also brings vulnerability. Lose control of satellites, and a modern military loses navigation, communications, weather forecasting, missile warning, and targeting. In even a modest conflict, that would be paralysis.

The greatest paradox is that orbit promises omniscience, yet it demands humility. No system, however well engineered, is immune to disruption. A commander who assumes uninterrupted data flow risks complacency. Those who train for outages, deception, and loss of timing have a better chance of thinking clearly when screens go blank.

This chapter uncovers how militaries are learning to command from a place they cannot touch, fill command posts that float above cloud and border, and trust machines they may never see. It traces how doctrine evolves when the high ground is literal, how communications adapt when adversaries fight in silence, and how commanders learn to wage war with ghosts of metal reflecting sunlight far above the Earth.

The deeper question lingers: if orbit becomes command's new heart, what happens when it falters? Who leads when control signals fall quiet, sensors blind, and the silent allies in the sky no longer answer?

Space order of battle

When a Russian satellite began shadowing a commercial communications platform in geostationary orbit, analysts at multiple operations centres noticed something odd. Its trajectory placed it uncomfortably close to antennas serving allied militaries in the Middle East. The intruder slowed, drifted, adjusted attitude, and matched the target's orbital slot. Nothing exploded, no weapon fired. Yet within days, a coalition of air and naval units had changed communications plans, redirected traffic through alternative satellites, and deployed mobile terminals to forward bases. Orders flowed, aircraft flew, ships manoeuvred—all because a spacecraft hundreds of kilometres above the equator had crept too close. The episode never made headlines, but it revealed a simple truth: the space domain already has an order of battle, and militaries are learning to fight within it.

For much of the twentieth century, space was a technical back-office—remote sensing for intelligence agencies, encrypted links for heads of state, weather forecasts for pilots. The notion of *space forces* sounded like science fiction. Yet today, most advanced militaries operate distinct space commands, organised not as support bureaus but as combat arms. Their remit spans intelligence, navigation, communications, missile warning, space control, and the defence of orbital infrastructure. In war rooms where admirals and air marshals once dominated, space officers now sit as peers, not guests.

This institutional shift did not arise from ambition but from necessity. Modern military operations depend on satellites so thoroughly that no service, however powerful, can fight effectively without them. A naval destroyer needs satellite links for beyond-horizon targeting. An armoured brigade requires real-time positioning and blue-force tracking. An air force relies on orbital weather feeds to plan sorties and precision navigation to deliver munitions. Space is not a boutique capability; it is the scaffolding of modern command.

The first task of a space order of battle is simply to make this dependence visible. In joint operations centres, screens once reserved for air sorties now show orbital tracks. Liaison officers translate spacecraft telemetry into operational decisions: *this satellite's coverage window closes in eight minutes; shift surveillance to the next pass.* Behind them sit planners responsible for protecting the constellation—avoiding collisions, responding to anti-satellite threats, and coordinating manoeuvres. The lexicon of battle is expanding: orbits are theatres, conjunctions are hazards, and lasers are weapons without smoke.

An integrated order of battle goes well beyond monitoring. The most capable militaries treat satellites as manoeuvring assets—not fixed stars, but units that can be tasked, repositioned, and cross-linked. When a theatre commander needs synthetic aperture radar coverage of an emerging threat, a space cell evaluates which satellites can tilt or adjust orbit to capture it. If a communications link is jammed, the cell reroutes traffic through alternate constellations or switches frequencies. The logic is identical to redirecting an aircraft or repositioning artillery, but the units act silently and without airfields.

This orchestration—the fusion of orbital effects with land, sea, air, and cyber—is transforming joint warfare. A fighter pilot in contested airspace no longer waits for a distant headquarters to confirm targeting. Instead, satellites detect a missile battery, downlink coordinates to a ground fusion cell, which validates them using drone imagery and dispatches updates through protected satellite communications directly to the cockpit. The pilot's display changes in seconds. The line between sensor and shooter collapses.

Perhaps the most underrated component of the space order of battle is the joint targeting cell—small teams where orbital specialists collaborate with cyber analysts, naval intelligence officers, artillery planners, and air controllers. Their craft is not launching rockets but matching global sensors to local needs. They decide which satellite will map flood zones after a cyclone, which will monitor a convoy at night, and which can be temporarily loaned to a partner nation during a crisis. These cells blend commercial and military assets in ways that challenge old doctrine: a private Earth-observation firm may deliver imagery faster than a government satellite, and a foreign ally may have better weather coverage of a battlefield than any domestic asset. Power lies with those who can choreograph the full orchestra, not merely play their own instrument.

Still, the order of battle in space differs from the air or sea in one important respect: there is no front line. Satellites owned by rival states cross paths peacefully every day. Orbits intersect, sensors stare at each other, and payloads collect data over cities and oceans alike. In such a world, deterrence looks strange. A spacecraft that approaches too closely to another may be probing, shadowing, spying—or simply drifting. Intent is hard to judge. Space commands, therefore, develop playbooks that mirror submarine operations: track silently, analyse patterns, assign probabilities, and prepare responses that may never be acknowledged.

This ambiguity makes integration with cyber forces indispensable. A satellite's anatomy is partly physical and partly digital. Its survival depends on encryption, command authentication, ground-station security, and hardened networks. Some militaries embed cyber units within space commands, treating jamming, spoofing, and intrusion attempts as battles in their own right. A compromised satellite may not explode visibly; it may simply drift a few degrees off course, misreport weather data, or deliver corrupted timing signals. In a precision-dependent battlefield, such subtle sabotage can be as damaging as a missile.

Land forces feel this convergence most acutely. Infantry platoons carry satellite radios for beyond-line-of-sight communications; artillery batteries depend on GPS-guided shells; logistics units coordinate convoys with satellite tracking. For them, the space domain is not distant but intimate. A space command officer sitting continents away can influence whether a dismounted squad receives a warning of improvised explosives ahead, or whether a drone finds a wounded soldier in darkness. When adversaries jam positioning signals, ground commanders request alternatives: inertial navigation updates from satellites, timing corrections from protected services, or even tasking of commercial beacons.

Naval integration is older but becoming more complex. Ships now rely on constellations that link surface vessels, submarines, and maritime patrol aircraft. Anti-ship missiles use satellite guidance. Ballistic missile defence at sea depends on space-based early warning. Navy officers in joint cells think in seconds: if a satellite detects a launch, which ship can intercept? If a carrier group sails into a communications blackout, can a satellite relay its targeting data through cross-links without touching vulnerable ground stations?

Air forces, meanwhile, depend on space for precision timing, route planning, and sensor fusion. A stealth aircraft avoiding radar may still rely on a satellite-borne infrared system to detect missile launches. Tankers coordinating mid-air refuelling use satellite links to orchestrate complex choreography. When a space asset fails, sorties must divert, loiter, or cancel. Thus air commands embed space liaisons who ensure orbital effects are baked into daily flight plans.

And above all domains sits the logic of missile warning. Space commands run constellations that detect launches, track trajectories, and cue interceptors. Here, integration is existential: a warning that arrives thirty seconds late may cost thousands of lives. Joint doctrine now drills seamless data sharing between satellites, radars, airborne sensors, and cyber analysis platforms. A space order of battle is therefore not only about enabling combat but preventing catastrophe.

Yet, despite institutional progress, tensions persist. One school of thought argues that space forces should remain a supporting element, quietly ensuring the rest of the military fights efficiently. Another insists that space is now a separate theatre requiring independent doctrine, service culture, and strategic planning. The debate is not semantic; it determines budgets, training pipelines, and the authority of commanders during crises. A fully independent space service may prioritise orbital resilience over tactical support to ground units. A subordinate space command may lack the autonomy to respond quickly to threats. Nations are still experimenting.

The integration challenge grows sharper as commercial firms join the battlespace. Militaries now rely on privately owned communications and Earth-observation constellations that obey business models, not orders. A joint targeting cell may use commercial synthetic aperture radar to find a mobile missile launcher, but that imagery passes through civilian ground stations and cloud servers. State actors cannot simply commandeer these services without legal and diplomatic repercussions. Space commands therefore maintain contracts, priority agreements, and contingency frameworks to ensure access during conflict. The order of battle is not purely uniformed anymore; it is an uneasy partnership.

The reliance on allied constellations adds another layer of complexity. A coalition fighting far from home may depend on a partner nation's satellite for reconnaissance. That dependency carries risk: political shifts, export controls, or operational disagreements can jeopardise access. In this sense, space commands must practise diplomacy as much as strategy. They run liaison teams, standardise formats, and create joint tasking procedures that allow multi-national forces to share orbital data securely without compromising secrets.

A sophisticated order of battle also demands readiness for loss. Satellites age, malfunction, or face hostile action. Militaries incorporate rapid launch, on-orbit spares, and shuffle plans to compensate for gaps. Just as air wings maintain reserve aircraft, space commands maintain replacement spacecraft—now often small satellites that can be lofted quickly on commercial rockets. Resilience is no longer optional; it is doctrine.

Training is where this doctrine becomes human. Space officers attend war colleges, not just engineering campuses. They wargame scenarios where timing signals are corrupted, where imagery is delayed, where a co-orbital threat stalks a critical satellite. They learn from pilots, submarine captains, and cyber specialists. In turn, those colleagues learn how orbital assets can rescue a failing mission or fail without warning. Jointness becomes cultural, not merely procedural.

At its heart, the space order of battle is about perception and control. Nations that can see the battlefield from orbit, communicate through resilient links, and connect those signals to ships, soldiers, aircraft, and digital defences enjoy a formidable advantage. They shorten reaction times, multiply force, and blunt surprise. They can project power without escalation, gather intelligence without overflight, and coordinate allies across oceans.

Yet this advantage is fragile. A constellation is not armour-plated. It is a web of radio waves, processors, solar panels, and trust. A clever adversary does not need to blow anything up; it can interfere, confuse, dazzle, deny, or impersonate. If a commander relies too completely on orbit, they risk paralysis the moment silence descends.

That tension drives experimentation. Some militaries push towards distributed constellations—hundreds of small satellites difficult to target. Others focus on hardened spacecraft with powerful cybersecurity and manoeuvre margins. Some emphasise autonomy in orbit, allowing satellites to reconfigure or self-heal under duress. Others invest in space-to-space communications that bypass vulnerable ground infrastructure. These choices shape the emerging order of battle as surely as fleet composition shaped naval power.

The more satellites matter, the more tempting it becomes to threaten them. Thus a final paradox: building an order of battle in space invites competition, even conflict. Militaries hope that showing competence will deter attack, yet offensive capabilities grow in parallel. The officers who plan orbital operations know that the next crisis may be silent, anonymous, and quick—a manoeuvre too close for comfort, a burst of interference, a cyber breach. They prepare quietly for a domain where escalation may be hard to read and harder to reverse.

What does it mean to command forces that orbit above borders, visible to all yet belonging to one? How do states maintain stability in a domain where every movement can be interpreted as threat or routine? The answers are still forming in the minds of the people who sit in those joint cells, watching dots glide across screens—silent, fragile, and decisive.

C2 in a vacuum

A satellite under attack makes no sound. There is no crack of gunfire, no plume of smoke—only telemetry that begins to look wrong. A reaction wheel spins harder than it should. The radio link flickers. Commands take a fraction longer to acknowledge. In the war rooms beneath concrete, engineers exchange glances. Has the antenna been dazzled? Is the uplink being spoofed? Or is this merely solar weather tugging at the fragile chain of control? Space does not announce its dangers. It offers silence, ambiguity, and the unnerving possibility that you have already lost command before you notice anything at all.

That is why command and control for satellites is one of the most delicate arts in modern warfare. Unlike aircraft or ships, a spacecraft cannot hear its operators. Everything depends on the flow of signals: instructions uplinked, telemetry downlinked, encrypted handshakes affirming identity. Cut those lines and a satellite becomes an expensive stone, tumbling through orbit, blind and deaf. The paradox of space power is that the most advanced systems rely on the most fragile medium—thin strands of radio waves stitched through the vacuum.

This vulnerability has shaped the architecture of modern space control. Early constellations often talked only to the ground. If a jammer blanketed a region or a ground station went dark, operators could do little but wait. Today, resilient constellations build webs of cross-links, allowing satellites to pass commands among themselves like a relay team. If one node cannot hear Earth, it asks its neighbour. A spacecraft in the Pacific might route its traffic through a partner over Europe, which reaches another over Africa, which finally finds a ground antenna outside the interference zone. The constellation becomes a nervous system with multiple paths to the brain.

Cross-linking does more than preserve contact; it changes strategy. A satellite that senses suspicious interference may warn its peers. If a spoofed command tries to impersonate ground control, other nodes can refuse to authenticate it. In some systems, spacecraft share updates about space weather, orbital debris, and hostile approaches. The more autonomous these constellations become, the harder it is to isolate any one satellite. The attacker must silence the network, not the node—a far higher bar.

Yet control cannot be ceded entirely to automation. Operators must still send orders and receive data, and ground stations remain essential choke points. That makes them targets. A well-placed missile strike on a major control facility could cripple communications for dozens of satellites, not by touching them in orbit but by severing the link to Earth. For that reason, militaries disperse control nodes across continents. Some sit in mountains, others in desert bunkers, a few aboard naval vessels or mobile trailers. Each carries encrypted hardware and trained crews capable of assuming control if primary sites are compromised. A fly-away terminal can be packed into a cargo plane, flown to a remote airstrip, and reconstitute command within hours—a quiet form of resilience that few civilians ever see.

But jamming is not the only threat. Spoofing—a falsified signal masquerading as legitimate—may be more insidious. If an operator cannot trust what they hear, the entire architecture falters. To counter this, satellites rely on layers of authentication, from cryptographic keys to frequency-hopping patterns and time-synchronised handshakes. Some commands require redundant confirmation from multiple ground centres. Others must match a satellite's own internal predictions before they are executed. A spacecraft that receives an implausible order—such as firing thrusters into a collision—should reject it. This is not merely a technical safeguard; it reflects a philosophical shift: in space, mistrust is a form of survival.

Even genuine signals can be corrupted in transit. Solar storms induce noise. Atmospheric scintillation distorts radio waves near the horizon. A signal that is perfectly formed at the transmitter may arrive torn and garbled. Engineers design modulation schemes that can survive such turbulence, encoding commands in patterns that remain readable even when damaged. Error correction, spread-spectrum transmission, and adaptive coding all serve one purpose: preserving clarity in a hostile medium. A satellite that misunderstands a command can break an entire constellation. Precision is not optional; it is the currency of control.

Communication pathways have multiplied. Space-to-ground radio links are the backbone, but some militaries explore optical communication—laser beams between satellites or down to terminals. Lasers are harder to jam and far narrower in beam, reducing interception risk. Yet they demand exquisite pointing accuracy; a slight misalignment and the link vanishes. Clouds can block them, dust can scatter them. As with every space technology, advantages come with trade-offs.

Ground infrastructure remains as critical as rocket engines. Antennas track satellites across the sky, scheduling precious minutes of contact. Behind them sit network operations centres where officers monitor telemetry, detect anomalies, and coordinate manoeuvres. These centres resemble a fusion of air-traffic control and submarine command: constant vigilance, high stakes, limited windows for decision. A satellite in low Earth orbit may pass overhead for eight minutes. In that brief span, operators must upload tasks, download data, and check the spacecraft's health. Miss the window, and the next chance may be hours away. Time, in this domain, is merciless.

The tempo of operations accelerates when threats loom. If a rival satellite manoeuvres towards a sensitive asset, controllers may send evasive instructions—small burns to adjust orbit, changes in attitude to reduce vulnerability. But thrusters have finite fuel. Every defensive movement must be weighed against long-term mission life. The satellite becomes a chess piece with limited moves. Command and control is therefore as much about restraint as reaction.

Some nations adopt a doctrine of silent running. They reduce radio chatter, allowing satellites to operate on pre-planned sequences. The less the spacecraft transmits, the less it can be tracked or targeted by electronic surveillance. Yet silence is dangerous. If an anomaly occurs while the satellite is out of contact, the gap between incident and response widens. Autonomy becomes both shield and risk.

The rise of commercial space complicates everything. Militaries now depend on privately owned constellations for imagery, navigation augmentation, or backup communications. But commercial ground networks follow business priorities, not wartime doctrine. A disruption at a civilian data centre can ripple into military operations. To mitigate this, governments negotiate priority access, secure control channels, and require firms to maintain redundant sites. Still, tension persists: commercial satellites may serve customers in rival states, and militaries cannot simply revoke access without political cost. Command and control becomes a negotiation, not a given.

Cyber intrusion represents a subtler threat. A spacecraft's control software is built by human hands, often incorporating commercial libraries and third-party components. If malware infiltrates the ground network, it can tamper with commands, corrupt telemetry, or mask an ongoing attack. Some operations centres treat incoming satellite data as untrusted until verified. Encryption helps, but cannot eliminate insider risk. Thus space C2 inherits every vulnerability of terrestrial computing—with the added constraint that a single corrupted packet can alter a spacecraft's trajectory.

There is also the challenge of attribution. When a link degrades, operators ask: is this a solar flare, accidental interference, or deliberate jamming? The vacuum does not answer. A cautious commander cannot escalate on guesswork, yet hesitation may invite further boldness from an adversary. Space C2 teams cultivate analytical forensics: measuring signal-to-noise ratios, comparing antenna patterns, correlating events across different satellites. They operate like detectives piecing together a silent crime scene. Their conclusions can shape diplomacy as much as warfare.

Some systems pursue graceful degradation—keeping partial functionality under stress. If a high-bandwidth link is jammed, the satellite switches to a narrow emergency channel. If encryption keys are compromised, it rotates to backups. If ground stations go offline, it stores data temporarily, then dumps it when a window reopens. In the language of engineers, the spacecraft is *fault tolerant*. In the language of operators, it is alive.

Yet even the most resilient architectures face moral and strategic dilemmas. Perfect autonomy could, in theory, allow satellites to defend themselves—jamming back, manoeuvring aggressively, or disabling hostile sensors. But such behaviour risks escalation without human judgement. Militaries debate where to place the boundary: enough autonomy to survive sudden attack, but not so much that machines take decisions meant for statesmen. This tension echoes throughout the history of warfare, but in orbit the consequences are amplified. A satellite that mistakes a routine proximity operation for a threat could trigger a cascade of reprisals.

The human dimension of space C2 is often overlooked. Controllers train for years, mastering orbital mechanics, encryption protocols, antenna operations, and emergency recovery. They drill scenarios where everything that can go wrong *does*—from dual ground-station loss to corrupted memories aboard the spacecraft. They learn to trust their instincts when telemetry looks "wrong in a way we haven't seen before." Some veterans speak of satellites as personalities: one that sulks in high temperature, one that resists calibration, one that responds sluggishly in eclipse. These quirks matter in crisis. Machines may operate in a vacuum, but command is always human.

And the future grows more complex. As constellations swell from dozens to thousands of satellites, manual control becomes impossible. Artificial intelligence may soon manage routine tasking, routing, and anomaly detection. A constellation could reconfigure itself under attack, shifting roles among satellites, prioritising missions, and choosing communications paths autonomously. The commander becomes conductor rather than operator—guiding intent, not micromanaging actions. But AI introduces its own fragility: opaque decisions, adversarial manipulation, unforeseen failure modes. Trusting an algorithm to control a national asset is not a casual step.

Even with perfect automation, the vacuum will still demand humility. A stray piece of debris can tear an antenna, a cosmic ray can flip a bit, a miscalibrated clock can corrupt navigation signals for millions of receivers. Command and control will remain, at its core, a dialogue between fallible humans and fragile machines, stretched across light-seconds of emptiness.

The more nations depend on orbital systems, the higher the stakes become. A lost satellite can cripple communications, blind reconnaissance, or degrade missile warning. In peacetime, that means confusion. In crisis, it can invite catastrophe. So militaries rehearse silent hours—operating without GPS, without satellite comms, without early warning. They learn to fight blind, not because they want to, but because they might have to.

Perhaps the most unsettling truth is this: in space, control is never total. Every command arrives from afar, delayed by physics, vulnerable to interference. Operators must assume that something, somewhere, is trying to break the chain. The vacuum offers no mercy—only a test of whose systems endure the longest.

Can a constellation remain coherent when the world beneath it burns, when jammers howl, when ground stations fall silent? Can a nation still command its orbital eyes and ears when every signal is suspect? The answers will define future wars in ways few civilians yet understand.

Targeting cycles reimagined

A convoy creeps along a mountain road, headlights killed, tarpaulins masking the outline of what rides beneath. Ten years ago, that might have been enough to buy a night's safety. Today, a radar satellite in polar orbit sweeps the pass, its synthetic aperture painting vehicles even through cloud and darkness. A ground analyst watching on a tablet approves a tasking request. Minutes later, another spacecraft in a different orbital plane is retasked for a second look. Within the hour, artillery on a distant ridgeline receives precise coordinates. The road was quiet; the sky was busy.

Modern targeting has become a story of compressed time. It once took days to detect, verify, plan, and strike a target. Now the ambition is measured in minutes. The military lexicon speaks of "sensor-to-shooter loops" as if war were a circular machine, humming with data. But a loop is the wrong image; it is more like a web—mesh networks of satellites, drones, analysts, and firing units, each node able to trigger action when the picture is clear enough to justify it. Space sits at the heart of that web, transforming inconstant signals into precise opportunity.

The remarkable shift is not only technical; it is conceptual. During the Cold War, satellites were strategic instruments: slow, precious, and heavily scheduled. Now they are tactical. Commercial constellations in low Earth orbit circle the planet every ninety minutes, each pass another chance to catch a fleeting target. Militaries subscribe to imagery as if it were cloud storage, pulling scenes on demand. A general no longer waits for a national asset to complete its orbit; he pings a commercial provider and asks which satellite will be overhead next. Space has become a service, not a spectacle.

Synthetic Aperture Radar (SAR) is a striking example of this new logic. Unlike optical imagery, SAR does not care about weather, darkness, or camouflage nets. It reads shape and movement in the language of reflections. A truck hidden under foliage still reflects a pattern. Tracks on wet ground leave signatures. Even decoys can betray themselves: metal resonates differently from plywood under radar illumination. When tasking orders arrive, SAR satellites adjust their pointing angle or dwell time to sharpen detail. They do not wait for the sun.

Speed is the first weapon. In a conventional intelligence cycle, imagery might be collected at dawn, downlinked hours later, processed on secure servers, and finally distributed to units in the field. By then, the convoy has moved. Today, the pipeline shortens. Some constellations downlink directly to mobile terminals in theatre. Algorithms flag anomalies without human prompting: a bridge that is suddenly gone, a pattern of vehicles that was not there yesterday, a ship that left harbour under a false name. Analysts then use the second weapon: fusion.

Fusion means knitting different sensors into a single story. SAR might provide location and motion. An optical satellite confirms the vehicle type. A signals-intelligence payload detects a communications burst from a nearby relay. A small commercial satellite—one of hundreds—passes overhead minutes later and provides a thermal image. None of these alone offer certainty. Together, they anchor a decision. This is why joint targeting cells increasingly resemble financial trading floors: multiple feeds, constant updates, rapid judgement.

The ethos has changed: rather than exquisite platforms every few hours, militaries want persistent eyes every few minutes. Commercial firms oblige with proliferated constellations—hundreds of inexpensive satellites instead of a handful of costly ones. If one is jammed or destroyed, others fill the gap. This redundancy shrinks the window in which a target can hide. A missile launcher pausing between firings might once have blended into civilian traffic. Now, analysts watch its behaviour across time: where it hides, where it refuels, whether its signature matches known units. Patterns betray intention.

Such rapid loops depend on command and control architectures able to ingest data at speed. In some operations centres, analysts sit beside artillery officers and air controllers. When a contact is confirmed, the fire plan triggers automatically: the nearest platform—whether aircraft, ship, or ground battery—receives coordinates and engagement rules. The satellite feed is not an end in itself; it is a precursor to effects. In the most advanced doctrines, space is merely the high vantage from which decisions accelerate.

Yet velocity brings risk. If a machine flags an image and a human misreads it, weapons may strike the wrong target. False positives linger like ghosts in the system. Militaries therefore grapple with a new tension: how to exploit speed without abandoning caution. Some impose layered confirmation: two satellites must agree, or one satellite plus a drone, or imagery plus signals intelligence. Others rely on confidence scoring—the higher the certainty, the fewer steps required. But no safeguard is perfect. The fog of war is not banished by orbital light.

Commercial involvement introduces further complexity. Private firms can receive tasking from multiple customers. A small state may request satellite imagery of an adversary's airfield. Hours later, a rival does the same. Who decides priority? Who ensures neutrality? And what happens when a military wants imagery of a region where a commercial provider has corporate interests or regulatory obligations? The battlefield now passes through civilian servers, hosted in data centres that may sit thousands of miles from any uniformed commander.

Export controls try to shape this behaviour. Some nations allow high-resolution imagery to be sold broadly; others restrict it to allies. A company with global clients must navigate political fault lines: it might have to deny imagery to a paying customer because of sanctions, or blur sensitive installations to satisfy national regulators. Meanwhile, militaries want assured access: guaranteed tasking rights, priority downlink, pre-reserved bandwidth. Negotiations become quiet battles of their own—commercial interests on one side, strategic demands on the other.

Rewrite the targeting cycle and you rewrite deterrence. If a leader knows that every movement of armour, every redeployment of missiles, every sortie from an airbase could be captured within minutes and sent straight to a firing unit, traditional brinkmanship becomes harder. Surprise dwindles. Deception must evolve. Adversaries respond with decoy convoys, inflatable aircraft, false radio chatter, and manipulated heat signatures. They seed the data stream with digital noise, hoping analysts chase phantoms. The counter-move is pattern analytics: machines that learn the rhythm of deception and flag what does not fit.

There is also the political dimension. Rapid tasking works both ways. A state can use commercial imagery to prove a violation—say, an attack on civilian infrastructure or a breach of a ceasefire. It can share pictures with allied capitals or the press before an adversary can deny. Satellites become witnesses, not just scouts. And because their data is commercial, it can be shared publicly without compromising national assets. Diplomacy gains a new lever: transparency at speed.

Still, this reliance on orbital data has vulnerabilities. Jamming can blind a satellite's SAR instrument or disrupt downlink pathways. Cyber intrusion can corrupt imagery, altering pixels to hide a target or fabricate one. An adversary might flood the system with meaningless tasking requests, overwhelming bandwidth. And every rapid loop relies on ground terminals—small antennas in trucks or on rooftops, quietly downloading intelligence. If those are suppressed, the constellation's eyes have no voice.

Some militaries prepare for a harsher world: one in which satellite imagery is intermittent or contested. They train to fight with degraded data, to plan strikes with uncertain coordinates, to accept a slower loop. Yet no commander willingly returns to the age of waiting days for verification. The taste of instant intelligence is intoxicating.

The philosophical shift runs deeper. Traditional warfare prized mass: more tanks, more aircraft, more artillery. The new paradigm prizes cognition:

who sees first, who understands fastest, who can turn observation into action before the opponent moves. Space is not just high ground; it is acceleration. The side that shortens the loop might end a fight before the other knows it has begun.

A future targeting cycle may rely less on human interpretation. Machine learning systems already classify vehicles, track ships, and flag anomalies without fatigue. Given enough training data, they might forecast behaviour—predicting where a missile launcher will move next based on past patterns. Commanders could pre-empt rather than chase. The loop becomes a spiral, tightening with each observation.

But autonomy raises uncomfortable questions. If an algorithm mistakes a civilian vehicle for a military one, who is accountable? If a rapid loop executes too fast for human veto, does deterrence erode into automation? States will struggle to balance speed with responsibility. The temptation to delegate judgement to machines will grow, especially when adversaries do the same.

What is clear is that the battlefield no longer waits for sun or sky. Commercial satellites shrink the Earth into a monitored surface, where movement leaves trails, heat leaves fingerprints, and patterns betray intent. Strategic surprise has not vanished, but it has narrowed.

If tomorrow's conflict hinges on who can see, decide, and strike the fastest, then the orbiting cameras are not just observing war—they are shaping it. Will speed sharpen clarity, or will haste multiply mistakes? And when every army watches every road, what does it mean to hide at all?

Resilience at the edge

The hillside was quiet except for the low hiss of a generator. The strike had come an hour earlier: three missiles, a plume of dust, shattered concrete. The brigade's headquarters compound—its antennas, its fibre, its air-conditioned server room—was a crater. Yet thirty minutes later, a folding dish was angled at the sky from the back of a pick-up truck. A field laptop blinked to life. Within minutes, messages were flowing again: tasking orders, satellite imagery, logistics updates. The war moved on, because the link was back. In the age of orbital command and control, resilience no longer lives in steel bunkers and fixed stations. It rides in rucksacks and steel cases, spread across landscapes like seeds that refuse to die.

For decades, militaries trusted large ground stations: fenced compounds bristling with parabolic dishes, guarded by concertina wire and concrete revetments. They were impressive, indispensable—and increasingly vulnerable. Fixed infrastructure says exactly where to aim. A state with long-range missiles or loitering munitions needs only a handful of coordinates to blind an adversary's satellites. Worse, cyber attackers do not need a missile at all. A single breach in a ground station's control network can corrupt satellite tasking or seize a spacecraft's command channel. The enemy does not need space supremacy; they simply need to sever the link between sky and soil.

Resilience at the edge is the antidote to that fragility. It is the philosophy of dispersion: if every node can be attacked, then multiply the nodes until no attack can silence them. Instead of a handful of gleaming antenna farms, imagine dozens of small dishes scattered across safe houses, trucks, shipping containers, even ships at sea. Some are active; others sleep until needed. They pull down commercial imagery, upload new tasking, rekey satellites under cyber threat, and restore command after a strike. The network breathes.

The principle sounds simple. Its implications are profound. For one, the classic distinction between strategic and tactical sites dissolves. A platoon with a fly-away terminal can perform tasks once reserved for national-level centres. They can request satellite reconnaissance of a nearby valley, receive encrypted messages from a theatre commander, or re-establish timing signals for precision munitions. The antenna that hides under camouflage netting by day might be more important than the monumental radome hundreds of kilometres behind the front.

Commercial technology accelerates this shift. Portable phased-array terminals—no heavier than a suitcase—can track multiple satellites at once, hopping beams as constellations pass overhead. They do not require precise mechanical pointing; they steer electronically, adjusting in milliseconds. A team on foot can deploy one, align it via built-in GPS, and start downloading secure data. Some militias and special forces units carry terminals disguised as innocuous equipment, blending redundancy with deception. Resilience is not just robustness; it is ambiguity.

Yet mobile nodes alone do not solve the problem. They need power, mobility, and a communications backbone that survives disruption. Militaries experiment with solar-backed battery kits, ultra-efficient radios, and terminals built into vehicles that move constantly to avoid targeting. Others use civilian infrastructure to their advantage: small ground relays hidden in industrial estates, rooftop antennas disguised as satellite

TV dishes, fibre backhauls running through commercial networks. In conflicts where every obvious target is struck, survival comes from being unremarkable.

Some nations go further: they build "resilience layers" of ground access. A satellite may downlink first to a hardened base, but if that base goes dark, it fails over to a mobile team. If that team is jammed, it can route through a maritime terminal on a naval vessel. If that vessel is out of range, a partner nation's ground station takes the next pass. In the most advanced systems, the satellite itself makes the choice, dynamically selecting the best downlink path. Humans never have to intervene; the network heals itself.

Resilience also requires independence from single suppliers. If a commercial provider suffers cyber attack or political pressure, militaries want alternatives ready to activate. Some sign pre-arranged contracts with multiple satellite operators. Others deploy software-defined terminals that can switch frequency bands and protocols, talking to different constellations on demand. The antenna does not care whose spacecraft is overhead; it cares only that one is.

This redundancy reshapes strategy. If ground segments are dispersed and survivable, an adversary seeking to blind a nation must attack dozens or hundreds of sites. Each strike risks escalation. Each cyber intrusion must remain stealthy across a fractured landscape. The cost of disabling the constellation rises dramatically. And because many of these terminals operate on commercial networks, attacking them risks collateral effects on civilian systems. What was once a straightforward military objective becomes a political gamble.

Still, dispersion is not a cure-all. Mobile terminals can be detected: through heat signatures, radio-frequency emissions, or human intelligence. A pickup-mounted dish transmits just enough energy for an adversary's electronic warfare teams to triangulate. Some states deploy drone swarms that sniff for emissions and mark targets for artillery. Others use cyber implants placed in commercially sold ground equipment, waiting for activation signals. Resilience is not invisibility; it is the art of making the network too agile to pin down.

That agility drives new doctrine. Units train to deploy terminals under fire, to relocate every few hours, to conceal power sources, to encrypt traffic even if satellite layers fail. Engineers build terminals that can operate on degraded bandwidth, passing only the most essential commands. Even if imagery is lost, timing signals for GPS-guided weapons might survive. If telemetry is jammed, a satellite can switch to cross-linked communications with its peers, routing control messages around contested ground.

Not all resilience is physical. Some is legal and diplomatic. States negotiate hosting agreements with allies, allowing satellites to be controlled from foreign bases if home infrastructure is hit. In peacetime, this looks like redundancy. In war, it becomes strategic insurance: a link chain that spans borders and survives even when the homeland burns. But diplomacy introduces new vulnerabilities. Host nations may impose restrictions on the kinds of operations they support. A political dispute may freeze access. Resilient design must anticipate human volatility, not just technical failure.

The sharper edge of resilience lies in automation. Constellations increasingly operate with high autonomy: they maintain station, avoid debris, and follow pre-programmed response plans when commands are lost. If a ground operator cannot reach a satellite, the spacecraft might continue surveillance missions according to a priority list stored onboard. It may even rendezvous with a friendly satellite for crosslink control. The constellation behaves like a flock—individual birds disrupted, but the group still flying.

There is a philosophical shift here: resilience becomes survivability by diffusion, not protection by fortification. The old logic of space warfare imagined a decisive blow—strike the ground nodes and the satellites become silent. The new logic envisions a swarm of terminals, an adaptive network, a constellation that keeps speaking even when individual voices are muted. This frustrates adversaries and complicates deterrence. If a state cannot reliably blind another's space architecture, can it ever gain advantage? Or does resilience stabilise conflict by reducing the incentive for a knockout punch?

Yet proliferation invites complacency. If every unit can deploy a terminal, commanders may forget the vulnerabilities that remain. A convoy with a satellite dish is a target even if the link is encrypted. A civilian ground node, pressed quietly into service, could bring legal blowback if struck. And redundancy is expensive. Every spare terminal, every hidden base, every alternative fibre path costs money and manpower. Nations with deep pockets will build layered resilience. Smaller states may find themselves with a single fragile chain, no matter how clever the doctrine.

The commercial world again complicates the picture. Many militaries rely on private networks for backhaul, hosting, and data processing. A missile may miss a ground station, but a cyber attack on a data centre halfway around the world might still cut the link. Engineers speak of "cloud resilience"—mirrored architectures, auto-scaling servers, encrypted gateways—but clouds have geopolitical boundaries. Data housed in one jurisdiction may suddenly become inaccessible in a crisis if regulators intervene or borders close digitally. Space resilience is terrestrial risk wearing a cosmic mask.

Where does this end? Perhaps in extreme dispersal. Imagine ground segments woven into everyday infrastructure: public buildings, telecom towers, merchant ships, scientific stations, rail depots. Any of them might serve as a node, activated only when the constellation requests it. An adversary would face not a single communications hub but a nationwide substrate. Striking it would be indiscriminate, legally fraught, and politically suicidal. Even the most aggressive strategist would hesitate.

Or perhaps the answer lies in space itself. Laser crosslinks, inter-satellite routing, and autonomous tasking reduce dependence on ground segments altogether. A constellation might run for days without touching earth, passing commands between spacecraft and downlinking only when safe. Resilience becomes orbital, not terrestrial. But such autonomy raises its own anxieties. A network that can operate without human oversight begins to look like an actor in its own right.

The irony is that the weakest part of a space architecture is not the satellite; it is the human on a hillside, crouching beside a folding antenna, fingers numb, waiting for a secure handshake to complete. Resilience at the edge is a triumph of human ingenuity, not just engineering. It is the refusal to let a single crater end a conversation.

If war in space is ultimately a war about information, then the last mile—the ground link, the quiet dish, the field laptop—is everything. The constellation sees, but the terminal speaks. And in the shadows of ruined bases and jammed networks, that tiny voice decides whether space remains a weapon, a shield, or an empty sky.

When the next conflict seeks to silence satellites, will it succeed? Or will resilience at the edge steal victory from the teeth of destruction, one folding dish at a time?

Training and doctrine

The screen went black first. Then the clocks jumped. Navigators glanced at their wrists, only to find the seconds refusing to advance in unison. Precision-guided systems began drifting from their targets. No missile fell, no satellite exploded, yet the brigade knew it was blind. In the command tent, an officer whispered the question that mattered: *is this training, or are we under attack?* The answer was both. The exercise had simulated the loss of timing and communications, and the point was brutal in its simplicity. Space systems fail quietly. When they do, only those who have practised chaos keep fighting with purpose.

Modern militaries were long accustomed to rehearsing tank battles, submarine duels, and dogfights in the sky. But rehearsing the invisible domain—silence, latency, corrupted coordinates, ghost signals—demands a different imagination. Training for space-enabled conflict is not about theatrical explosions; it is about subtle degradations of trust. A satellite's downlink slows by half a second, and an air defence battery misjudges an incoming threat. A navigation signal is jammed in one sector, and an armoured column drives into a minefield it believed was cleared. The enemy might never appear in the sky, yet the battlefield snaps under invisible pressure. Good doctrine prepares soldiers for this: fight when seeing less, decide when knowing less, survive when timing dies.

Wargaming is the crucible. Some exercises are grimly realistic: operators watch their satellite feeds degrade, commanders lose the map overlays they rely upon, targeting cycles stretch from minutes to hours. Officers trained on crisp digital clarity must rediscover tactics their predecessors took for granted. They relearn how to call in fires from paper maps, how to coordinate movements with hand signals and couriers, how to make decisions when the data stream flickers. Such discomfort is intentional. A generation raised on persistent overhead surveillance and satellite-guided manoeuvre must be reminded that confidence is not a substitute for resilience.

Red teams make the lessons sharper. They sit behind closed doors with laptops, radio transmitters, and a grim sense of creativity. Their mission is to break trust: to inject false coordinates, jam timing signals, mimic friendly callsigns, or corrupt the targeting feed just enough that commanders doubt their own systems. Every weakness uncovered in training is one less gift to an adversary. Red teams are the loyal enemies militaries pay to expose their complacency. A successful red cell does not merely disrupt; it humiliates. It forces doctrine writers to ask why a brigade panicked when the satellites went dark, why the fallback procedures were dusty, why so few knew how to operate without orbital advantage.

Simulation laboratories take the work even further. Engineers build digital replicas of constellations, ground networks, and adversary tools. They can run a virtual war in real time: jamming attacks, cyber intrusions, kinetic strikes, even debris clouds drifting across orbital planes. Operators sit at real consoles, reacting to alarms that feel authentic because, in some sense, they are. A simulated satellite tumbling in low orbit forces a decision about de-orbiting, collision avoidance, or crosslink rerouting. The only difference between exercise and reality is that once the lesson is learnt, someone presses reset.

Doctrine evolves through the scars of these rehearsals. In the past, space was treated as a support domain—a strategic enabler for navigation, reconnaissance, and communications. Today, militaries accept that space is contested, and doctrine must assume degradation from the first hour of conflict. Some nations publish guidance that every unit should prepare to operate under "denied, degraded, and disrupted space environments". That phrase is not a slogan; it is a forecast. A commander who assumes perfect satellite service is gambling with lives.

This shift changes procurement. Engineers favour redundancy: multi-constellation receivers that can use GPS, Galileo, BeiDou, or GLONASS; anti-jam antennas; inertial backups; star trackers that let missiles navigate even when all timing signals die. Training exercises force units to test those systems under real stress. If the anti-jam mode knocks bandwidth down to a trickle, can a drone pilot still navigate? If encrypted timing packets arrive late, will artillery units refuse to fire or improvise manual solutions? Doctrine must answer these questions before war does.

Philosophically, training in the space-enabled battlefield is training in humility. Humans are astonishingly dependent on unseen infrastructure. Soldiers today trust satellites the way their grandparents trusted compasses. When that trust fractures, decision-making becomes psychological as much as technical. Commanders must learn to detect deception, to know when a data feed is lying, to operate with partial truths. Some exercises deliberately seed fake intelligence into scenario feeds, teaching officers that information abundance can be as dangerous as scarcity.

Commercial technologies add another layer. Militaries increasingly rely on private imagery providers, commercial satcom beams, and cloud-based services. Training therefore includes negotiating loss of those services. What if a commercial operator is hacked during a crisis? What if legislation blocks access? Units practice switching rapidly between networks, using fallback constellations, or routing through allied terminals. Doctrine that ignores the commercial layer is fantasy.

Not all training is dramatic. Some of the most important lessons come from small-scale drills: a platoon practising deployment of a mobile terminal under fire; a naval crew rehearsing manual celestial navigation; fighter pilots learning approaches when satellite-based landing aids are jammed. These mundane skills are lifelines. When satellites falter, civilisation's digital conveniences unravel, and militaries are not spared. The soldier who can navigate by paper and stars holds a quiet advantage.

Internationally, joint exercises reveal cultural and doctrinal contrasts. Some nations prioritise offensive space capabilities and train aggressively in jamming and cyber operations. Others emphasise protection: dispersion, encryption, and redundancy. When allies train together, differences become visible. A country that assumes constant satellite ISR may be shocked when a partner designs an operation expecting nothing but radio silence. Harmonising doctrine across alliances is difficult, yet essential. In conflict, an army cannot wait for a partner's satellites to wake up.

The most interesting frontier is cognitive training. In a world where synthetic imagery can be generated in minutes, and fake radio signals can mimic friendly units, situational awareness becomes fragile. Wargames now include deepfake reconnaissance: images doctored to hide a convoy or show a phantom bridge. Officers must learn to doubt what they see and demand corroboration from multiple sources. Decision-making under deception becomes a core skill.

Yet doctrine must walk a fine line. If militaries over-emphasise degradation, they risk paralysis and constant suspicion. If they over-emphasise technological trust, they risk humiliation when systems fail. The art lies in balance: trust technology enough to use it, distrust it enough to survive its betrayal.

This raises a deeper question about human-machine relationships. In advanced forces, algorithms perform satellite scheduling, target recognition, collision avoidance, and crosslink routing. Sometimes the system knows best. But doctrine must define when to override automation, and training must prepare humans to intervene without choking the machine's efficiency. An operator who never practises manual control will hesitate when automation misbehaves. Hesitation kills.

The most sobering exercises simulate catastrophe: a debris cloud wipes out half a constellation; cyber teams seize satellite control; a solar storm blinds ground receivers. In these nightmares, doctrine is stripped to its bones. Can the military function without space? Can it navigate by inertial sensors alone? Can it fight blind for days? The units that have answered "yes" do so because they have rehearsed failure until it feels routine.

Training for space conflict is training for a world where nothing works as promised. It prepares soldiers to think like adversaries, to improvise like engineers, and to distrust their own screens. It is uncomfortable, stressful, occasionally humiliating—and utterly necessary. Space has no mercy for the unprepared. It does not announce when timing is wrong or imagery is doctored. It simply watches as human assumptions crumble.

So the rehearsals continue: the black screens, the corrupted timing, the vanished signals. Soldiers curse, commanders adapt, doctrine evolves. Somewhere, between the alarms and the silence, militaries learn how to fight when the sky betrays them. The question that lingers is unsettling: in a future war where satellites fail and deception thrives, who will adapt fastest—the side with bigger constellations, or the side that has already practised losing them?

Chapter 8

Markets as Battlefields

In the summer heat of a launch site, a rocket stood silent on its pad, gleaming with corporate logos and national flags. Television cameras framed the event as a celebration of science and ambition. Few viewers noticed the unremarkable payload: a communications satellite for broadband services. Fewer still realised that the next available launch slot was more than a year away, and that the satellite it was replacing—faulty, flickering, losing power—served both rural schools and an armoured brigade. When schedules are tight and the queue is long, orbital access becomes a quiet form of power. A delayed launch can reshape a battlefield without firing a shot.

Economies often look bloodless on the surface: spreadsheets, shipping manifests, quarterly statements. Yet in space, every procurement decision echoes with strategic consequence. A nation that controls launch services holds a choke point. A company that supplies radiation-hardened chips can decide who builds satellites fast enough to stay ahead. Insurance premiums tilt design choices; licensing regimes reshape innovation; sanctions reroute entire supply chains overnight. Markets, for all their veneer of neutrality, can be as decisive as missiles.

Consider the supply chains that run from cleanrooms to launch fairings. A spacecraft is assembled from thousands of components, many sourced from specialised vendors who operate at the edge of physics: radiation-resistant memory, precision gyroscopes, star trackers capable of surviving a decade in orbit. When only one company manufactures a key component, a war for procurement is a war for time. If that factory suffers sanctions, sabotage, or simple bankruptcy, entire industries stall. Satellites on drawing boards become mock-ups gathering dust. Nations that once imagined autonomy discover dependence.

The dual-use dilemma adds moral weight to these cold mechanics. Commercial broadband beams keep villages online and hospitals connected, but they also carry encrypted orders to a mechanised brigade. A weather satellite maps crops and refugee camps, yet its data also guides drones. Civilian services and military needs are entangled. When a commercial constellation is asked to reposition satellites to support troops, is it a neutral business serving customers—or a participant in conflict? Markets have become fronts where public and private responsibilities blur.

Sovereignty, once measured in territory, now includes supply chains. Governments speak of "strategic autonomy" and invest in domestic launch vehicles, navigation systems, and imaging satellites. A nation that depends on a foreign provider for timing signals risks paralysis if relations sour. Some states have learned this the hard way: a delayed export licence, a sudden embargo, a denied spare part. Procurement is not a mundane budget line; it is a national security doctrine written in contracts.

Sanctions and standards exert pressure without smoke or fire. When a country is barred from importing high-resolution sensors, it cannot build satellites that match rivals. When regulators impose strict debris mitigation rules, manufacturers shift factory lines and software stacks. Legal frameworks that appear technocratic become instruments of geopolitical shaping. They decide who gets to play in orbit and who must watch from below.

This chapter follows those threads: the pricing of launch slots, the brittle chains of components that cross borders, the uneasy marriage of consumer markets and military needs, the race for sovereign capability, and the quiet force of standards and sanctions. Each reveals how space economics is not merely about profit, but about leverage, access, and power. Satellites do not reach orbit by policy alone; they travel on rockets built in markets that obey currencies, contracts, and competition.

Some readers might expect warfare to unfold in the sky. Here, it unfolds in factories, insurance offices, export-control tribunals, and boardrooms deciding where to open the next assembly line. The battlefield is scattered across stock exchanges and supply chains, where national strategies hide behind procurement codes.

The deeper tension is simple and uncomfortable: space has been sold as the triumph of open markets, yet the stakes are unmistakably strategic. As more nations and firms enter the sector, the race will be shaped as much by who can buy, build, and insure a satellite as by who can shoot one down. Sometimes the decisive battles are fought not by admirals or generals, but by procurement officers, risk analysts, and export regulators.

Turn the page, and the polite language of commerce begins to sound like strategy. In space, money is a weapon—subtle, enduring, and often more powerful than force.

Pricing access to orbit

There are few scenes more revealing than a launch manifest pinned to a control room wall. Names of satellites are scribbled in pencil, erased, and rewritten as schedules slip and payloads queue. Spaceflight looks like a triumph of engineering, but beneath the plume of exhaust lies something older and more familiar: a market. In this market, buyers haggle for the most precious commodity of all—time. A satellite that waits on the ground is a satellite that does not navigate ships, relay orders, or warn of storms. One delayed launch slot can ripple across a battlefield, a supply chain, or a national economy. The difference between launching in June or September might determine who sees first, who responds first, and who wins.

The paradox is stark. Space has never been more crowded with launch providers, from national agencies to agile commercial firms. Prices are lower than two decades ago. Rideshare options allow small satellites to hitch on larger rockets. Yet access remains constrained. Rockets explode; components fail inspection; weather misbehaves; range safety windows close. Every disruption cascades. A replacement imaging satellite stuck in a warehouse cannot track troop movements. A failed launch can cripple an entire constellation until another vehicle is ready, insured, certified, and scheduled. Orbit may be vast, but the queues to reach it are narrow.

Behind every manifest lies a hierarchy shaped by law, money, and quiet strategy. Government payloads often receive priority, especially when they carry national security missions. Commercial customers negotiate for margins and backup options. A small scientific satellite may be bumped for a defence payload requiring immediate deployment. In theory, the market treats all buyers as equals. In practice, the power dynamics are unmistakable. Launch capability is soft influence; pricing and availability become a shield or a lever, depending on who controls them.

Consider the commercial ride-share trend: dozens of satellites bundled beneath one fairing, each paying a fraction of the cost of a full rocket. The model is elegant—until one customer's late delivery holds up the entire stack. The cheapest ticket carries hidden risk: someone else controls your schedule. For firms operating satellites with short lifespans or critical missions, waiting six months can erase competitive advantage. For militaries depending on space-based support, delay can be perilous. Some states quietly buy backup launch options, paying a premium for the right to leap ahead of the queue. In emergencies, speed becomes worth more than cost, and pricing shifts from predictable to psychological.

Reusable rockets promised to democratise access, and to some extent they have. Prices dropped; cadence increased. But even reusability has limits: turnaround time, inspection, crew availability, and competing customers. There are only so many pads, so many windows, so many ground teams qualified to handle complex missions. Launch is not an assembly line. It is choreography on the edge of physics, and every misstep sends satellites back to the warehouse. Nations seeking sovereignty in space know this too well. Those without domestic launch capability find themselves negotiating in a seller's market, one where contracts and geopolitics intermingle.

This scarcity drives innovation and resentment. Some companies build constellations of dozens or hundreds of satellites to insure against losses. If one fails, another takes its place. Others develop miniature spacecraft that can launch on smaller, more frequent rockets. Militaries explore "responsive launch"—small boosters capable of placing satellites into orbit on days' notice. The ambition is clear: remove the bottleneck. Yet even responsive launch depends on infrastructure, legal permissions, and manufacturing pipelines that are themselves fragile. Speed is not only about rockets; it is about the systems behind them.

The strategic implications are profound. In terrestrial warfare, supply lines determine victory. In orbital operations, launch markets are supply lines. A country unable to replace a damaged satellite quickly may lose critical communication links, navigation accuracy, or intelligence feeds. An adversary who can replenish constellations at speed gains resilience. Launch pricing becomes a shadow tool of statecraft. Subsidies to national launch providers, export controls on engines or software, and strategic partnerships with foreign firms are not mere commerce—they are policy.

Logistics shapes power quietly. Sometimes a payload slot becomes a diplomatic gesture, offered to an ally in need. Sometimes it becomes pressure, withheld until concessions are made. The marketplace makes these transactions look mundane: invoices, payload integration schedules, paperwork. Yet each is a component of a global architecture of influence. Spacefaring nations understand this well. Ambitious newcomers learn quickly. Those stuck waiting on the ground grasp it most painfully.

There is a philosophical tension at the heart of this market. Space was imagined as open, borderless, and equal: a domain where laws of physics trumped laws of politics. But rockets are built in nations, with components sourced from alliances or adversaries, and their schedules reflect power. The pricing of access to orbit reveals a truth often hidden by the romance of exploration: space is not a frontier; it is a marketplace governed by scarcity and strategy.

New technologies may shift the balance. Fully reusable vehicles, air-breathing first stages, in-orbit servicing to extend satellite lifespan—each promises to loosen the bottleneck. Yet as access expands, demand grows faster still. Surveillance networks grow denser. Broadband constellations scale from hundreds to tens of thousands. Earth observation firms propose fleets capable of imaging every square metre hourly. Each new need adds stress to the queue.

Perhaps the future holds abundance. Perhaps launch becomes routine, like booking cargo on a transoceanic flight. Or perhaps scarcity will persist, and with it the politics of delay, priority, and exclusion. If aerospace history teaches anything, it is that every technological breakthrough births new dependencies: new materials, new engines, new software, each with its own vulnerability.

The next time a rocket lifts from its pad, consider not only the spectacle, but the quiet struggle behind it. Which customer waited longer? Which state secured a strategic slot? Which competing satellite remains grounded, its mission slipping away with each passing orbit of its rivals? Launch markets decide these fates in invoices rather than gunfire, but the consequences can be just as lasting.

Some battles are loud. Others are booked months in advance, paid for by procurement officers, and fought with scheduling spreadsheets. The most decisive wars in space might not be waged in the sky at all—they may be fought on the launch calendar.

Supply chains of space

A satellite can be designed in a meeting room, simulated in software, even built in a cleanroom—yet a single missing component can freeze the entire enterprise. The paradox feels almost absurd: a billion-pound national system, halted by a chip the size of a fingernail, sourced from a single vendor thousands of miles away. Space hardware is glamorous in the abstract, but on the factory floor it resembles something far more fragile: a chain of dependencies where strength is measured not by what works, but by what fails.

The fragility became painfully clear when semiconductor shortages rippled across global industry. Car factories paused, phone launches slipped, and satellites waited unfinished on assembly benches. Radiation-hardened processors—niche devices capable of surviving the punishment of orbit—were among the hardest hit. The firms that manufacture them are few, their production runs small, and their supply constrained by strict export controls. If one foundry goes offline, a constellation's next generation might be delayed for years. A weapon needs steel; a spacecraft needs silicon. In space, the rarer commodity is often the chip.

The deeper one looks, the stranger the web becomes. Many satellites intended for sovereign missions carry components designed in one country, fabricated in another, assembled in a third. A tactical imaging platform purchased by a defence ministry may include power systems from Sweden, solar arrays from Germany, star trackers from Canada, and encryption modules from the United States. A single export licence revoked, a sanction tightened, or a factory fire can scatter timelines. States that imagined space as a realm of autonomy discover instead a world of interdependence.

Software introduces another layer of risk. A spacecraft might rely on open-source drivers, commercial middleware, and proprietary flight code stitched together over years. The supply chain is no longer only physical—it is digital, and digital chains can be poisoned quietly. A library update introduces a bug; a vendor discontinues support; an unpatched vulnerability lingers in an onboard processor. In low Earth orbit, mistakes propagate in silence until a sensor freezes or a bus controller loops. Engineers have long feared mechanical failures. Now, they fear dependencies.

The problem is not limited to satellites. Launch vehicles depend on avionics, guidance computers, inertial measurement units, and rad-hard processors. Ground stations rely on specialised antennas, encryption modules, and timing hardware. Many of these parts are sourced from single suppliers with years-long lead times. Nations that trumpet "independent access to space" often mean independent rockets—not independent supply chains. True sovereignty would require entire ecosystems: fabs, testing labs, software vendors, optical manufacturers, and precision machine shops. Very few countries come close.

Yet supply chains are not only about scarcity; they are about leverage. When a state controls the export of key components—radiation-hardened chips, high-resolution sensors, precision gyroscopes—it controls who can build what. Export controls are tools of strategy as much as of regulation. They shape alliances by enabling partners and denying rivals. A state may allow a close ally to import secure communication modules while blocking others from obtaining the same. In the abstract, this is compliance. In practice, it is power.

Commercial firms sit in the middle. They source parts wherever they can, often from global vendors with no military mission in mind. But once their satellites become dual-use—supporting humanitarian mapping one day and battlefield intelligence the next—their suppliers inherit the politics. Some firms quietly design swappable hardware to avoid single-vendor bottlenecks. Others maintain shadow inventories: critical components purchased years in advance, stored under controlled conditions, ready for crisis. The accounting departments may wince, but the strategy is sound.

Some states take a different approach: accept fragility and compensate with numbers. Instead of building a handful of exquisite satellites with complex components, they build hundreds of smaller, simpler platforms using commercial-grade parts. The philosophy is blunt: if one fails, another takes its place. What was once a vulnerability—limited radiation tolerance, shorter lifespan—becomes a disposable feature. It is the logic of distributed systems brought to the heavens. But even this model needs chips, radios, solar cells, and thrusters. The bottlenecks simply multiply.

The human factor matters too. Skilled technicians who assemble space hardware are scarce. Specialist welders, cleanroom assemblers, and space-qualified test engineers cannot be hired off the street. When a country loses that workforce—through retirements, migration, or lack of investment—it loses capability. Factories can be rebuilt faster than expertise. A warehouse full of parts is useless without the people who know how to integrate them.

There is a philosophical discomfort running through these realities. Space has been portrayed as a symbol of mastery: the place where nations prove their technological confidence. Yet the more sophisticated the mission, the more vulnerable it becomes to small, unglamorous links in the chain. A satellite that can automatically dodge debris cannot dodge a global shortage of magnetorquers. A launch vehicle capable of precision landing cannot launch without a certified flight computer. Sophistication is the enemy of resilience unless the supply chain is equally advanced.

Some propose radical redesigns. Open-hardware avionics. Standardised satellite buses. Modular components where one supplier can swap for another. Spacecraft built from commercial off-the-shelf electronics wrapped in shielding rather than relying on scarce rad-hard parts. These ideas are gaining traction, but they remain constrained by testing requirements, long certification cycles, and cautious regulators. Space is unforgiving, and mission failures are expensive.

Others look to policy rather than engineering. Tax incentives for domestic component production. Shared facilities for testing and hardening. Consortiums of states pooling supply chains to avoid overdependence on any single nation. The logic echoes the old maritime world: no navy sails without a shipyard, no merchant fleet without ports. Space is becoming an ocean of its own, and supply chains are its harbours.

There is no easy answer. Independence is expensive. Dependence is risky. Redundancy is the only real defence, but redundancy costs money and time. As constellations scale into the thousands, the demand for components will strain suppliers already operating at capacity. Add geopolitical tension and export regulation, and the future of space manufacturing becomes a strategic puzzle rather than an engineering challenge.

Perhaps the most revealing question is this: who controls the bottlenecks? Not who builds rockets or launches satellites, but who builds the one irreplaceable part—the secure oscillator, the hardened CPU, the cryogenic valve—that everyone needs. In a world where power follows supply, the companies that make these parts are silent kingmakers. They sit far from launchpads and camera flashes, yet the fate of missions, constellations, and sometimes wars rests in their production schedules.

Satellites orbit freely, but the industry that sustains them is anchored to Earth—fragile, interconnected, and shaped by forces most users never see. The next breakthrough in space might not be a rocket or spacecraft at all. It might be a factory. Or a chip. Or a new way of designing around scarcity itself.

The dual-use dilemma

A broadband satellite over a warzone does not know it is over a warzone. Its beams land blindly, spilling connectivity across fields and cities, hospitals and command posts alike. A child may use it to download homework. A brigade may use it to coordinate artillery fire. The hardware is indifferent; the politics are not. From orbit, civilian and military needs blur until the distinction becomes almost philosophical. That ambiguity is the essence of the dual-use dilemma.

When commercial space companies began offering global services—navigation, imaging, broadband—few imagined that their infrastructure would become so tightly woven into national security. Yet the logic was inevitable. If a constellation can stream a lesson to a remote classroom, it can stream encrypted maps to an infantry team. If a commercial imaging system can track deforestation with weekly revisit, it can track armoured convoys with daily cadence. The same satellites that power supply chains and agriculture can reconstruct the outline of a battlefield. In orbit, market demand built capabilities that defence ministries once paid billions to develop for themselves.

For militaries, this convergence is a gift. Buying imagery from private constellations is faster than tasking a dedicated reconnaissance satellite. Leasing bandwidth from commercial broadband networks is cheaper than operating state-owned systems. Commercial platforms offer global footprint, frequent refresh, and rapid innovation—qualities defence procurement rarely delivers. In conflict, commanders rarely care who owns the satellite so long as the feed arrives on time.

But the gift comes wrapped in complications. Once a commercial satellite supports military operations, however indirectly, it becomes a legitimate intelligence target. The adversary need not destroy it; disrupting service can be enough. Jamming a civilian broadband beam to silence a military communications link also knocks schools and hospitals offline. A state that would hesitate to attack civilian infrastructure may hesitate less if the same infrastructure provides tactical advantage to its opponent. The line between civilian and combatant assets collapses, yet international law strains to draw it back.

Commercial firms know this tension well. They sell services to humanitarian agencies and financial companies, but their biggest customers are quietly defence ministries. Some sign agreements to provide imagery or communications during crises; others avoid explicit military ties but accept the revenue when it arrives through intermediaries. The temptation is clear. Defence budgets are steady, long-term, and willing to pay for high-end capabilities. Venture investors like predictable cashflow. Shareholders appreciate government guarantees. The market rewards dual-use technology.

Still, boardrooms have limits. A company that markets itself as a builder of peaceful infrastructure faces reputational risk if its satellites appear to tip the balance of a war. Executives must decide whether to prioritise neutrality, national allegiance, or commercial logic. Some choose silence. Others quietly restrict services in certain regions, disable specific functions, or apply geofencing to avoid escalation. None of these choices are morally clean. Denying service can cripple civilians alongside combatants; granting service can strengthen one side in a conflict the firm never intended to touch.

Governments exploit this ambiguity. They lean on private companies to provide access, sometimes formally through contracts, sometimes informally through expectation. A company headquartered within a nation's borders finds it difficult to decline support when its own military asks for bandwidth or imagery. Export controls add another layer: a firm may be free to provide high-resolution pictures to a European agriculture bureau, but forbidden from selling the same product to a foreign defence ministry. Legal compliance becomes geopolitical alignment.

There is a deeper structural issue. In many countries, commercial space firms outperform defence equivalents. They launch more often, innovate faster, and refresh constellations on consumer timescales rather than bureaucratic ones. The state grows dependent on private actors not just for capacity, but for relevance. When the most capable imaging network is privately owned, the question of who decides how it is used becomes strategic. A prime minister may find that critical intelligence flows through a company rather than a ministry. That shifts power quietly.

The dual-use dilemma also disrupts arms control. Traditional treaties focused on weapons: missiles, warheads, interceptors. But what is the weapon when a commercial satellite's camera guides humanitarian logistics by day and artillery by night? A treaty that restricts military reconnaissance satellites ignores the fact that commercial analogues exceed the performance of many state programmes. Efforts to classify assets as "civilian" or "military" increasingly resemble an exercise in semantics.

Some argue that this blurring brings stability. Commercial services diffuse power: small states and NGOs gain access to capabilities once monopolised by superpowers. Transparency can deter aggression; monitoring can expose atrocities. When everyone can see troop movements, secret mobilisation becomes harder. On this view, dual-use satellites democratise situational awareness, making war less likely or at least less opaque.

Others see danger. If a private firm withdraws service during a conflict, military planners may interpret it as a hostile act. If a company provides support to one side, the other may strike back—digitally or physically. A commercial ground station attacked by malware becomes collateral in a geopolitical struggle, yet insurance policies and legal frameworks are not written for this world. Shareholders did not sign up for cyber skirmishes with nation-states; engineers did not expect to harden their terminals against military intrusion.

Then there is the human dimension. Employees who joined a company to provide global internet may wake to find their work shaping the outcome of a war. Some become uneasy. Others feel pride. A few leave. When a firm's mission evolves from commerce to conflict support, corporate culture shifts. Casual decisions about bandwidth allocation or feature deployment acquire ethical gravity. Engineers are thrust into the moral geometry of conflict—without training, doctrine, or legal guidance.

The dual-use dilemma will intensify as constellations expand. Thousands of satellites providing global coverage make it impossible to isolate civilian from military activity. Data flows to whoever pays or persuades. Artificial intelligence will mine imagery for threats. Low-latency networks will carry encrypted tactical messaging with the same ease as streaming films. The infrastructure of everyday life will become the infrastructure of deterrence and warfare.

The uncomfortable truth is that dual-use cannot be undone. The commercial revolution in space has made advanced capabilities ubiquitous. The real question is how societies manage the ambiguity. Should companies adopt explicit policies governing military use of their services? Should states mandate neutrality or compel support? Should there be transparency requirements—declaring when imagery or bandwidth aids combat operations? Each answer carries risk: too much disclosure invites targeting; too little invites mistrust.

In the end, the satellites themselves remain indifferent. Their beams fall evenly on schools and brigades, hospitals and headquarters. It is humans—not hardware—who decide how that power is used. The dilemma is not technical. It is political, ethical, and unresolved, suspended in orbit like the constellations that gave it birth. The next conflict may show whether dual-use technology restrains violence or accelerates it. And commercial firms, long accustomed to thinking in terms of markets and customers, may discover they have become actors in something far older and far darker: the calculus of war.

Sovereignty by procurement

A nation can lose control of its space assets without a single missile being launched. It only needs to lose access to someone else's launch pad, someone else's navigation signal, someone else's satellite bus, or someone else's encrypted uplink. Space dominance has never been solely about who flies highest or sees furthest. It is also about who holds the receipts. Procurement—humdrum, bureaucratic, and often overlooked—is becoming a decisive theatre of sovereignty.

Many governments learned this the hard way. When geopolitical tensions rise, reliance on foreign launch providers becomes an unexpected vulnerability. A constellation operator may hold a spacecraft ready for orbit, only to discover that the next available slot on a trusted rocket is months away—and that the cheaper, quicker option lies in a jurisdiction now diplomatically hostile. A satellite stranded on Earth is a satellite that cannot detect missiles, relay communications, or validate timing signals. No general wants to plan operations around another nation's calendar. No finance minister wants the national banking system tied to an orbital asset that cannot be replaced on demand.

This is why launch capability has become a proxy for autonomy. Governments that once treated rockets as cold-war relics now see them as strategic lifelines. A domestically built launcher reduces political dependence and shortens the path from factory to orbit. It signals that critical infrastructure can be maintained even under sanctions, crises, or supply-chain disruption. Some countries pursue this aim through national champions; others subsidise private launch firms and guarantee them payloads. The physics of rocketry is unforgiving, but the politics of access is even harsher.

A similar logic drives regional navigation systems. The first global systems—GPS, GLONASS—were military projects, born from the quiet realisation that navigation is power. Whoever controls timing controls banking, transport, communications, and precision strike. For decades, most of the world relied on American or Russian signals. Then Europe built its own constellation, insisting that its economy and defence could not hinge on foreign goodwill. China followed with a full global system. India developed a regional network tailored to its borders. None of these projects were cheap. Yet they were cheaper than strategic dependence.

Navigation is only one example. Weather satellites affect agriculture and disaster response. Imaging satellites support border security and maritime policing. Communications satellites knit together national broadcast networks, ministry backbones, and transcontinental fibre gaps. If these functions rely entirely on foreign operators, sovereignty becomes porous. A state may find that its meteorologists are blind, its coast guard deaf, or its emergency responders isolated—all because a contract was cancelled or a ground station was severed from a foreign satellite.

Procurement is not merely about buying hardware. It shapes entire industrial ecosystems. When a government commits to domestic launch, domestic manufacturers follow. When it funds national imaging satellites, universities expand their space engineering capabilities. When it mandates secure national communications networks, cryptographic firms and antenna suppliers flourish. Sovereignty, in this sense, is cumulative: each procurement decision builds or erodes national capacity.

This carries its own tensions. Domestic space industries must compete with global giants whose scale reduces cost. A national launcher may struggle to match commercial pricing, especially if its primary rationale is strategic rather than economic. Some states accept higher prices as the cost of autonomy. Others pursue hybrid strategies, maintaining at least one domestic rocket while freely using foreign ones in peacetime. A few place their hopes in reusable launchers, small-satellite rockets, or air-launched systems. Sovereignty is a spectrum. It can be full or partial, symbolic or functional.

Payloads follow a similar spectrum. A surveillance satellite can be bought off the shelf or built in-house. A telecom satellite can be leased rather than owned. A nation can rent broadcast capacity from a commercial operator rather than launch its own. Each choice trades efficiency against control. Leasing makes sense for cash-strapped governments, but it also places critical communications in corporate hands. Buying a satellite outright provides autonomy, but demands a domestic ground segment, orbital rights, and an insurance regime that can withstand failure.

Historically, only superpowers had the luxury of choice. Today, smaller states are acquiring their own space assets, sometimes through clever procurement rather than indigenous development. A country might contract a foreign factory to build a satellite, but require technology transfer and local assembly. It might partner with universities for mission planning, or use commercial ground stations while training its own operators. Sovereignty can be purchased in instalments: first capacity, then knowledge, then independence.

Yet the drive for autonomy has unintended consequences. If every region builds its own navigation system, interference risks rise. If every state insists on domestic launch, markets fragment and duplication spreads. Efficiency yields to geopolitics. The sky becomes crowded with national pride and political insurance. But from a strategic viewpoint, redundancy is a feature, not a flaw. No nation wants to discover that a rival's export ban has knocked out its communications. The world's most advanced militaries think the same way: distribute, diversify, harden.

There is a deeper psychological dimension. Space carries symbolic weight. Launching one's own satellite is a declaration that a nation has moved beyond being a consumer of technology. It signals that it has joined a club once occupied by only a handful of players. Space is a stage on which sovereignty is demonstrated—not through speeches or treaties, but through hardware that works. It is no accident that new spacefaring nations broadcast their launches live and emblazon the rockets with national colours. The message is clear: our interests reach beyond our borders.

For defence planners, sovereignty by procurement is more than symbolism. In crises, they assume foreign partners may be distracted, reluctant, or compromised. A nation that relies entirely on allies for satellite imagery may discover that those allies prioritise their own theatres. A government that depends on foreign launch providers may see its replacement satellite postponed if global supply tightens. Worst of all, a hostile state might compel a supplier to cut service. The absence of a single contract clause can become an act of coercion.

This is why procurement strategies increasingly include sanctions resilience. Firms relocate production lines to avoid export restrictions. Alliances build multi-vendor supply chains. Some states stockpile critical components—radiation-hardened chips, reaction wheels, thrusters—much like they stockpile fuel. Launch providers diversify propellant sources and manufacturing sites. Even ground antennas are being modularised so they can be shipped and reassembled quickly if a base is threatened. Sovereignty, once a constitutional term, now has a logistics department.

Yet full autonomy is impossible. Satellites require global tracking networks, orbital debris monitoring, and international frequency coordination. Launch windows depend on shared airspace and maritime zones. Constellations rely on foreign components, foreign software, foreign insurance. Even the most ambitious national programmes ultimately depend on a web of shared infrastructure. Sovereignty, in space, is never absolute. It is negotiated—quietly, pragmatically, and continuously.

That is the paradox. Nations chase autonomy precisely because they are interdependent. The more they need space, the more they fear losing access to it. The more commercial the sector becomes, the more governments feel compelled to exert control. The procurement officer, once a paper-pushing bureaucrat, has become a gatekeeper of national power. The factory floor has become a strategic frontier.

As more countries enter the club of spacefaring states, sovereignty will be measured not only in who can launch, but in who can replace. A satellite in orbit is useful; a satellite factory on the ground is power. The next decade will test whether the global market remains open, or whether launch and payloads become instruments of pressure and reward. When nations demand sovereignty by procurement, they are not merely buying rockets and satellites. They are buying freedom from dependence—and hoping that, if the world fractures, their sky remains their own.

Sanctions and standards

A satellite can be born in one country, tested in another, fuelled in a third, launched from a fourth, and operated over dozens. Yet the entire chain can be halted by a single line in an export regulation or a change in sanctions law. Space may advertise itself as borderless, but its hardware and software are deeply entangled with national rules. The most powerful weapon in orbit is often not a missile. It is compliance paperwork.

Consider a small firm that designs radiation-hardened processors for satellites. Its engineers care about transistor counts, thermal envelopes, and radiation tolerance. Its executives care about something far more abstract: where each wafer was fabricated, which national laws govern its sales, and which customers might turn a commercial payload into a military asset. One signature added to a sanctions list can turn yesterday's customers into today's liabilities. A simple component—no larger than a coin—can suddenly become a controlled technology whose export requires a licence, an audit trail, and diplomatic discretion. The marketplace bends around these rules. Companies re-route supply chains, move factories across borders, and reconfigure ownership structures simply to keep selling.

This is where law and strategy quietly intersect. Sanctions are not merely punishments; they are instruments of industrial redirection. When a nation is barred from acquiring high-grade imaging sensors, it is being denied more than a piece of glass. It is being denied the ability to see, track, and target. When launch providers are prohibited from exporting to certain destinations, replacement satellites are delayed and intelligence gaps widen. The sanctions are economic, but the effects are military.

Standards work just as subtly. Deciding which encryption algorithms a satellite may use, which frequency bands require registration, or which components must be traceable is ostensibly about safety and interoperability. Yet every standard is also a gate. Those who meet it enter, those who cannot are kept out. Emerging space powers often discover that building a rocket is only half the challenge; persuading others to accept its telemetry, coordinate its spectrum, and recognise its frequency filings is the other half. Without regulatory acceptance, a rocket becomes a museum piece.

Firms respond in pragmatic ways. Some split into subsidiaries so that "clean" divisions can serve compliant markets while "restricted" divisions operate under tighter control. Others move assembly to neutral countries that can trade with both sanctioned and sanctioning states. A few redesign entire satellites to use only components sourced from politically safe jurisdictions. The hardware may look identical, but its supply chain has been scrubbed of risk. This shift is expensive, yet cheaper than losing access to global customers.

The most striking changes are often in software. Many states now treat certain code as a defence article, subject to export approval. A satellite operator that updates its onboard encryption, adds anti-jamming measures, or improves autonomous manoeuvring may find the new code classified for military relevance. Algorithms that predict orbital conjunctions, optimise ground contact windows, or identify radio-frequency interference can all fall under dual-use restrictions. As a result, firms sometimes freeze software features—not for lack of innovation, but for fear of bureaucratic entanglement.

Sanctions ripple outward. Imagine a constellation builder whose flight computers rely on a specialised chip produced by a single vendor in a country suddenly placed under export scrutiny. The firm must redesign its board, retest its radiation tolerance, re-certify the flight computer, and possibly delay an entire launch campaign. Each delay carries financial penalties, lost market share, and—if the satellite supports national security—operational risk. Sanctions imposed on one jurisdiction can therefore warp the business plans of companies continents away.

Standards have similar downstream effects. When regulators tighten debris mitigation rules—requiring satellites to deorbit within a shorter timeframe or carry collision-avoidance capability—manufacturers must add propulsion, upgrade software, or pay higher insurance premiums. These changes alter design choices, launch mass, and business models. Small satellite operators, especially, find themselves squeezed: either comply with costly standards or lose access to key markets and ground stations. Innovation bends to the rulebook.

There is a philosophical tension here. Space was once imagined as humanity's shared frontier. In practice, it is governed by the same logic as traded goods and controlled technologies. Some argue that weaponising access to components or launch services undermines openness and fuels division. Others argue that sanctions are necessary: without them, adversaries would simply buy their way into orbital advantage. Both views are correct, depending on whose security is at stake.

Historically, space sanctions were blunt instruments. They were aimed at stopping nuclear proliferation or restricting missile technology. Today, they are scalpel-precise. A nation might be barred not from space entirely, but from high-resolution optics above a certain threshold. A company might freely sell communications satellites, but require approval if the payload includes encrypted telemetry. Some governments even require "know-your-customer" diligence for earth observation firms, ensuring images are not quietly transferred to hostile actors. The language resembles finance more than flight dynamics.

These rules shape geopolitics. When one bloc restricts a technology, another develops a domestic alternative. Investors flock to firms promising "sanctions-proof" supply chains. Countries form regional clusters of manufacturing to reduce vulnerability. Some launch providers design rockets that never cross certain controlled thresholds so they can sell globally without triggering export regimes. Others build super-heavy vehicles precisely because their customers are governments that want strategic lift without dependence on foreign fleets.

Yet sanctions are double-edged. Overuse can accelerate self-sufficiency in rivals. A state barred from buying optical sensors may build its own. A company denied access to Western semiconductors may invest in domestic fabrication. Paradoxically, sanctions that seek to limit capability can sometimes stimulate it. The long-term outcome is not simply containment, but technological bifurcation: two or more parallel ecosystems that do not share parts, software, or standards.

Standards face their own dilemmas. If rules diverge—one region demanding on-board propulsion for every satellite, another accepting passive disposal—operators are forced to design for the strictest regime or fragment their product lines. Common standards lower cost and enhance safety, but they require trust between competitors. When trust collapses, standards become weapons.

Still, there is a quiet optimism beneath the bureaucracy. Many engineers, regulators, and insurers understand that debris, interference, and unsafe operations threaten everyone. Shared minimum requirements for end-of-life disposal or collision avoidance are emerging not because diplomats love agreement, but because insurers hate ruinous claims. Economic self-interest may do more for orbital safety than treaty negotiation ever did.

Ultimately, sanctions and standards tell a story about power: who exercises it, who complies with it, who resists it, and who adapts around it. They reveal a truth often missed in discussions about rockets and satellites. Space is not only a contest of physics, bravery, or innovation. It is a contest of legal frameworks, procurement strategies, and regulatory leverage. Nations that cannot defeat a rival in orbit may still constrain it on the ground—by limiting what it can buy, where it can build, or who will insure it.

Some future crisis will test these systems. A state may find that its constellation cannot be replenished because its components are trapped behind paperwork. A company may discover that its most advanced satellite cannot launch because a supplier fell under new restrictions. Or perhaps the opposite will occur: a sanctioned nation, forced to build from scratch, will emerge technologically stronger and less dependent than before.

The open question is whether these rules will evolve into a coherent global framework or fracture into competing spheres. Will common standards emerge from shared vulnerability, or will sanctions carve the space economy into isolated blocs? For now, the only certainty is that the path to orbit runs through a maze of regulations. Those who navigate it well will shape the future of space—not through thrust or payload, but through the quiet power of compliance.

Chapter 9

Deterrence Without Gravity Wells

A strange transformation is underway. The oldest logic of deterrence—credible punishment, clear signalling, and the management of fear—has left the missile fields and naval bastions and drifted into orbit. Yet space offers none of the intuitive guardrails that once steadied nuclear strategy. There are no borders in low Earth orbit, no secure territories, no oceans to patrol. Satellites cross every nation's skies in minutes. Weapons can masquerade as a benign inspection craft. And a single act of destructive force risks poisoning the environment for everyone, attacker and victim alike. Deterrence in space is not just a military puzzle: it is a philosophical one. How do you threaten harm without destroying the very commons you rely upon?

For all the talk of space becoming "the next battlefield," most states know that an orbital firefight would be an act of self-harm. Debris does not respect strategy. The shards of a shattered spacecraft swipe across friend and foe alike. This peculiar fragility creates a paradox: capability must be shown to be believed, yet destruction must be avoided to be credible. The harsh truth is that it is far easier to build a weapon that works once than a weapon that signals without wreckage. Space deterrence therefore leans toward subtler forms of strength—redundancy, dispersion, manoeuvre, resilience—rather than explosive demonstration. It rewards the quiet engineer more than the swaggering general.

This chapter examines that shifting architecture of influence, where satellites are defended not by armour but by numbers, mobility, and ambiguity. Deterrence by denial has become the backbone of orbital stability. A nation that once relied on a handful of exquisite, vulnerable spacecraft now spreads capability across proliferated constellations, hardened uplinks, and distributed ground nodes. If an adversary cannot meaningfully cripple those systems, the incentive to strike erodes. A space force composed of hundreds or thousands of replaceable units—each small, cheap, and rapidly produced—undercuts the classic attack logic. Why swing a hammer if the target shatters into a problem without delivering victory?

Yet denial alone is never enough. Deterrence has always depended on signalling: showing what one can do without actually doing it. On Earth, this might take the shape of a missile test or a troop rotation. In orbit, destructive demonstrations are politically costly and environmentally reckless. Instead, states experiment with reversible interference—directed energy that blinds without breaking, jamming that annoys without annihilation, and proximity manoeuvres that say *we can reach you* without leaving debris in the sky. These are warnings disguised as irritation. They are calibrated to speak loudly but leave little physical trace. The line between reassurance and intimidation, however, is razor thin.

Complicating everything is entanglement. The global economy and modern militaries increasingly share the same satellites, the same communication beams, the same data relays. A single spacecraft may carry school lessons to a rural classroom in one moment and encrypted command data to a deployed brigade in the next. Knock out the satellite, and you do not only silence a defence network; you cut off hospitals, disaster relief teams, and farmers checking weather maps. This overlapping infrastructure makes traditional targeting logic treacherous. A strike intended as a limited message can trigger worldwide outrage or economic chaos. In space, the concept of "civilian collateral" expands far beyond borders.

To navigate these risks, states seek tools of escalation control. Some are diplomatic: hotlines between rival space commands, notifications of close approaches, shared orbital data, and pre-announced manoeuvres that prevent misread intentions. Others are technical: cryptographic authentication to avoid accidental spoofing, safety corridors for inspection satellites, telemetry formats that allow verification without revealing secrets. The purpose is not trust—trust is rare—but predictability. Even adversaries can agree that surprise in orbit is dangerous.

Yet the most corrosive element in space deterrence is ambiguity. Secrecy may feel like protection, but it often invites worst-case planning. When a satellite suddenly changes orbit with no explanation, intelligence agencies scramble to infer the motive. When interference hits a ground station and no one claims responsibility, suspicion fills the vacuum. A single misattributed event—a glitch mistaken for a cyberattack, a failed manoeuvre perceived as hostile—can ignite a cycle of retaliation. In a domain where proof is hard and denial is easy, imagination becomes a weapon.

Deterrence without gravity wells demands a different vocabulary. It favours resilience over invincibility, communication over bravado, and clever restraint over theatrical violence. The logic is not about scaring an enemy into silence. It is about making aggression pointless, escalation controllable, and misunderstandings rare. The stakes could not be higher. Satellites underpin timing, banking, navigation, weather prediction, disaster response, and global communications. The world does not simply *use* space. It depends on it the way lungs depend on air—quietly, constantly, unnoticed until threatened.

The pages ahead explore how this invisible structure of stability is built: through redundant constellations, reversible tools, diplomatic choreography, and a careful balance of transparency and secrecy. The puzzle is unresolved, and the future uncertain. What happens when more states—and private firms—field their own space forces? When proliferated constellations multiply by an order of magnitude? When the first deliberate attack tests whether restraint is myth or muscle?

The answers matter not just for generals and diplomats, but for anyone who relies on a phone, a ship, a power grid, or a weather forecast. Space deterrence is not a distant abstraction. It is the quiet architecture that keeps a fragile world from stumbling into catastrophe.

Credible punishment and denial

The old logic of deterrence rested on a blunt promise: if you strike me, I will strike you harder. That worked when cities were the targets and silos the assets. But it collapses in orbit. A satellite has no shockwave to fear, no rubble to sift. Its enemy is distance, velocity, and shards of metal travelling faster than rifle bullets. Worse still, a spectacular retaliatory attack risks poisoning the very orbital lanes your own forces depend on. The paradox becomes obvious the moment strategists run the numbers: how do you threaten punishment without destroying the commons you need to operate in?

A quiet answer is emerging, and it does not rely on vengeance at all. Instead of threatening an adversary with fire, spacefaring nations are increasingly shaping their constellations so that attacks do not work. Redundant spacecraft, dispersed ground stations, hardened command uplinks, and proliferated low Earth orbit (LEO) networks turn space from a brittle architecture of a few exquisite assets into a web of replaceable nodes. Deterrence by denial, once a footnote to classical theory, is becoming the central pillar of stability above the atmosphere.

The logic is brutally simple. If an attacker cannot meaningfully damage a system—or can do so only at disproportionate cost—aggression loses its value. A decade ago, the space orders of battle of major powers resembled fine jewellery: small in number, priceless in capability, and fragile under pressure. Knocking out a handful of satellites could blind a military, stall global communications or undermine missile warning. Today, rising numbers of states and companies are moving in the opposite direction. Constellations of hundreds or thousands of smaller spacecraft, each with modest individual capability but tremendous aggregate capacity, make that fragility harder to exploit.

Proliferated LEO constellations are the emblem of this shift. A surveillance or communications network once depended on a few satellites parked in high orbits, each one a single point of failure. Now, in many mission areas, those hulking flagships are being supplemented—or replaced—by swarms. For an attacker, the maths is unforgiving. One anti-satellite missile might remove a single node, but dozens replace it within minutes. Even if the attacker launches a coordinated strike, the constellation recoheres, routing around losses like a biological organism healing from a wound. The days of "silver-bullet" satellite kills delivering decisive advantage are fading fast.

Redundancy is not just about numbers; it is about agility. Small satellites can be produced quickly, launched cheaply, and manoeuvred frequently. Some operators quietly maintain on-orbit spares—silent spacecraft that wait in reserve, ready to take over when a neighbour fails or is attacked. Others rely on responsive launch capabilities, the space equivalent of battlefield surgeons: a damaged constellation can be patched in days or weeks rather than years. In deterrence terms, this undermines the attacker's calculus. Why strike if your victory dissolves before the propaganda can be drafted?

Then there is hardening. Some satellites now carry directional antennas resilient to jamming, protected command modules resistant to cyber compromise, and shielding against electromagnetic pulses or radiation bursts. Hardened uplinks, encrypted telemetry, and authentication protocols reduce the chance that a spoofed command signal can hijack an entire mission. None of this is glamorous, and most of it remains invisible to the public. But it reflects a profound shift in philosophy: the race is not to build the most powerful spacecraft, but the most survivable system.

Dispersion completes the triad. Militaries once controlled satellites from a small number of large ground stations—easy targets for missile strikes or cyber attacks. Increasingly, they spread their infrastructure into distributed footprints: mobile terminals hidden in forests, antennas on ships, fly-away kits that can be unpacked beside a runway or highway. In wartime, these pop-up ground nodes restore links even after primary bases are damaged. Dispersion also complicates classic coercive strategies. If command and control can migrate across continents and platforms, no attacker can be confident that a disabling blow has landed.

All of this leaves adversaries with an unenviable choice. They can invest immense resources in attacking a constellation that will not stay crippled, or they can escalate to more destructive—and politically catastrophic—forms of violence that risk debris showers and global outrage. Denial forces them to question whether the juice is worth the squeeze. It is not moral restraint that slows a would-be aggressor. It is arithmetic.

Critics sometimes argue that denial alone lacks grandeur. It feels defensive, even cowardly. They ask: what about deterrence by punishment? Where is the fear? Yet credible punishment still matters, though it looks different in space. A nation need not shatter satellites to impose costs. It might seize ground terminals, sanction suppliers, or degrade adversary constellations with reversible interference. Such measures can be dialled up or down without orbital shrapnel. They can be demonstrated without scarring the heavens.

Still, denial remains the cornerstone because it aligns incentives. It does not require an opponent to believe in your courage—only in your engineering. A dispersing, self-healing constellation says, in effect: *Attack if you wish, but you will not win.* That message resonates even between rivals who cannot speak openly. It lowers the temperature, discouraging risky gambits and accidental escalation. It also encourages more responsible behaviours: if satellites are cheap to replace, states are less tempted to shoot them down to make a point.

There is a deeper philosophical shift too. Classic strategic thought put deterrence in the realm of psychology—leaders assessing rivals' motives and bluffing bravado. In the orbital age, physics intrudes. Denial rests on orbital mechanics, signal routing, and manufacturing capacity. It is a technical form of restraint: stability engineered, not negotiated. When a constellation spans every latitude and reconnects after every strike, even hot-headed strategists face reality. Vengeance becomes irrelevant; control of the commons becomes the priority.

Yet there are limits. Not every satellite can be proliferated. Missile-warning spacecraft, deep-space tracking sensors, and some secure communications platforms still depend on large, exquisite assets. Their loss would be felt keenly. Denial does not eliminate vulnerability; it redistributes it. The most advanced actors hedge their bets: a few indispensable spacecraft hardened to the highest possible standard, surrounded by flocks of sacrificial, quickly rebuilt counterparts. This layered architecture is messy, but realistic.

Another tension lies in the economics. Redundancy and hardening cost money. Emerging space nations may struggle to field vast constellations or hardened ground networks. They worry—legitimately—about a future where only wealthy powers can afford deterrence by denial, leaving poorer states exposed. If stability depends on distributed capacity, what happens when only a handful of actors can distribute at scale?

There is also the problem of interpretation. A proliferated constellation can be read two ways: a shield, or a net. Some see it as defensive architecture; others fear that such constellations, especially with dual-use imagery or communications payloads, blur the line between civilian infrastructure and military command. In crisis, an opponent may perceive denial not as restraint but as preparation for offensive action. The psychological element never disappears entirely.

Still, denial's greatest strength is that it does not rely on trust. It is mathematical, mechanical, and visible through a telescope. A nation can lie about intentions, but it cannot fake the presence of 700 satellites in polar orbit. It cannot bluff a constellation of hidden ground terminals that spring back to life after an attack. In a world thick with suspicion, transparency of capability becomes a quiet stabiliser.

For all the elegance of the theory, denial remains an experiment in progress. The next armed conflict that touches space—whether directly or indirectly—will reveal whether proliferated networks truly blunt aggression or merely complicate it. Will a determined attacker abandon kinetic strikes in favour of cyber sabotage or ground assaults? Will reversible jamming become the favoured instrument of coercion? Or will denial force adversaries into unexpected restraint, recognising that space has become too complex to dominate by force?

The answer will not be found in press releases or war college seminars. It will be written in the orbital charts after the first real crisis: whether constellations flicker, then reform; whether debris clouds remain rare; whether attackers learn that striking space brings little reward. Denial is the ultimate message without fireworks: resilience as deterrent, persistence as warning, engineering as insurance.

For now, its power lies in undermining certainty. No planner who faces a proliferated, agile architecture can promise quick victory in orbit. That hesitation—small but potent—may be the most valuable commodity in modern deterrence. Whether it holds when pressure mounts remains to be seen, and the world will watch carefully. If denial succeeds, space may stay dangerous but not uninhabitable. If it fails, the silent lanes above Earth could become a scrapyard of shattered ambitions.

Signalling restraint

The first time a nation proved it could kill a satellite, the world learned it not from a press release but from a cloud of shrapnel. In 2007, thousands of fragments bloomed across low Earth orbit after a direct-ascent interceptor obliterated a weather satellite. The message was unmistakable: we can do this. The problem was equally clear: doing it poisoned space for everyone. The demonstration signalled power, but it also signalled recklessness. In the years since, major space powers have been wrestling with the same dilemma: how to show capability without leaving scars.

Deterrence in orbit requires communication. Silence invites miscalculation; secrecy invites paranoia. Yet every test, manoeuvre, or hint of strength risks inflaming tensions in a fragile environment where a single collision can ripple for decades. States have therefore begun to develop a different grammar of signalling—gestures that convey resolve while avoiding debris, reversible actions that warn rather than wound, and transparent behaviours that reduce the chance of accidental war.

Some signals are quiet but unmistakable. A satellite that shadows another at close range is not subtle. Proximity operations are a form of orbital body language: I am watching; I can follow; I can reach. When a spacecraft from one nation drifts alongside a rival's reconnaissance satellite, the message is not friendly curiosity. It is a demonstration of manoeuvrability, tracking, and intent. Yet proximity leaves no rubble behind. Unlike a missile strike, the spacecraft can back away, break off, or open a channel explaining its presence. The move is provocative, but it remains reversible.

Electronic warfare offers an even clearer example. A satellite's signal can be jammed, its data link drowned in controlled noise, or its downlink stepped on by a neighbouring transmitter. Such interference is temporary, difficult to attribute without investigation, and often deliberately limited. For a state that wants to show teeth without biting off a limb, reversible interference is a calibrated warning: we can degrade you, but we have chosen not to destroy. The danger, of course, lies in ambiguity. A jam may be a signal—or it may be a covert attack. Without communication, a warning can look like sabotage.

Some militaries experiment with a subtler form of signalling: demonstrating defensive capability rather than offensive aggression. A constellation may reveal its resilience during exercises, rapidly rerouting traffic after a simulated outage, rolling to backup frequencies, or deploying ground-based terminals after a cut uplink. These rehearsals say, in effect: *You cannot black us out.* By broadcasting survivability instead of threat, states reshape deterrence. They hint that any attack would fail, not that a retaliation would devastate. It is a colder, more technical form of messaging—and often a more stabilising one.

The rise of reversible effects fits this pattern. Rather than blowing a spacecraft to pieces, a system might momentarily blind an imager with laser dazzling, corrupt telemetry for minutes at a time, or saturate radar with carefully modulated pulses. The target recovers. No debris. No permanent loss. But the signal is unmistakable. States increasingly see value in such temporary measures. They offer a ladder of escalation, with rungs spaced far below catastrophic violence. Each rung is a message: *We see you; we can touch you; do not force our hand.*

This is restraint as strategy, not virtue. Spacefaring powers are acutely aware that a debris-generating conflict would be a self-inflicted wound. Weather forecasting, banking, navigation, intelligence, humanitarian coordination—all rely on the same orbital highways. A war that shatters satellites endangers civilians, neutral states, and the attacker's own spacecraft. The taboo against debris is therefore not altruistic; it is survivalist. The most sophisticated actors do not want to glide through wreckage of their own making.

But restraint must be seen to exist if it is to stabilise. That requires openness. When nations announce missile-warning tests or proximity drills in advance, they are not being courteous; they are reducing the chance of panic. Transparency becomes a signalling tool: "We are testing manoeuvres, but not preparing to strike you." Some governments share orbital ephemerides or alert others to potential conjunctions. The subtext is clear: we are not hiding. Secrecy may protect sensitive capabilities, but it can also produce ghosts—imagined threats, misunderstood manoeuvres, phantom attacks.

There are moments when signalling restraint becomes an act of diplomacy. Consider the difference between a state that quietly builds anti-satellite weapons in secrecy and one that publicly renounces debris-producing tests. The latter is not naïve; it still has other tools—cyber, jamming, proximity operations—but it signals that it will not poison the environment. This kind of commitment reassures allies, calms jittery rivals, and narrows the space for paranoia. A pledge against debris is not a disarmament measure; it is a statement of sophistication.

Yet restraint has its own dangers. A state that signals too gently can be ignored. A reversible effect that goes unnoticed teaches nothing. And sometimes a demonstration intended as a warning is interpreted as weakness. This is the delicate balance: signal enough strength to deter, but not enough to trigger escalation. It is the kind of chess played silently, in vacuum, at 7 kilometres per second.

Some analysts worry that reversible measures normalise interference. If jamming becomes a routine signal, does it encourage tit-for-tat harassment? If dazzling becomes a preferred warning, will space be filled with temporary blinding contests? The line between signalling and aggression can blur quickly. What looks to one actor like a gentle nudge may look to another like the opening shot of a covert war. Restraint does not solve distrust; it only reduces the cost of misunderstanding.

There is also the philosophical question of visibility. A missile test that destroys nothing still sends a loud message. A proximity manoeuvre must be observed to matter. A jammed signal must be recognised as deliberate interference. States have to assume their signals will be seen, correctly interpreted, and properly contextualised. That is a fragile assumption. In a crisis, fear can distort perception; intelligence officers can misread intent; politicians can imagine threats where none exist.

The risk of escalation remains. In a tense environment, the difference between a warning and a provocation may be a single interpretation. If a satellite brushes too close and a rival pilot miscalculates, the restraint of proximity operations becomes irrelevant. If a jam is misattributed or mistaken for permanent sabotage, a reversible action may trigger irreversible retaliation. Signalling without debris avoids one kind of escalation, but it introduces another: escalation through confusion.

Still, there is no sensible alternative. The world cannot return to theatrical displays of destruction. The orbital commons are too valuable to treat as a stage for war. And yet quiet capability must be shown somehow. The middle path—signals that leave no shrapnel—offers the least bad route. It is deterrence through demonstration, not devastation.

Some states experiment with even softer signals: notifications of new launch sites, open-source technical documentation, routine invitations to observe space tracking exercises. They telegraph competence without menace. Others pursue cooperative norms, proposing shared rules against debris, codes for proximity operations, or hotlines for orbital incidents. These efforts are not sentimental; they are strategic infrastructure. If actors cannot speak clearly, their satellites will speak for them—and not always deliberately.

A peculiar irony sits at the heart of signalling restraint: the most powerful message may be the quietest one. A constellation that shrugs off interference without fanfare, a satellite that calmly reroutes after a spoofing attempt, a ground station that reappears hours after a strike—these actions tell an adversary that escalation earns little. The signal is not: *We will punish you.* It is: *You cannot defeat us.* That form of communication is profoundly stabilising.

Over time, restraint may become the currency of power in space. Nations that can demonstrate capability without collateral damage gain credibility. Actors that rely on loud, reckless tests invite diplomatic backlash and strategic isolation. The future of space security may depend not on who has the strongest weapon, but on who has the finest control over it.

The unanswered question is whether restraint can survive genuine crisis. In wartime, the pressure to escalate—to strike first, to blind sensors, to cripple communication—can override decades of careful signalling. Will commanders remember the value of reversible effects when lives are at stake on the ground? Will politicians accept temporary interference rather than demand a decisive knockout? The theory of restraint has not yet met the stress of sustained conflict.

Until that day, signalling remains a fragile art. It is communication through orbital manoeuvres, controlled interference, transparency, and promise. It is the practice of showing strength while leaving nothing broken in your wake. And it sits at the centre of a strategic paradox: to keep space peaceful, actors must sometimes demonstrate how they could make it dangerous.

Whether humanity can balance that paradox will decide the shape of the skies for generations. Restraint is rational, but rationality is a thin shield under pressure. The hope is that the signals sent today—quiet, reversible, and precise—teach future rivals something essential: that power in space does not require shattering it.

Entanglement risks

A decade ago, a European weather satellite suffered a quiet software fault. For a few hours, the image stream vanished. Data feeds broke. Forecast models stalled. The outage was inconvenient, not catastrophic. Yet what startled officials was not the blackout itself, but the ripple that followed: aviation planners lost wind charts, emergency managers missed storm updates, and commodity traders grumbled that price models had frozen. Nothing military had been touched. No adversary was involved. But a single glitch in orbit revealed something uncomfortable—civilian life and national security now ride the same satellites.

Modern space infrastructure is a web without neat boundaries. Broadband constellations serve schools on weekdays and military brigades on weekends. Earth-observation satellites map deforestation in August and track armoured columns in September. Navigation signals guide farmers sowing crops and missiles steering to targets. There is no bright line between civilian and military utility. The same spacecraft that beams textbooks to remote villages can also deliver encrypted orders to special forces. Entanglement is not a by-product of space expansion—it is its defining feature.

This blurring complicates the logic of conflict. In older forms of war, targets were dressed in uniform: airbases, missile silos, radar stations. Destroying them inflicted harm only on an opponent. But an attack on a dual-use satellite risks collateral damage to neighbours, allies and neutrals who depend on the same network. A state may wish to disrupt an adversary's communications, yet doing so could black out rural clinics, merchant shipping or disaster warning services across an entire region. The legal definition of military necessity has never been comfortable with such spill-over; in space, spill-over is the rule, not the exception.

One of the starkest illustrations came from Eastern Europe in 2022. Commercial broadband networks, contracted for civilian purposes, became central to military command and control. Terminals rode in ambulances and armoured vehicles; antennas linked headquarters to frontline units. When interference surged before hostilities began, villages lost connectivity alongside soldiers. The line of attack blurred: was it a strike against military communications, or a disruption of civilian life? And if the same satellite beams served users in neighbouring countries, what obligations existed to protect them?

The vulnerability runs both ways. A commercial constellation owned by a private firm may find itself suddenly entangled in geopolitical conflict. Operators become reluctant participants in national strategy, deciding whether to geofence coverage, throttle data, or share imagery with governments. In theory, these systems are neutral. In practice, their decisions tilt battlefields. A company that supplies humanitarian broadband today may supply encrypted tactical links tomorrow, simply by switching software profiles. Neutrality evaporates at the speed of configuration.

States once imagined they could wall off military satellites from civilian networks—separate fleets, separate frequencies, separate control. That illusion has faded. Many nations lack the budget to duplicate capabilities. Some rely on commercial imagery for intelligence, leasing tasking rights from private operators. Others depend on consumer navigation signals because their sovereign systems are incomplete or vulnerable. Even the most technologically advanced powers use shared ground stations and rented satellite phones. Entanglement is structural, not accidental.

This creates a moral hazard. If every useful satellite performs civilian and military functions, an attacker can justify striking almost anything. "Dual-use" becomes a label applied retrospectively, after the debris has already scattered. The norms of proportionality and discrimination struggle to survive in a sky where harm is diffuse. A missile aimed at an adversary's surveillance satellite might disrupt maritime tracking, aviation routing, or earthquake response for half a planet. Whose suffering counts in the calculus of war?

Diplomacy responds slowly. International law offers principles, not clarity. The Outer Space Treaty forbids placing weapons of mass destruction in orbit, but says little about the subtler weapons that disable infrastructure without explosives. Export controls regulate sensitive technologies, but not operational decisions by private firms. And the speed of commercial innovation outpaces treaties by decades. Lawyers can argue whether a cyber intrusion against a satellite is an "attack"; meanwhile, the farmers awaiting GPS-timed irrigation simply lose their signal.

The entanglement problem deepens with scale. Thousands of small satellites now operate in tight constellations. They cannot be disabled one by one without turning low Earth orbit into a shooting gallery. Striking a few craft might degrade service for millions. Striking many would create debris fields that imperil all operators, friend and foe alike. The cost of escalation rises with density—not because military systems are robust, but because civilians sit directly beneath the line of fire.

There is another, subtler form of entanglement: data. Commercial imaging firms provide open-source intelligence visible to anyone with a browser. Human rights groups track forced labour camps; analysts monitor missile deployments; journalists verify atrocity locations. An adversary who wishes to hide cannot simply shut down the satellites without silencing global transparency. To blind their enemy, they must blind the world. That calculation stays some hands—but not all.

Policy-makers wrestle with grim trade-offs. Do they nationalise critical commercial assets to ensure command and control? Do they mandate redundancy across multiple providers? Do they fortify ground stations and fibre routes shared between broadcasters and defence ministries? None of these measures erase entanglement; they merely cushion its shock. A hardened signal path still carries weather alerts alongside military orders. A redundant constellation still sends banking timestamps alongside missile warnings.

Some propose carving protected humanitarian bands—orbital channels reserved for civilian uses, shielded by international agreement. But how would enforcement work? A satellite cannot be painted white like a hospital ship. A frequency cannot be visually identified. And a belligerent could always claim that hostile forces were exploiting "civilian" satellites for military ends. The fog of war drifts easily into vacuum.

The core tension is philosophical. Space was once imagined as a domain of clean separation: military satellites for war; civilian satellites for peace. That world never existed. Instead, humanity built systems of extraordinary utility, then layered strategic reliance on top. The entanglement is not a flaw—it is evidence of success. Global navigation works precisely because it is universal. Earth-observation helps farmers and generals alike. In trying to separate these threads, we confront the reality that shared infrastructure is a feature of modern civilisation.

Yet the more shared the infrastructure, the higher the stakes when it is threatened. A state contemplating interference must weigh the wrath of neutral countries whose banks, airports, and hospitals depend on the same beams. Even reversible effects—spoofing, jamming, dazzling—risk collateral harm. A jammed frequency may spill across borders; a dazzled imaging satellite may miss floods or fires. Containment is nearly impossible.

This entanglement might, paradoxically, deter reckless escalation. Knowing that an attack would punish bystanders, not just enemies, can restrain decision-makers. But that restraint relies on rational leaders, clear attribution, and a shared understanding of consequences. None of these are guaranteed. Misattribution is easy in the fog of electronic warfare. If a navigation signal flickers, who is to blame—the adversary, solar weather, a software bug? When civilians suffer, politicians look for villains.

The hardest question sits like a stone at the centre of strategic planning: how do you fight in space without harming everyone else? Militaries have answers on paper—precision interference, reversible effects, selective targeting of military-only systems—but the physics do not cooperate. Beams scatter. Networks interlock. Users crowd the same spectrum. Even a perfect attack can have imperfect consequences.

For now, nations live with this uncertainty. They entangle because the efficiencies are irresistible. Shared satellites are cheaper, faster to launch, and easier to upgrade. Private operators innovate at a pace governments cannot match. To decouple civilian and military infrastructure would require a revolution of budgets and bureaucracy that no state appears willing to fund.

So we continue to build a world where a school in one country shares a communications satellite with a submarine in another. We applaud the efficiency, celebrate the connectivity, and quietly dread the vulnerability. Entanglement has become the price of progress.

Whether this price is sustainable depends on decisions yet to be made. If states craft norms that protect shared infrastructure—hotlines, transparency, pre-announced tests, commitments against debris—they may blunt the worst risks. If they treat dual-use satellites as disposable, the next conflict could blind not just militaries, but entire societies.

Some future strategist will face a terrible choice: strike the satellite and silence hospitals, or hold back and watch the battlefield tilt. In that moment, entanglement becomes not an abstract policy problem, but a human one. The real danger is not that satellites serve both peace and war. It is that humanity has forgotten how tightly its fate is tied to the machines above.

Escalation control

In 2020, a Russian inspector satellite drifted unusually close to a Western military spacecraft. Analysts watched its trajectory tighten: a silent, gliding approach in the dark. Neither side fired. No lasers, no jammers, no debris.

Instead, a diplomatic note arrived, and the Russian satellite backed away. The manoeuvre—provocative but reversible—became a test of restraint. It was also a reminder that in orbit, the line between signalling and sabotage can be measured in kilometres, not explosions. A misread intention, a missed hotline call, and the world might have woken to a cloud of fragments circling Earth for decades.

On land, armies can amass visibly. At sea, fleets can shadow each other over open water. In the air, contrails betray patrols. But space strips conflict of all these cues. Satellites whisper across vacuum. Their manoeuvres are silent arcs of mathematics. Intentions must be inferred from orbital dynamics, propulsion budgets, and the paranoid logic of adversaries. When a spacecraft fires its thrusters, no one hears the burn—yet everyone watches the path. In this domain of quiet movements and high stakes, escalation control is less about treaties on paper and more about managing perceptions under the cold geometry of orbital mechanics.

The challenge is stark: how do nations avoid stumbling into a cosmic Cuban Missile Crisis? Traditional deterrence assumed visible warning. In space, the warning can be a single manoeuvre—an inspector sidling closer to a navigation satellite, a servicing vehicle matching inclination with a rival's reconnaissance asset, a sudden change in pointing angle that hints at a laser. Each of these can be read as hostile. Each might be innocent. Without channels of clarification, uncertainty becomes provocative all by itself.

Hotlines are supposed to stop the spiral. Their history is long; diplomats love the symbolism of a direct line. Yet the mechanics matter more than the metaphor. A hotline must be monitored, answered quickly, and staffed by officers who understand the technicalities of space operations. A call at 03:00 explaining an unplanned thruster burn is useless if it reaches a switchboard clerk who cannot distinguish a collision avoidance manoeuvre from a covert rendezvous. Escalation control demands competence on both ends of the line.

Some states publish *NOTAM*-style alerts before major manoeuvres, announcing orbital changes, satellite servicing missions, or potential conjunction avoidance. These notices serve the same function as pre-announced missile tests: they reassure others that the event is routine, not an ambush. Transparency has strategic value. It shrinks the space in which paranoia can grow. But transparency also carries risk. Revealing plans can expose vulnerabilities—timing, fuel margins, operational cycles. Adversaries may exploit what diplomats share. Thus, nations ration openness, revealing just enough to keep tempers cool, but not enough to forfeit advantage.

Commercial operators complicate this further. Their satellites are manoeuvring constantly—raising orbits, dodging debris, repositioning to meet market demand. Militaries monitor these movements, but the intentions behind them are commercial, not strategic. How should a defence ministry interpret a foreign satellite sharing a similar ground track to a sensitive asset? Without context, even coincidence becomes suspicious. Some governments encourage companies to publish ephemerides and updates, turning commercial space tracking into a confidence-building measure. Others withhold data, arguing that secrecy protects intellectual property and outwits adversaries. The result is a patchwork of uneven transparency, a recipe for misunderstanding.

The logic of escalation control in space shifts the burden from weapons to behaviour. Kinetic anti-satellite tests are rare today not because they are technologically hard, but because they are politically reckless. Debris would not merely strike an enemy; it would contaminate orbits for all. Hence the rise of reversible measures—jamming, dazzling, spoofing, interfering with data uplinks. These effects can be dialled back, denied, or disavowed. As signalling tools, they are subtler than missiles. Yet subtler actions are easier to misread. A jammed satellite could be suffering from solar weather. A spoofed signal might be accidental interference. Or it could be a warning shot. Attribution is rarely immediate. In the hours of analysis that follow, tempers can harden and escalation ladders shorten.

Some strategists argue that the best way to avoid misunderstanding is to demonstrate capability openly. Show the world you can disable a satellite without debris. Publish footage of proximity operations. Conduct inspection missions under international observation. Capability revealed is capability normalised—less mysterious, less threatening. Others counter that demonstration invites copycats; better to cultivate ambiguity. The philosophical gulf is wide: one side trusts clarity, the other trusts deterrence by opacity.

Orbital transparency tools—public trackers, academia-run telescopes, hobbyist radars—offer a civilian layer of de-escalation. When amateurs publish satellite positions online, the shadows shrink. It becomes harder for states to interpret routine operations as covert aggression. Yet transparency cuts both ways. If everyone can see manoeuvres, everyone can design counters. And in a crisis, public information may fuel nationalist narratives faster than diplomats can de-escalate. The very tools that calm peacetime anxieties might inflame wartime fears.

The peculiar physics of orbit make escalation asymmetric. A manoeuvre that looks small—a 10-metre shift, a minor inclination change—can carry enormous signalling weight. If a satellite approaches within a few kilometres of a rival, lawyers scramble to interpret whether that constitutes interference. If two spacecraft match orbits for days, speculation erupts about docking, capture, or covert sabotage. Every step invites interpretation. Mistakes are magnified by altitude.

Nations have experimented with more formal confidence-building measures: data-sharing centres for space situational awareness; bilateral agreements to notify of close approaches; shared simulation exercises to rehearse crisis response. These are valuable, but thin. They depend on political goodwill and continuity. A change of government, a cyberattack on a tracking centre, a diplomatic feud—each can erase months of progress. Space is unforgiving; mistrust fits neatly into its silence.

The deeper truth is that escalation control is psychological. It requires leaders to imagine how their moves appear to adversaries, not how they intend them. A burn that saves a satellite from debris might mimic the trajectory of an attack posture. A communications blackout caused by a ground station failure may look like covert jamming. Escalation control demands humility: the acceptance that one's own actions are not self-explanatory.

Ironically, the most stabilising behaviour may be dull routine. Predictable operations—regular orbit raising, standard servicing protocols, annual debris-removal tests—build patterns that others can recognise. Surprise, even benign surprise, is destabilising. In a sky full of sensitive electronics, stability looks boring by design.

Yet boredom is not a natural condition in a rapidly militarising domain. More nations are launching manoeuvrable satellites. More constellations crowd low Earth orbit. More dual-use craft blur the lines between commercial and defence roles. The skies grow louder with traffic and quieter with communication. When something goes wrong—and it will—the ability to pick up the phone, explain intentions, and recalibrate perceptions will matter more than any satellite's shielding or propulsion.

Escalation control in space is not a luxury; it is survival. If a collision triggers retaliation, if a jammed signal hardens into suspicion, if silence is read as hostility, then the first shots of a space war may be fired by accident. And once they are fired, the debris will not distinguish between the flags on the hardware it strikes.

The hardest question lingers, unanswered: when the next provocative manoeuvre unfolds—whether by design, malfunction, or a rookie operator typing the wrong delta-v—will anyone trust the hotline enough to pick it up?

The cost of ambiguity

In February 2022, a European broadband satellite suffered a sudden outage. Technicians traced the disruption to a flood of malicious traffic. To the public, it looked like routine cybercrime. To several defence ministries, the timing—coinciding with a major land invasion—looked anything but routine. Analysts began to ask whether the disruption was deliberate sabotage, a probing operation, or a warning shot. The culprit was not immediately clear. The outage hit terminals used by civilians across multiple states, not just the country under attack. Insurance questions piled up. Lawyers argued over contracts. Militaries quietly prepared responses. For days, the world lived under the shadow of an unanswered question: *was this accident, collateral damage, or a strategic signal?* The uncertainty did not de-escalate. It accelerated worst-case assumptions.

Ambiguity has always haunted security policy, but in orbit it is amplified. Space systems sit at the intersection of civilian infrastructure, commercial competition, and sensitive military missions. When something goes wrong—a jammed link, a drifting satellite, a navigation glitch—adversaries rarely assume coincidence. Secrecy and strategic ambiguity might offer tactical advantage, but they also create fertile ground for paranoia. The more opaque a state's space posture, the more imaginative an opponent's threat models become.

This risk is not theoretical. When governments classify the capabilities of manoeuvrable satellites, they hope ambiguity will deter rivals from testing boundaries. Yet secrecy can also backfire by leaving rivals to fill in the blanks. Intelligence analysts are paid to think pessimistically; when information is scarce, they substitute inference for fact. A spacecraft that appears to shadow another may be performing a routine calibration, but to an external observer without insight into intent, the pattern can resemble stalking. The manoeuvre itself becomes a message, whether intended or not. In a domain where every satellite is dual-use by design—navigation supports civilian logistics and precision-guided munitions alike—clean lines of interpretation are almost impossible.

The logic of worst-case planning is simple: if a nation cannot prove that an anomaly was benign, it plans for the possibility it was hostile. When a military communications satellite suffers interference, commanders must decide whether it was solar weather, an equipment fault, or jamming. Waiting for certainty can mean losing an escalation step. Acting on suspicion can spiral a crisis. In a world of classified capabilities, misattribution is not a possibility—it is a constant risk.

Secrecy also undermines diplomacy. Hotlines exist to clarify ambiguous events, but states rarely admit uncertainty. A nation might know that a rival's satellite drifted close due to malfunction, but acknowledging that insight would reveal intelligence sources: ground radars, optical sensors, signals intercepts. So diplomats speak vaguely. The other side hears evasion. Answers raise questions faster than they resolve them.

Commercial activity adds further noise. A manufacturer might withhold technical specifications of propulsion systems to protect intellectual property. But without that data, space traffic management models become less reliable; conjunction warnings become more frequent; operational payloads must manoeuvre more often. Every unnecessary burn looks tactical, not technical. The suspicion lands on the operator, not the spreadsheet. Ambiguity breeds cost at every tier—from risk premiums to diplomatic bandwidth.

Some governments embrace ambiguity deliberately. They argue that hiding capabilities complicates an adversary's targeting calculus. Ambiguous assets must be treated as potentially armed or potentially vital. A rival contemplating aggression must assume the worst. In theory, uncertain cost deters bold action. In practice, it often encourages pre-emption. If planners believe a foreign satellite might carry a high-energy laser, waiting to find out could be fatal. The logic that protects can also provoke.

There is another price: domestic politics. Secrecy erodes public trust. When unexplained space incidents occur—unexpected outages, lost satellites, silent manoeuvres—citizens sense that officials are not telling the whole story. Transparency is rationed through press releases. In democracies, defence spending and space policy rely on public consent. Ambiguity is a fragile foundation for legitimacy. It frays quickly under scrutiny.

Even allies suffer. Coalition operations depend on shared awareness of capability and intent. When partners hide orbital capabilities, coordination falters. A nation might move a reconnaissance satellite for a classified mission, inadvertently obstructing allied sensors. Without context, allies assume interference or negligence. What begins as justified secrecy ends as coalition distrust.

There are practical limits to ambiguity anyway. Amateur trackers, university telescopes, and commercial radar networks have eroded the monopoly on orbital knowledge. Movements once considered secret are now measured and posted online within hours. The crowd has partial transparency even when governments choose opacity. This shifts ambiguity from *what happened* to *why it happened*—a more dangerous form, because intention is harder to prove than trajectory.

Some states have attempted controlled transparency: publishing ephemerides, notifying of close approaches, disclosing limited capabilities. These gestures can stabilise expectations, but they require consistency and credibility. A sudden lapse—an unannounced rendezvous, a classified launch—erodes the trust built over years. Ambiguity is always cheaper to create than to repair.

The paradox is stark. Spacefaring states prize secrecy because satellites are strategic assets. But those same states depend on stability in orbit—stable markets, stable alliances, stable deterrence. Ambiguity corrodes stability by magnifying imagination. And imagination, in security affairs, skews dark.

Consider attribution. A navigation outage affects civilian shipping and military logistics alike. If one state believes the outage is hostile interference, and the other believes it is a technical glitch, escalation dynamics diverge. Each interprets the other's silence as evidence of guilt. Retaliation becomes a rational hedge. In conflict, minutes matter. Orbital incidents unfold faster than crisis diplomacy can decode them.

Nor is the cost solely strategic. Ambiguity raises insurance premiums, inflates launch contracts, and scares investors. Firms building dual-use systems must plan for legal and reputational exposure if their satellites are implicated—fairly or not—in hostile acts. The commercial ecosystem pays for political shadows.

The most unsettling cost is psychological. When ambiguity thrives, leaders make decisions in fog. Cognitive bias fills gaps: mirror-imaging, threat inflation, confirmation bias. A commander who expects interference sees it in normal telemetry. A diplomat who distrusts an adversary interprets routine silent periods as malicious jamming. Ambiguity weaponises human nature.

Some strategists insist that secrecy has always been a currency of power. But in space, secrecy is not just hiding capability—it is hiding context. And context determines whether a manoeuvre is stabilising or inflammatory, whether an outage is tolerated or avenged. In a domain with no margin for debris or delay, context is not optional. It is the difference between restraint and escalation.

Yet full transparency is impossible. No state will publish every thruster burn, every test, every software update. No intelligence service will disclose what it can see or infer. The real challenge is to decide which shadows are tolerable. Which capabilities can remain ambiguous without inviting fear? Which actions must be accompanied by explanation?

A final, unsettling thought lingers over every classified spacecraft and every unexplained anomaly: the next incident might not allow time for clarification. If a navigation constellation drops offline over multiple continents, or a military satellite suddenly tumbles, who will assume coincidence? When the stakes are sky-high and seconds matter, can any nation afford to treat ambiguity as a feature rather than a fatal flaw?

The cost of opacity may not be measured in headlines or treaties, but in the day a misread signal turns hesitation into action.

Chapter 10

Lessons from Recent Crises

A convoy of armoured vehicles once vanished into a rural treeline, the sort of disappearance militaries relied on for decades. But the concealment lasted less than an afternoon. A satellite owned not by a government, but by a commercial imaging firm, caught the tyre tracks burned into the frost. Hours later, analysts on the other side of the planet matched the pattern to a known brigade, and the images circulated across diplomatic channels and social media simultaneously. That single snapshot did more than expose a movement; it demonstrated a new balance of power in information. Truth was no longer the monopoly of intelligence agencies. Civilians could watch a war from orbit.

In recent conflicts, satellites used for agriculture, insurance, shipping, and broadband found themselves thrust into geopolitical theatre. Their operators never planned to become actors in global crises, but space does not ask permission. When a nation fires a missile or moves a fleet, sensors in orbit—commercial as much as military—record the event with relentless impartiality. For governments accustomed to controlling the narrative, this new transparency cuts both ways. It deters atrocity and propaganda, but it also erodes secrecy, accelerates blame, and sometimes reveals what one side would rather keep hidden.

This chapter looks at crises not because they are dramatic, but because they are clarifying. Conflict is a stress test. It strips away diplomatic slogans, exposes the strengths and failures of technology, and shows where real resilience lies. Satellites that spend most of their lifetimes beaming broadband to rural schools may suddenly become strategic assets when jamming begins. Imagery companies that normally count warehouses and forests find themselves mapping artillery positions. Shipping trackers originally meant to verify insurance claims start identifying sanction evasion fleets. A humanitarian corridor can depend on timely weather data, and an evacuation route may hinge on radar imaging that slices through cloud and smoke. Quietly and consistently, space systems shape life on the ground.

Commercial imagery became a force multiplier. A public armed with pictures from orbit refuses to be gaslit by official statements. When a strike hits a city, pixels reveal the crater before diplomats open their mouths. When a convoy edges towards a border, the world sees its length, direction, and tempo. What once required spies and classified briefings now arrives as subscription data. Analysts in think tanks and universities used the same feeds as militaries, narrowing the distance between experts, journalists, and curious citizens. This diffusion of access challenged governments that relied on ambiguity. If a state wished to deny involvement, it needed a better plan than silence.

But transparency offered no immunity. Communication satellites faced direct attack, both subtle and overt: uplink jamming, cyber intrusion, and interference timed to coincide with ground offensives. Instead of collapsing, networks adapted in real time. Terminal firmware was rewritten, beams were retuned, and fleets of ground antennas switched to alternative channels. The lesson was stark: in space, resilience is not merely hardware but software agility and operator ingenuity. Modern constellations behave like organisms—reactive, learning, sometimes even predicting the next strike.

At sea, a different form of visibility mattered. Tankers tried to slip through sanctions by changing flags, faking ship names, or switching off their transponders. Radar satellites, AIS receivers, and imagery sensors worked together like pieces of a puzzle. Analysts traced routes through narrow straits, compared hull shapes, and caught vessels in the act of disappearing. The world of maritime deception grew more sophisticated, but the tools for piercing the fog kept pace. For the first time, sanction enforcement was partly crowdsourced: hedge funds, NGOs, and investigative journalists parsed orbital feeds with a zeal once reserved for naval intelligence.

Yet satellites were not merely eyes for governments and watchdogs. They kept civilians alive. When floods cut off roads, radar satellites mapped the deluge hour by hour, guiding aid trucks around collapsing bridges. In warzones, humanitarian agencies used imagery to identify safe corridors through contested cities. Weather satellites forecast storms that could drown refugee camps. What looks like a cold stream of gigabytes on a control console translates, downstream, into convoys of food, medicine, and evacuations.

Still, even in this new age of transparency, silence endured where satellites could not see. Cloud cover blinds optical imagers. Smoke and dust blur signatures. Militaries deploy decoys, inflatable armour, and elaborate camouflage. Some communications interference blends skillfully into background noise, making culpability hard to pin down. The world sees more than ever, but not enough to answer every question. Open-source intelligence is powerful, yet it can be gamed. The gaps matter as much as the revelations.

The deeper insight emerging from recent crises is that space has become a contested commons. Commercial operators find themselves adjudicating between governments, deciding whether to restrict access, prioritise bandwidth, or modify coverage footprints. States now vie not only for satellites but for the loyalty and compliance of firms that own them. The boundary between neutrality and participation has thinned. When a broadband signal helps evacuate civilians, it may also assist a brigade. When a company provides imagery to an NGO, it might simultaneously inform a military planner. Intentions blur, consequences accumulate, and liability becomes a geopolitical concept rather than a contractual one.

The crises of the past decade revealed how fragile—and how adaptive—the orbital ecosystem has become. Even when satellites withstood jamming, ground stations became targets. Even when imagery exposed disinformation, propaganda mutated to exploit uncertainty. Every gain in transparency produced a countermeasure. Every countermeasure sparked a new innovation. The lesson is neither triumphalist nor pessimistic. It simply shows that space, once the backdrop to conflict, is now woven into its conduct.

This chapter asks what these recent crises teach us about the future. If commercial satellites can expose troop movements, what happens when both sides assume they're being watched? If broadband terminals survive hacking through software updates, what does that imply for the pace of cyber warfare? If ships can be tracked across oceans by radar and algorithms, what remains of plausible deniability? And if every humanitarian effort depends on orbital insight, how will relief agencies cope when satellites become targets?

The answers are complex, and they will not comfort anyone who wishes for clean divides between war and peace, civilian and military, public and private. But clarity is not the same as simplicity. The lessons of recent crises sharpen our understanding of what space can do, and what it cannot. They remind us that satellites are not spectators; they are participants, sometimes unwilling, sometimes decisive.

The pages that follow examine these lessons in depth—not as distant observations, but as lived realities for the people who operate, protect, and depend upon the systems circling overhead. The world has already seen what happens when geopolitics and orbit collide. The next crisis will not repeat the last, but it will rhyme. Knowing the pattern may be the best defence we have.

Commercial imagery in conflict

The first tanks did not announce themselves with thunder or dust. They were discovered by a university researcher in a dim office thousands of kilometres away, scrolling through satellite pictures intended for crop forecasting. The columns—dark shapes threading along a frost-bitten road—stood out only because the shadows betrayed their length. Within hours the images circled the globe. Journalists published them, diplomats brandished them, and intelligence agencies quietly confirmed what the pixels already declared. An invasion that was meant to be deniable became undeniable, not because a spy risked their life, but because a commercial imaging satellite happened to pass overhead.

This is the paradox at the heart of modern conflict: the most revealing eyes in war now belong to companies whose business models revolve around agriculture, insurance, infrastructure, and disaster relief. Their satellites were never designed to expose troop movements or trace armoured brigades, yet they have become instruments of global accountability. History once relied on intelligence leaks, declassified briefings, or carefully choreographed press conferences to show what armies were doing. Today, a subscription to a commercial imagery provider can deliver more clarity than a dozen diplomats.

The implications are profound. Commercial imagery shapes narratives before governments can spin them. When a missile strike hits a city, the crater and debris are visible from orbit long before official statements race to shape the story. When a convoy takes a supposedly secret route, the tyre tracks unwind across satellite mosaics for anyone patient enough to stitch them together. Public analysts—some retired generals, others freelance cartographers, some simply curious citizens—assemble near-real-time assessments from commercially available feeds. The monopoly on seeing has fractured.

In past wars, journalists had to trust military escorts or wait for censored briefings. Now they publish comparative before-and-after imagery: a school on Monday, rubble on Tuesday. The evidence does not rely on trust; it is plainly visible. This shift unsettles states that once leaned heavily on ambiguity. Denial becomes difficult when a crater's geometry can be measured in pixels and geolocated with street-level accuracy. The result is an information environment in which governments must respond to evidence, not speculation.

But commercial imagery does more than shape stories. It shapes targeting. Militaries, especially those without constellations of their own, learned to watch the same feeds as journalists and researchers. An artillery battery hidden under camouflage might evade a reconnaissance drone, but it may not escape a constellation of high-resolution satellites circling in polar orbits. The latency is short; the revisit rate relentless. Commanders in the field now pore over imagery from companies headquartered continents away, paying for snapshots in the middle of battle.

One conflict showed how quickly this could change outcomes. Artillery positions were spotted by open-source analysts, who published coordinates online. Militias saw them, so did citizens, and so did militaries. Within hours counter-battery fire struck at precisely those grid squares. The chain of discovery no longer depended on classified pipelines or satellite dishes perched on bunkers. It depended on bandwidth, credit cards, and a community of volunteers willing to annotate rooftops and trenches.

Critics worry that this democratisation of surveillance is reckless. What happens when amateurs misidentify a target? What if an image, misinterpreted, leads to escalation? These concerns are not trivial. A blurred shape on a satellite photograph can be a tent, a truck, or a civilian shelter. Analysts who publish too quickly risk turning rumour into consequence. And yet, the alternative—total opacity—has its own dangers. Photographs that live in secret archives can be selectively interpreted or withheld. Commercial imagery limits the room for fabrication. It offers a common reference point on which arguments must be anchored.

Still, even transparency has blind spots. Many satellites in commercial fleets rely on optical imagery, which clouds, forest canopy, or smoke can negate. During intense fighting, militaries learned to use weather forecasts as camouflage plans, waiting for storms or fog to reposition assets. Fires and industrial smoke obscured factory complexes. Sometimes, the most critical movements occurred during short windows of darkness between revisits. Commercial satellites are powerful, but they are not omniscient.

This is where synthetic-aperture radar (SAR) constellations entered the picture. Unlike optical sensors, SAR sees through clouds and darkness by emitting microwaves and analysing the reflections. These images can detect trucks in forests, ships under cloud cover, and in some cases even shallow trenches or tyre ruts. The data is technical, often grainy, but devastatingly useful. Analysts learned to pair optical imagery with radar maps, revealing patterns invisible to either alone. A convoy might hide from cameras, but not from the roads they crushed beneath their weight.

Commercial SAR exposed naval secrets as well. Ships that switched off their transponders were still visible, caught mid-ocean by bursts of radar. Fleets manoeuvring at night found themselves mapped by journalists and NGOs. Maritime deception—fake flags, renamed hulls, ghost fleets—became harder to sustain. Sanction evasion that once relied on gaps in radar coverage now left digital footprints. Even when governments remained silent, the satellites spoke.

The uncomfortable truth is that commercial operators became geopolitical actors whether they wanted to or not. When a company released images proving that civilian homes were destroyed by artillery, the story cascaded into diplomatic chambers. Governments requested, sometimes demanded, access to higher-resolution scenes. Some firms agreed; others held back, wary of being drawn into conflict. Neutrality grew complicated. A satellite operator that withholds imagery might be accused of aiding one side. A company that supplies it might face retaliation in cyberspace or in regulatory arenas.

This tension surfaced starkly when imagery of troop build-ups contradicted official statements. Diplomats claimed exercises; satellites showed cross-border logistics. Commercial providers, lacking political filters, simply sold their data. The public judged for itself. The ability to refute propaganda with a single photograph altered the tempo of crisis diplomacy. Leaders could no longer use fog and distance as excuses. They were accountable to a world that could see.

Yet there is a deeper philosophical shift. Conflict is no longer solely about force; it is about perception. Commercial imagery blurs the line between intelligence and public record. Citizens become observers, analysts become participants, and militaries become performers on a global stage. The psychological effect matters: when armies know they are seen, their behaviour changes. Deception grows subtler. Atrocities become harder to hide. The performative aspect of war increases, as each action is judged not just by adversaries, but by international audiences equipped with evidence.

This does not guarantee moral restraint. Some actors simply deny what the world can see. Others retaliate not by changing behaviour, but by targeting the satellites themselves. In recent crises, communication networks experienced jamming and cyber attacks for providing imagery that exposed battlefield failures. Companies patched firmware overnight; ground antennas shifted beams; constellations evolved. The battlefield extended into cyberspace and orbit, where the goal was not only to move tanks but to manage eyes.

An extraordinary development followed: hobbyists entered the arena. Citizen cartographers, open-source investigators, and data scientists built tools to ingest commercial imagery and create detailed maps. Trained only by curiosity, they catalogued missile impacts, tracked armour, and flagged potential war crimes. Their work became citations in government briefings and evidence in international courts. The moral burden of knowledge expanded. No state could claim ignorance when hundreds of independent reviewers held photographic proof.

All this points to a future in which no conflict will go unseen. Even the poorest nations can purchase single scenes of satellite imagery. Insurgents, humanitarian groups, journalists, financial firms—each becomes a node in a decentralised surveillance web. This redistribution of sight alters strategy. Concealment must be active, not assumed. Camouflage becomes an art revisited in the age of orbiting cameras. Deception strategies evolve: inflatable decoys, holographic nets, heat signature masking. The cat-and-mouse game that once played out on the ground now unfolds in the heavens.

Yet the greatest transformation is not technical but psychological. For the first time, ordinary citizens can watch war unfold from above. They can see burned villages, shattered bridges, floating oil slicks, massed artillery, and the dust trails of fleeing vehicles. The emotional distance that once separated the public from the front line shrinks. Images carry moral force. They provoke outrage, empathy, pressure, and consequence. A government deciding to shell a port knows that commercial satellites will document every crater.

But transparency also tempts overconfidence. What happens when imagery is misinterpreted? What if a blurred shape is taken for a missile battery and leads to escalation? The world has not yet resolved how to manage disputes born of open-source intelligence. There is no arbitration board for ambiguous pixels. States may weaponise uncertainty, planting false interpretations or distributing doctored imagery. Truth becomes contested, even when the camera does not lie.

Commercial imagery in conflict reveals a new world of distributed intelligence. Non-state sensors now rival national capability, and their neutrality has become as consequential as their technology. Companies once concerned only with profitability now find themselves deciding who gets access to orbital truth. Their databases have geopolitical gravity.

The next conflicts will not be private affairs. Satellites will watch, algorithms will analyse, and citizens will judge. Every tank, every convoy, every crater has an audience. Whether this leads to accountability or escalation is uncertain. But one fact remains: secrecy has been demoted. The sky has too many eyes, and they answer to many masters.

SATCOM under fire

The first warning was silence. A forward operating unit, accustomed to a constant stream of satellite-fed messages, suddenly found its terminals unresponsive. Weather was clear, power was stable, but the screens froze. Somewhere beyond the horizon an adversary had opened an invisible tap of energy—just enough interference to smother the link. For a few minutes there was nothing to do but wait. Then, as abruptly as the outage began, the terminals flickered back to life. The constellation had reconfigured itself, hopping beams and rerouting traffic across fresh frequencies. What might have crippled a brigade in the past had become a brief inconvenience.

This small episode captures a profound shift: satellite communications are no longer delicate lifelines that snap at the first sign of deliberate disruption. They are becoming resilient, adaptive, self-healing networks. And yet their growing importance makes them irresistible targets. Adversaries jam, spoof, probe, and hack because modern militaries depend on space-based communications for everything from close air support to logistics. To attack SATCOM is to reach a long, unseen hand into the heart of battlefield command.

Jamming is the oldest and most visible method of interference. A ground transmitter, aimed roughly at the satellite or ground terminal, floods the signal with noise. The physics are simple, the execution crude, but the effect can be devastating. In recent conflicts, jamming teams drove to hilltops, extended antennas, and smothered entire sectors of SATCOM coverage. The goal was not total blackout—just enough disruption to sow confusion. Soldiers suddenly lost access to mapping apps, drones went silent, and commanders could not transmit new orders. Even in a world flooded with digital devices, a few kilowatts of radio energy can paralyse a brigade.

But jamming is noisy in every sense. Sensors detect it quickly, satellites notice the interference, and ground networks triangulate the source. For the attacker, it carries a signature—an admission of involvement. That is why subtler methods have surged to the fore.

Spoofing replaces silence with deception. Instead of cutting the link, a malicious transmitter imitates it. A terminal receives false timing packets or corrupted navigation data. A drone, trusting counterfeit commands, may drift off course. A ground station, unaware that the signals are forged, may update software with poisoned data. Spoofing is stealthier than jamming; it may linger undetected for hours. In the spectrum, a clever spoofer hides like a pickpocket in a crowd.

Cyber intrusion is stealthier still. SATCOM networks are, after all, computers that talk through space. Their ground stations, antennas, routers, and modems run firmware. Their control centres patch software, authenticate keys, and manage access lists. An attacker who infiltrates these components can distort, delay, or disable communications without transmitting a watt of radio energy. In one crisis, hackers breached commercial terminals used by both civilians and military units. The outage was sudden, global, and humiliating. Engineers scrambled to rewrite firmware and push patches over the air. For weeks, technicians carried laptops into the field, manually restoring service to antennas that refused remote recovery. The lesson was unmistakable: a satellite can survive orbital radiation, but its weakest point may be a factory default password.

To counter these threats, SATCOM architecture has evolved. Constellations now proliferate in low Earth orbit, offering redundant paths and narrow beams that are harder to jam. Terminals hop frequencies, steer electronically, and sense interference. If one node falls silent, the network rebalances. For decades satellites were rigid, monolithic platforms; now they are programmable routers above the sky, able to reshuffle routing tables on demand.

The firmware battle may be the most crucial of all. When a commercial operator discovered that ground terminals were being probed by a foreign intelligence service, its engineers wrote a defensive update in hours.

Overnight, thousands of antennas rebooted, closing backdoors and raising encryption strength. The counterattack was not a missile or a drone—it was a software patch.

Yet even resilience has limits. Wide-area jamming can swamp entire bands, overwhelming agile waveforms. A cyber intrusion that slips past authentication can take weeks to cleanse. Adversaries experiment with "surgical" jamming, targeting only the frequencies used by specific drones or command nodes. Others deploy mobile interference units disguised as civilian vans. The battlefield of SATCOM is not in orbit alone; it sprawls across towns, forests, and digital infrastructure.

Civilian systems play a surprising role. armies often rely on commercial SATCOM, either for surge capacity or for redundancy. This creates uncomfortable dependencies: a terminal used by a farmer in peacetime may carry battlefield data during war. When adversaries jam a commercial satellite's beam, they may disrupt hospitals, banks, container ports, and emergency services. A single interference campaign ripples across societies that never expected to be combatants.

This raises a philosophical tension. Who owns resilience? Military SATCOM is often hardened, encrypted, and redundant. Commercial SATCOM, cheaper and faster to deploy, prioritises availability over defence. But when commercial terminals become wartime assets, the boundary between civilian communications and military infrastructure dissolves. Engineers in corporate offices find themselves as critical to national security as officers in forward command posts. The decision to patch a vulnerability, reroute a beam, or throttle capacity becomes a strategic choice with geopolitical consequences.

Governments have taken notice. Some require providers to maintain rapid patching capabilities. Others demand that terminals support encrypted channels and frequency agility. Regulatory agencies, once concerned mainly with spectrum licensing, now ask how quickly an operator can recover from cyber attack. Insurance markets evaluate resilience with actuarial precision: an operator unable to withstand targeted jamming may lose its underwriting.

Still, the offence adapts. Portable jammers proliferate on grey markets. Malware kits circulate in hidden forums. Even amateurs experiment, sometimes unintentionally, with devices that cause satellite interference. A fisherman's poorly tuned transmitter once disrupted a port's SATCOM for weeks. Every unprotected terminal is a potential vector. Every misconfigured antenna is a doorway.

What follows is a contest of agility. The fastest side wins—not necessarily the strongest. If a network can detect jamming in seconds, hop to a clean frequency, tighten its side lobes, and switch to alternative relays, the attack fizzles. If an operator can push firmware updates across thousands of terminals overnight, a cyber intrusion becomes a short-lived embarrassment rather than a strategic wound. In modern war, resilience is rarely a static condition; it is a race.

And yet, a deeper question lingers. What happens when every step toward resilience prompts adversaries to escalate? If hopping waveforms are too hard to jam, might an attacker disable ground stations with cyber attacks? If terminals are hardened, might adversaries turn their attention to undersea cables or terrestrial relays? SATCOM sits inside a larger ecosystem, and pressures on one part inevitably leak into others. The battlefield is no longer bounded by terrain; it is systemic.

The frequency spectrum, once considered mundane, has become contested space. Engineers speak of it with the seriousness of officers planning artillery fire. Algorithms allocate channels dynamically, squeezing signals between interference spikes. Antennas form nulls—zones of silence—aimed at jammers. In some cases, satellites cooperate as a swarm, handing off traffic mid-transit to evade detection. The clarity of the old world—one satellite, one link, one beam—has shattered into fluid complexity.

There is also a psychological dimension. Units that once trusted SATCOM blindly now train for its absence. Commanders rehearse orders delivered by runners, drones preloaded with mission data, or ground networks that spool up when space links go dark. Paradoxically, the more central SATCOM becomes, the more militaries try to live without it—if only for a moment—so they do not collapse when the spectrum turns hostile.

The next generation of threats will be quieter still. Cyber attacks that rewrite routing tables, jamming patterns that mimic harmless interference, spoofed signals that lull operators into complacency. A well-executed intrusion may leave no trace but hesitation: a commander waiting for confirmation, unsure if what they see is real. The invisible battlefield of SATCOM becomes a theatre of doubt.

Yet the story is not one of fragility. It is one of adaptation. The most remarkable victories are not visible in photographs or parade grounds.

They happen when a constellation shrugs off a jamming attempt, when a terminal reboots itself with fresh firmware, when a packet finds its way through a maze of interference and lands in the hands of a soldier who needs it. War has always been a contest of wills; now it is also a contest of bandwidth and ingenuity.

The silence that opened this story—the sudden blackout of SATCOM—was once the harbinger of catastrophe. Today, it is merely a signal that the network is fighting back. The constellations are watching, the code is learning, and the spectrum is alive with contest. The true question is not whether SATCOM can survive under fire. It is how long the offence and defence can dance before the battlefield shifts again.

Maritime shadows

It began with a blank patch of ocean. Analysts monitoring tanker movements noticed a vessel vanish just after exiting a congested strait. Its transponder, previously broadcasting position every few seconds, went dead. No storm. No mechanical fault. Just silence. Days later, the same ship reappeared thousands of kilometres away, its tanks mysteriously lighter, reporting a route that made no sense. Somewhere in that blind corridor, crude oil had changed hands, sanctions had been evaded, and every regulatory authority had been outmanoeuvred. What once required fleets of patrol aircraft and naval surveillance was orchestrated through a single act: the quiet flick of a switch that turned off an Automatic Identification System transmitter.

Ships are not supposed to disappear. The law of the sea, imperfect as it is, presumes transparency. AIS beacons broadcast a vessel's identity, course, and speed, enabling collision avoidance and operational safety. Tankers the size of skyscrapers do not pass unseen. That principle held when AIS signals were monitored by coastal stations and the traffic was predictable. But satellites changed the equation. Constellations catch AIS pulses across the globe, from deep ocean to polar ice. The world's shipping lanes, once hidden behind the horizon, became visible like arteries on a medical scan. Turning off a beacon ceased to be an inconvenience; it became a conspicuous signal in itself.

The disappearance of a ship, marked by a sudden drop in its AIS transmissions, is not merely suspicious—it is a data event. Analysts build statistical baselines for how tankers behave: typical speeds, refuelling intervals, port calls, draught changes. Anomalies stand out. A tanker loitering in open water may be waiting for an illicit transfer. A cargo vessel slowing to a crawl may be rendezvousing with another hull. Patterns of life exist even in the middle of nowhere.

The cat-and-mouse game between transparency and concealment now unfolds with orbital eyes. AIS signals, once too sparse for global coverage, are stitched into real-time maps. Where the beacon dies, synthetic aperture radar steps in. Radar does not care about darkness or cloud cover; it paints ships as bright metal signatures on a rippling sea. A vanished tanker may hide its identity, but it cannot hide its hull. Vessels caught playing in the margins—broadcasting false positions, phantom identities, or deliberate gaps—find themselves illuminated by satellites that have no patience for maritime lies.

The sanctions regime against rogue states and sanctioned networks has turned the ocean into a chessboard. Instead of storming ports, enforcement agencies monitor algorithms. They correlate AIS gaps with radar tracks, infrared plumes, and historical behaviour. Ships in the "dark fleet" develop new techniques: switching off AIS, swapping transponders, repainting hull numbers in remote anchorages, or conducting ship-to-ship transfers at night. Yet every manoeuvre leaves fingerprints. The hull shadow seen by radar contrasts with its supposed location. A sudden change in a vessel's draught hints at cargo transfer. Satellite imagery catches deck cranes extending or hoses connecting two tankers side by side.

Maritime tracking is no longer a chore of sailors with binoculars; it is data science at planetary scale. Companies ingest AIS streams, radar sweeps, weather models, optical frames, and port logs into generative models that flag suspicious behaviour. When a tanker vanishes for 72 hours near a known transfer hotspot, the warning lights flash. Banks, insurers, and customs authorities respond. Flags are downgraded. Premiums rise. The entire financial ecosystem surrounding shipping tightens around vessels that misbehave.

This transparency has strategic implications. During conflicts, warships may prefer to stay unseen. They may operate without AIS, relying on radar silence and decoys. But commercial satellites detect wakes and thermal plumes. A carrier group cannot cross an ocean without satellites spotting the churn of its escorting destroyers. Even submarines, supposedly the most secretive tools of naval power, sometimes betray their presence through indirect signatures—long-range magnetic anomalies, disruption of marine life patterns, or simply the need to surface near busy sea lanes. The shadows at sea grow shorter with every additional satellite launched.

The irony is that both criminals and coastguards draw from the same technological well. A smuggling network will use commercial imagery to scan for naval patrols. A national intelligence agency will use the same imagery to track the smugglers. The ocean, once ruled by states, is becoming a contested information space where small actors can buy insights once reserved for superpowers. Where secrecy once privileged navies with reconnaissance satellites, now activists trace illegal fishing fleets and journalists expose arms transfers with nothing more than subscription services and analytical skill.

The philosophical stakes are higher than they appear. Seas have always reflected power. The ability to ship goods, enforce embargoes, or deploy fleets is an extension of sovereignty. But sovereignty presumes knowledge. If a state cannot track vessels in its waters, it loses control. If it cannot hide its own vessels, it loses deterrence. Absolute transparency is a nightmare for covert operations but a boon for enforcement. Absolute opacity is the reverse. Modern surveillance creates a strange middle ground: a world where hiding is possible but noticeable, where tracking is powerful but imperfect, and where the truth of maritime behaviour lies in patterns, not single events.

Consider the global sanctions on oil-exporting pariah states. Before satellites expanded AIS reach, tankers switched flags, forged documents, and rebranded mid-sea without consequence. Today, analysts detect shell companies that buy aging tankers, register them under permissive jurisdictions, and conduct ship-to-ship transfers in remote gulfs. The transfers are often captured accidentally by radar satellites scanning for environmental change. A suspiciously stationary vessel leaves a bright echo. Two hulls, touching gently, create a distinctive signature. A few days later, one sails to a sanctioned port, the other to an unsuspecting refinery on a different continent. The deception is clever; the data trails are patient.

Yet, even as transparency spreads, ambiguity persists. AIS signals can be spoofed. A vessel can broadcast a location hundreds of kilometres away. Deep-learning algorithms detect the mismatch between claimed position and satellite observations, but a high-end spoofer can mimic route patterns that appear plausible. Intelligence agencies invest heavily in unpicking such fabrications. Their analysts weigh probabilities: is the vessel's behaviour physically possible? Does its claimed speed match its class? Does its wake length match its broadcast velocity? The ocean becomes a probabilistic map, not a simple grid.

Commercial firms often become the unexpected referees of maritime disputes. When one nation claims a tanker violated sanctions, another may counter with AIS logs showing compliance. Independent satellite companies publish imagery that settles the argument. Journalists break stories that governments would rather keep quiet. The power dynamic shifts: truth in maritime affairs no longer belongs solely to the state.

Still, there are darker uses. Some states track tankers not to enforce sanctions but to undermine competitors. If an adversary depends on oil imports, monitoring its tanker traffic gives early warning of shortages. During crises, a state might buy up satellite capacity to watch choke points. Financial traders exploit the same data to predict commodity price swings. Warships shadow merchant fleets under the guise of maritime security, but their real mission is surveillance.

A fleet is not just steel and sailors; it is data. Every course change, every port call, every drop in speed feeds into predictive models. War planners simulate blockade scenarios not with paper charts but with real-time satellite feeds. They see which routes serve which ports, where tankers cluster, where supply lines are most fragile. The strategic value of this information is immense: to know where a rival's economy breathes is to know where to choke it.

And yet, there is a counterpoint. Satellite visibility cannot resolve intent. A tanker meeting another at sea may be conducting legitimate bunkering. A warship near a strait could be on routine patrol. Transparency does not eliminate ambiguity; it sharpens the stakes of interpretation. In a crisis, a misread image could push a nation to believe an attack is imminent. Open-source intelligence moves faster than diplomats. The risk is not merely that someone hides; it is that someone is seen and misunderstood.

In the margins of the world's oceans, imaginative adaptations appear. Smugglers experiment with AIS transponders aboard small decoy boats that broadcast the identity of larger tankers. Fleets travel in loose convoys, sharing identities to muddy the water. Some cruise at unusual speeds to confuse prediction models. Others paint over identifying features visible to optical imaging. Every tactic is a temporary shelter; the surveillance net tightens a little more each month.

The open ocean is vast, but satellites are multiplying faster than ships. Costs fall. Resolution improves. Machine learning turns torrents of radar imagery into searchable databases. The days when a vessel could slip across the equator unseen are ending. In their place emerges a world in which transparency is the default, evasion the risk, and the sea—once the freest domain—becomes a monitored archive of behaviour.

Yet nothing in this system is guaranteed. A conflict that disables key satellites could return regions of the ocean to darkness. Nations that once relied on space-based maritime awareness would find their visibility shrinking. Shipping lanes would become uncertain again. Insurers would panic. Navies would patrol blindly. And the silence—so comforting to smugglers and so dangerous to fleets—would return.

This possibility haunts strategists. The surveillance of oceans depends on fragile infrastructure hundreds of kilometres above the Earth. Fleets rely on technology that adversaries know how to target. Transparency, like trust, is delicate. The maritime shadows may have shrunk, but they have not disappeared. And if the satellites ever blink out, the world will feel the loss immediately—in markets, in security, and in the uneasy knowledge that the sea remembers how to hide.

Humanitarian corridors

The children were meant to be safe. Buses had been arranged, white flags raised, and the route negotiated. Yet the convoy never arrived. Roads that officials believed to be passable were, in reality, submerged under metres of water. A bridge that looked intact in ground reports had already collapsed, swept away by floodwaters churning invisibly beneath the surface. The failure was not malicious; it was informational. The people planning the evacuation were blind. Hours later, a synthetic aperture radar satellite passed overhead. Its image showed the truth: the corridor was gone, replaced by a temporary inland sea. Relief workers adjusted their plans, but the delay had cost lives.

Humanitarian corridors are not just lines on a map; they are promises. To civilians trapped between advancing armies, flooded valleys, or shattered infrastructure, a corridor is the slender path between despair and survival. The difficulty lies in making those promises real. The ground may be hostile. The weather may shift. Bridges may be bombed, roads mined, or rivers blockaded with debris. In every disaster—natural or man-made—information becomes at least as important as manpower. Satellites have become the unseen guides steering people through danger.

The most straightforward is weather forecasting. A military convoy can risk poor visibility; a humanitarian one cannot. Relief aircraft need reliable data on cloud ceilings and wind shear. Ships carrying medical supplies need to know which storm systems to avoid. Weather satellites track cyclones as they form, measure rainfall intensity, and estimate the likelihood of landslides on soaked mountainsides. What once required guesswork now happens in near-real time. During the 2021 flood crisis in central Europe, high-resolution radar satellites mapped the spread of inundation hour by hour. Relief agencies used those updates to redirect ambulances, reroute convoys, and identify islands of population cut off by waterways that did not exist the day before.

Yet weather only tells part of the story. When cities crumble under bombardment, the problem is not rain; it is rubble. Optical imagery can show where streets are blocked, which hospitals still stand, and where fires continue to burn. In Syria and Yemen, aid groups have used commercial satellite imagery to mark "safe" lanes for ambulances trying to reach besieged neighbourhoods. Sometimes those lanes lasted only days before artillery carved new scars across them. Every satellite pass was a chance to update reality.

Optical sensors, however, have a serious limitation: they cannot see through cloud. When storms or smoke obscure the ground, optical data becomes little more than a grey blur. Synthetic aperture radar fills the gap. It detects the shape of the land with microwaves that cut through darkness and haze. When the Goa floods swept across western India, radar satellites revealed which roads were still elevated above the deluge. Those dry corridors—unmarked, unplanned, and hidden from ground view—became lifelines. Evacuation teams relied on the images more than on local reports, which lagged and often contradicted each other.

Space-based mapping of destruction carries moral complexity. When a bombed bridge is identified from orbit, that knowledge can guide evacuation—but it can also be used to plan the next air strike. Some states refuse to allow satellite providers to share high-resolution data with humanitarian organisations, arguing that such imagery has dual-use potential. In conflicts where both sides use drones and artillery guided by satellite coordinates, even the most well-intentioned data becomes strategic. Relief workers find themselves depending on commercial vendors willing to take political risks, or NGOs that pool subscriptions funded by philanthropic donors.

InUkraine, volunteers analysing commercial imagery spotted armoured columns massing on roads that had been declared safe for civilian movement. Their findings ricocheted across social media, warning families to avoid corridors that were quietly becoming kill zones. That information was neither military nor governmental; it came from citizens with laptops. The democratisation of satellite imagery makes humanitarian relief faster—but it also complicates diplomacy. Government promises of safe passage become harder to enforce when civilians can see violations unfolding in near real time.

Flood mapping illustrates how satellite data turns chaos into geometry. When Pakistan suffered catastrophic monsoon flooding, millions were displaced. Entire districts vanished beneath water. Traditional road maps were worthless. Orbital sensors detected not only the extent of the flooding but the subtle gradient of the land beneath. From those slopes, algorithms predicted where the water would flow next. Aid agencies moved camps before they were inundated, positioned food stockpiles on higher ground, and warned convoys against roads that would soon be underwater. Such interventions sound mundane—drive here, not there—but in disaster zones, mundane choices are the difference between relief and catastrophe.

Sometimes the challenge is not water but dust. After major earthquakes, dust clouds obscure streets. Infrared imaging reveals where fires continue to burn, and thus where infrastructure is compromised. LiDAR, from airborne platforms or forthcoming satellite missions, can detect subtle changes in land elevation—signs of collapsed tunnels, unstable slopes, or new fault ruptures. Each layer of data tightens the map of risk.

Humanitarian corridors rely on trust. Civilians must believe that a route is safe. Aid organisations must trust that combatants will respect their passage. Satellite imagery becomes an arbiter of credibility. When a state insists it has not targeted evacuation routes, independent imagery can verify—or contradict—the claim. Truth becomes visible, even when bodies are not.

There is, however, a darker side. Belligerents study the same imagery, searching for patterns in humanitarian movement. An evacuation convoy moving at predictable times on predictable roads becomes a target. Aid agencies now stagger departure schedules, hide convoys beneath cloud cover, or request radar passes that can track terrain without revealing vehicle positions. The very transparency that makes relief possible can place civilians at risk if not managed carefully.

A global network of data providers, academic institutions, and volunteer analysts has emerged around this problem. They scrape satellite feeds, merge them with drone footage, and build live crisis maps. These maps guide not only vehicles but diplomacy. When a government claims it cannot open a corridor due to weather, satellite evidence may show clear skies. When armed groups claim they have withdrawn from a checkpoint, imagery may show their vehicles idling metres away. The humanitarian corridor is no longer just a negotiated promise; it is a monitored instrument.

In places where internet access collapses, SATCOM terminals bridge the gap. Relief convoys use satellite communications to request airlifts, coordinate with hospitals, and update weather conditions. When cyber-attacks knock terrestrial networks offline, satellite links carry life-saving messages. But terminals become targets too. A dish on a rooftop tells hostile actors where communications are being relayed. Humanitarian responders learn to move quickly, power equipment intermittently, and avoid lingering under clear skies where drones might be watching.

Space-based tools expose another uncomfortable truth: some corridors fail because they were never meant to succeed. Imagery has documented aid trucks held at border crossings even when roads ahead were open. It has shown "safe" corridors littered with shell craters. Civilians see these failures from the sky before they hear official denials on the ground. The moral authority that satellite imagery brings has begun to reshape humanitarian norms. False promises can be disproven publicly, and the world can watch without relying on propaganda-laden testimony.

Yet space is not omniscient. Clouds still hide villages. Forest canopies mask mass displacement. Urban warfare produces smoke plumes thick enough to blind optical eyes. Radar sees shapes, not intentions. In the fog of disaster, the difference between a refugee convoy and a military one can be subtle. A misinterpretation could be lethal.

Even where data is available, not all actors can afford it. High-resolution imagery remains expensive. Small NGOs may depend on lower-resolution feeds that cannot detect subtle threats, such as a washed-out culvert that will collapse under a lorry's weight. Democratising access to space-based insight remains unfinished work.

Nor is the technology immune to attack. Satellites can be jammed. Their data streams can be spoofed. A hostile actor could feed false imagery into public channels, rerouting convoys into traps. The more the world relies on orbital truth, the more tempting it becomes to corrupt that truth. Protecting humanitarian data becomes its own strategic priority, demanding encryption, authentication, and trusted custodianship.

Despite these vulnerabilities, the evidence is overwhelming: satellites save lives. They shorten the gap between disaster and response. They make planning empirical. They allow evacuation corridors to flex with changing terrain. They allow medicine to flow where it is needed, not where a map once said a road should be.

And yet the core tension endures. Humanitarian corridors must be flexible, adaptive, and informed by the best data available. But they must also be honoured. Technology cannot compel restraint; it can only expose its absence. The satellites may show a road is safe, but they cannot prevent a sniper from firing on it. They may map a river's retreat, but they cannot assure that a convoy will not be stopped by a checkpoint erected five minutes earlier.

Space-based insight has made the unseen visible. It has placed knowledge where ignorance once ruled. But the promise of a corridor is more than a prediction of safe passage—it is a pledge of humanity amid chaos. Satellites can draw the route, monitor the weather, and warn of danger. They cannot guarantee mercy. The question, hanging uncomfortably above every crisis, is whether the clarity offered from orbit will eventually force the world to honour the promises made on the ground—or whether those promises will remain hostage to the same brutality that satellites merely record.

What stayed hidden

The satellite crossed overhead at precisely the advertised time, cameras pointed towards a battlefield journalists could not reach. Hours later, analysts published high-resolution images on social media. They circled scorched craters, dotted the map with vehicle silhouettes, and declared they had captured the truth of the fight. Yet a week afterwards, a soldier who had escaped the town quietly corrected them: the armour had been gone for days. What the satellites had photographed were mock-ups—sheet-metal frames painted with thermal signatures, arranged to deceive the world. The sensors saw everything, and yet they saw nothing.

So much of modern conflict is built on the presumption that orbit makes deception impossible. The narrative says adversaries cannot hide; that open-source imagery unmasks every armoured brigade, every missile battery, every destroyed village. But the real story is more complicated. Space gives unprecedented reach, but its vision is neither permanent nor perfect. What satellites miss can matter more than what they reveal.

Clouds remain one of the oldest and most stubborn defences. A tank column concealed beneath overcast skies is invisible to optical sensors, no matter how sharp the lens. States have learned to manoeuvre assets in weather windows, exploiting satellite orbits that only revisit every few hours or days. In conflicts where a surprise assault might hinge on a few kilometres of movement, a short burst of heavy cloud can hide a brigade. Analysts can guess what is happening beneath the haze, but guessing is not verification. The opacity of the Earth's atmosphere becomes a tactical asset.

Synthetic aperture radar was meant to solve that problem, penetrating cloud, smoke, and darkness. It has, but with limitations. Radar sees shape and reflectivity, not intent. A radar return can tell you there is metal in a field; it cannot tell you whether it is a functioning tank or a hollow decoy. In Kosovo, Chinese and Yugoslav forces famously fooled NATO's radar-guided bombs with wooden aircraft. Today's decoys are more sophisticated, built with reflective materials that imitate radar signatures. Some emit faint heat to confuse infrared sensors. Others mimic the communications chatter of real units. In a world where imagery intelligence is widely available, deception has become industrialised.

Camouflage has advanced too. A vehicle under a thermal blanket appears as part of the landscape. Missile launchers are painted to mimic agricultural machinery. Some states deploy fake roads—paths carved in dust to suggest movements that never occurred. And beyond physical deception lies digital illusion. Adversaries can spoof radar altimetry data, flood analysts with deep-faked images, or seed false coordinates into public mapping platforms. The result is a battlefield where truth and falsehood travel in parallel, both amplified by the same open networks that were meant to democratise information.

Even when no one is lying, satellites still struggle to interpret ambiguity. Consider a convoy of trucks. A high-resolution image might show tarpaulin-covered vehicles moving at night. Are they carrying humanitarian supplies, anti-aircraft missiles, or nothing at all? Without corroboration, states fall back on suspicion. Ambiguity fuels worst-case planning. One state assumes the convoy hides weapons and prepares to strike. The other assumes the satellite is misreading a harmless supply column and risks escalation through misunderstanding. When orbital vision is uncertain, the space between what is seen and what is believed becomes perilous.

There is also the matter of time. Satellites do not watch continuously; they glance. Between passes, hours can stretch into opportunities. In those gaps, forces can disperse, dig in, or melt into civilian traffic. They can move weapons into hospitals, stage artillery inside abandoned warehouses, or relocate command posts beneath schools. By the time the next pass arrives, everything has changed. The image is accurate and outdated at the same moment.

States exploit revisit gaps with choreography. Decoys are assembled just before a satellite arrives, then dismantled minutes afterwards. Anti-air systems are rolled out only when needed and stored when they are not, reducing their visible footprint. Some forces build simulated heat signatures—small fires, heated water barrels, or electrified metal panels—to fool infrared sensors. When analysts look down, they see a location full of "activity", but the real weapons may be kilometres away.

Deception also thrives in infrastructure. Fibre-optic command cables are buried underground. Mobile rocket launchers operate from concealed culverts. Transport aircraft fly without transponders, using terrain-masking routes to avoid line-of-sight radar coverage. The more sophisticated commercial imagery becomes, the more creative the countermeasures. In some regions, adversaries have begun to interfere directly with the satellite data stream. Jamming uplinks, hacking ground receivers, or corrupting metadata can make imagery unreliable—or worse, subtly inaccurate.

There is a psychological dimension. Open-source intelligence has convinced societies that satellites expose all wrongdoing, always. When atrocities occur, the public demands images. But cloud, smoke, or timing may obscure the truth. Absence of evidence is mistaken for evidence of absence. Perpetrators exploit this, committing crimes during overcast days, burning villages at night, or using the cover of industrial haze. When no image appears, propaganda fills the vacuum. "If satellites did not see it," they argue, "it must not have happened."

Conversely, the accessibility of imagery can drive snap judgements. A single satellite photo suggesting a missile launcher near a civilian site may galvanise outrage, even if deeper context—concealed by roofs or shadows—tells a different story. The world is learning that seeing from above does not guarantee understanding.

Disinformation campaigns now incorporate orbital deception. Fake "satellite images" circulate online, created with generative models. They appear authoritative because people trust the aesthetic: the angle, the resolution, the grid coordinates. By blurring the line between real and fabricated orbital evidence, malign actors erode confidence in genuine imagery. If everything might be a fake, nothing can be proven—an inversion of the transparency satellites were meant to provide.

Even honest analysis falters under scale. Thousands of satellites collect petabytes of data. Human eyes cannot parse it all. Machine learning fills the gap, classifying shapes and predicting patterns. But algorithms are fooled by decoys too. A wooden tank painted with the right shadows can register as a threat. A missile launcher hidden beneath a tarpaulin might be dismissed as a truck. Training data struggles to keep up with adversaries who design deception specifically to defeat recognition models.

The most effective concealment is often banal. A missile moved at night under cloud cover. A radar array shut down during overflight. A command post relocated into an apartment block where distinguishing military and civilian becomes morally fraught. The invisibility is not technological—it is architectural, geographic, human.

And sometimes the gaps are simply unavoidable. Dense jungles hide movements that even radar struggles to penetrate. Mountain valleys block line of sight. Urban density creates overlapping shadows. Hurricanes, sandstorms, smoke plumes, and volcanic ash all turn satellites into blind observers.

For humanitarian actors, these gaps mean that routes believed to be open may be death traps. For generals, they mean adversaries can stage surprise offensives. For diplomats, they complicate attribution. A cyberattack on a satellite ground station may originate from a nation's territory—or from a rented server farm inside it. A jamming signal might be intentional—or a faulty transmitter.

The irony is stark: never in history has so much of the planet been watched from above, yet so much remains uncertain. Transparency is partial. Surveillance does not abolish ambiguity; it merely shifts its boundaries. The world sees more, but also doubts more.

The emerging tension is philosophical as much as strategic. If perfect vision is impossible, what does accountability look like? If imagery can be fooled, misread, or faked, how do societies distinguish truth from theatre? When states plan for war under the assumption that satellites see all, what happens when those assumptions fail at the worst possible moment?

The promise of orbital insight is not omniscience. It is probability. It reduces uncertainty without eliminating it. The gaps—whether born of weather, deception, or the simple limits of physics—remain spaces where strategy, manipulation, and tragedy unfold.

And as more nations and private actors join the competition to hide or reveal the truth from above, one question lingers: will the shadows shrink, or will the world merely learn to create better illusions beneath the gaze of a thousand unblinking eyes?

Chapter 11

Designing for Resilience

When the first fragments hit, the operators thought it was a telemetry glitch. Pixelated streaks, a momentary loss of lock, then silence. Minutes later, another satellite in the same orbital plane fell quiet. Screens filled with red alarms, automated scripts attempting reconnection, ground teams scrambling for alternatives. Somewhere above, a shattered defunct spacecraft had become a spray of lethal confetti, spreading faster than the operators could model. The constellation was built for efficiency, not punishment. It had never rehearsed this specific nightmare. And yet, in the end, most of the system survived—not because its satellites were invincible, but because its architecture had been designed to bend rather than break.

That lesson is becoming unavoidable. The space environment is harsh, contested, and deeply interdependent. Satellites suffer radiation hits, navigation spoofing, signal jamming, and orbital debris. Ground stations face cyber intrusion, power cuts, sanctions, and natural disasters. A single point of failure can jeopardise everything from broadband to banking. Against that backdrop, resilience—true, engineered resilience—is not a technical afterthought. It is the foundation on which every credible space capability rests.

Yet resilience is not a slogan. It is design philosophy. It means accepting fallibility and planning for it. In space, nothing is fully safe: rockets explode, solder cracks, solar storms surge, and adversaries probe for weaknesses. The question is not whether something will go wrong, but how gracefully a system can adapt when it does. That mindset has quietly reshaped space programmes around the world. Instead of assuming perfect operations, architects assume interruption. Instead of monolithic satellites, they consider proliferated constellations. Instead of pristine ground stations, they build mobile terminals, modular uplinks, and distributed control. The new ambition is less about preventing failure and more about surviving it.

This chapter follows that shift. It begins with the simplest building block: architectures that absorb loss without collapsing. Some systems degrade intelligently, shedding non-essential services to preserve vital ones. When bandwidth is contested or an adversary jams a link, they fall back to text-grade communications rather than going dark. In a crisis, being slow but alive is better than being fast and gone. That idea—graceful degradation—is changing how militaries and civil operators design everything from command networks to weather data feeds.

Then comes the central debate of the decade: proliferation versus protection. Should states field vast fleets of low-cost satellites, accepting attrition as a feature rather than a flaw? Or concentrate capability in a smaller number of hardened platforms, built like orbital fortresses? Ministries find themselves torn between cost, control, and credibility. A proliferated constellation can absorb hits but demands relentless production, launch cadence, and tracking. Hardened assets are formidable but few; lose one, and the strategic impact may be catastrophic. We will explore where that trade-off leads, and why both philosophies are reshaping procurement strategies from Washington to New Delhi.

Robustness is no longer only about the spacecraft. Ground segments—the invisible arteries of space systems—must be just as resilient. That means intelligent antennas that hop frequencies under attack, dispersed command centres that can be evacuated, and mobile terminals that arrive in theatre like fly-away kits. At the same time, satellites themselves grow smarter. Onboard processing filters data before downlink, reducing reliance on vulnerable ground paths. Edge AI identifies interference, blocks spoofed commands, and reconfigures payloads without asking permission. Autonomy, once a novelty, becomes insurance against isolation.

And resilience is not limited to communication and navigation. The chapter examines logistics in orbit: refuelling, servicing, and orbital tugs that extend life, reposition assets, and clear debris. In the past, satellites died where they were launched. Today, a spacecraft can be inspected, repaired, or towed, reshaping both commercial economics and strategic calculus. A nation that can refuel its birds has more than endurance; it has flexibility. Space starts to behave less like a disposable frontier and more like an operational domain where assets evolve instead of expire.

The chapter closes with a harder truth: some disasters cannot be fully tested. No engineer can stage a real solar superstorm. No wargame replicates a chain-reaction debris cascade with perfect fidelity. But operators try.

They run digital twins—software replicas of constellations that simulate failures, cyberattacks, and kinetic strikes. They hold tabletop exercises for what happens when ten satellites are lost in an hour, or when a malicious update locks thousands of terminals. Red teams break assumptions. Blue teams learn humility. The ultimate aim is psychological resilience as much as technological: to ensure that when the unthinkable arrives, it is not unanticipated.

Designing for resilience is as much about philosophy as hardware. It demands accepting that vulnerability is permanent; that space can never be sanitised or made safe; that complexity guarantees surprises. The systems built today will define how societies endure crisis tomorrow. Somewhere in the orbiting quiet, every nation faces the same question: do their systems fail catastrophically, or do they fail slowly and recover?

Turn the page, and the answers begin to take shape.

Architectures that survive loss

The first warning was not a blinding burst of static, but a subtle thinning of the data stream. Imagery packets arrived out of order, timestamps trailing by seconds, then minutes. Operators watched the bandwidth shrink, their dashboards filling with amber warnings as a hostile jammer swept across the theatre. The satellite itself remained healthy; the payload was still collecting imagery. The only thing dying was the link to Earth. And yet, the mission continued. The system, anticipating degradation, shifted from full-motion video to still imagery, then to low-bandwidth text reports. Analysts received coordinates and target classifications instead of pictures. It was not elegant, but it was enough. A network built to fail gracefully did not fail at all.

That is the difference between architectures that break and those that survive. For decades, space systems were designed as if loss were unthinkable—every mission planned around uninterrupted connectivity and flawless hardware. But space has grown crowded, contested, and deliberately hostile. Interference is routine, ground links are targets, and the spectrum is a battlefield. Satellites, once imagined as aloof machines beyond reach, are now within the envelope of cyber, jamming, spoofing, and kinetic attack. In this environment, resilience is not a luxury. It is the precondition for utility.

Graceful degradation begins with acceptance. Designers assume failure. They expect that bandwidth will be pinched, routing tables corrupted, and antennas dazzled. Rather than collapsing into silence, resilient networks shed complexity as conditions worsen. A broadband service that once delivered high-definition video can fall back to compressed imagery, then to still frames, then to raw telemetry. Militaries use similar principles in their tactical communications: when satellites are jammed, terminals revert to narrowband bursts; when positioning data is degraded, units switch to inertial navigation. These are not kludges. They are strategic decisions that preserve coherence when the environment turns poisonous.

One might ask why systems were not designed this way from the start. The answer lies in heritage. Traditional space missions relied on single satellites with single downlinks—expensive machines launched once a decade and operated like museum pieces. Their fragility was hidden behind the illusion of distance. As long as no-one was trying to harm them, redundancy felt wasteful. But the rise of proliferated constellations, commercial mega-networks, and adversaries with electronic warfare capabilities has made that illusion impossible to sustain. Modern operators do not trust permanence. They trust adaptation.

Graceful degradation is not merely a technical principle; it is a question of philosophy. Does a system have the humility to perform badly rather than not at all? Engineers dislike compromise. They are taught to optimise, to squeeze every bit of performance from a link budget or payload. Degradation feels like failure. Yet history shows that rigid systems—those that demand perfect conditions—are the first to die when circumstances change. In war, in disaster response, in everyday commercial use, the worst moment to discover that your architecture cannot shed load is the moment everything begins to break.

This process of shedding begins with prioritisation. Not everything matters in a crisis. Banking satellites can sacrifice video streams to preserve timing signals; navigation constellations can retain coarse accuracy while discarding augmentation data; remote-sensing platforms can transmit only metadata to protect the most time-sensitive intelligence. Critical functions float to the top, while luxuries sink. When done well, the user barely notices. When done badly, millions discover how quickly digital life can unravel when its orbital foundation crumbles.

Some of the most revealing examples come from nations that rely on small satellites. With limited power, modest apertures, and fragile links, these spacecraft cannot compete with heavy, military-grade platforms for raw performance. What they can do is fail gracefully. They share tasks across swarms, relay data through whichever node remains reachable, and store payloads onboard until a link appears. If weather blocks one ground station, another takes over; if a satellite is lost, its neighbours fill the gap. No single node is indispensable. Loss is assumed, absorbed, and forgotten.

Contrast that with legacy constellations built around a handful of exquisite assets. These are marvels of engineering: hardened, radiation-shielded, and protected by layers of command authentication. But they are few. A single anti-satellite strike, a cyber breach, or an unexpected subsystem fault can strip entire regions of capability. In peacetime, this risk feels abstract. In crisis, it feels existential. Militaries that once scoffed at commercial proliferated networks now study them, borrow from them, and quietly plan their own.

There is also a psychological dimension. Systems that degrade elegantly help decision-makers stay calm. When a terminal downgrades gracefully—switching from video to text, from text to coordinates—it signals that order remains. Commanders can make decisions. Crews can stay in the fight. Markets can function. Societies remain connected. The opposite—abrupt blackouts, inexplicable silence, cascading faults—breeds fear and miscalculation. In deterrence theory, perception is half the battle. A nation whose space services fade gently rather than shatter violently projects control.

Ironically, this gentleness relies on ruthless design. Engineers must decide, long before crisis, which functions live and which ones die. They rehearse outages, throttle traffic, and simulate conflict until the system reveals its breaking points. Some operators use digital twins: software replicas of constellations running accelerated timelines, where satellites are lost, antennas jammed, and ground stations taken offline. These synthetic disasters expose brittle assumptions that glossy PowerPoint slides never show. In these rehearsals, operators discover that certain nodes are overburdened, that switching protocols stall under load, or that users misinterpret degraded outputs. Better to learn in a simulation than in combat.

This approach has political implications too. Allies using shared space architectures must trust that degradation paths will not privilege one user group over another. Commercial providers selling bandwidth to both civilian and military clients must decide whose packets survive when the spectrum narrows. During recent conflicts, governments quietly negotiated with satellite operators to prioritise humanitarian traffic, medical data and air-traffic control. These decisions were technical in form but moral in substance.

There are limits to this philosophy. A network that can degrade forever risks mediocrity. If a system becomes so obsessed with surviving that it never performs optimally, it may not justify its cost. And graceful degradation cannot mask catastrophic failure. If a constellation loses half its satellites in an afternoon, no amount of clever throttling will maintain full coverage. But resilience is not perfection. It is probability. Every layer of redundancy, every fallback mode, every alternative route nudges survival chances higher.

Some architects argue that pre-defined degradation paths are not enough. They want autonomy: satellites that make their own decisions about what to transmit, to whom, and when. Machine learning already filters imagery in orbit, discarding clouds and sending only useful pixels. In coming years, satellites may decide which users get priority, which ground stations they trust, and how to route data around hostile interference. This is not science fiction. It is a rational response to latency, jamming, and contested ground infrastructure. If a satellite can think, it can survive.

Others fear the opposite—a future of over-automation where humans lose insight into how their systems behave under stress. What happens when an autonomous constellation misclassifies a ground station as hostile? Or when machine learning preserves military traffic but discards emergency broadcasts? Graceful degradation demands transparency. Users must know not only that the system is working, but how. The more complex a system becomes, the harder that promise is to keep.

Across the world, space agencies and defence ministries are re-writing specifications. No longer do they ask only "What is the peak data rate?" They ask, "What happens when we lose a satellite? When the spectrum is jammed? When we cannot reach our primary ground station? When the payload overheats? When debris forces a manoeuvre?" These questions once sounded defeatist. Now they sound like competence.

Perhaps the deepest shift is cultural. Engineers raised on perfection are learning to prize robustness. Operators once terrified of data loss are learning to live with it. And political leaders, who used to see outages as national embarrassments, are teaching their publics that resilience is measured not by avoiding failure but by outlasting it. Systems that have permission to fail elegantly turn disaster into inconvenience.

Somewhere above us, thousands of satellites glide silently across the night. Most will never experience a deliberate attack or catastrophic fault. But all of them inhabit a world where space weather surges, firmware ages, and hostile actors experiment with interference. The difference between systems that endure and systems that collapse is measured in how they respond to the first crack in the armour.

The question remains: will nations invest in architectures that survive loss, or cling to systems that demand perfection? The future will not wait for caution. The next degradation event is already on its way—somewhere, some link is thinning, some sensor drifting, some operator about to discover whether the system bends or breaks.

Proliferation versus protection

The argument began in a quiet conference room, not on a battlefield. A defence minister, holding a briefing paper that listed a thousand small satellites, asked a blunt question: "*Why should I trust swarms of tiny machines when I could build a handful of indestructible ones?*" Across the table, an engineer answered with equal bluntness: "*Because nothing is indestructible.*" That exchange captures one of the defining strategic debates of modern space power. Should nations spread capability across vast constellations of cheap, disposable nodes, or concentrate it in a few hardened, exquisitely protected systems? The choice is not merely technical. It is philosophical, financial, and deeply political.

For decades, governments bet on protection. Their satellites were singular objects of national pride—heavy, shielded, encrypted, launched on ceremonial rockets and placed in orbits from which they would reign for fifteen years. They were built to survive radiation storms, hostile jamming, and even debris strikes. But they were few. When a single platform carried an entire nation's early warning sensors or command-and-control channels, loss was catastrophic. The logic was elegant: harden what matters most. The flaw was simple: fragility concentrates.

Proliferation takes the opposite view. Instead of worshipping invincibility, it embraces abundance. It spreads sensors and relays across hundreds or thousands of low-cost satellites, each easily replaced. A hostile actor may disable a handful, but the constellation continues. Data routes around damage. The network heals itself. The enemy wastes time and resources striking targets that scarcely matter. In this worldview, survivability is statistical. Defence is achieved not through armour, but through numbers.

Yet the debate cannot be reduced to a slogan. Many cheap nodes and a few hardened assets speak to different visions of control, risk, and statecraft. The ministries that must justify spending face a dilemma: is it better to launch one multi-billion-pound satellite that does everything reliably, or to launch two hundred that do most things well enough? Treasury officials favour predictability; military planners fear single points of failure; intelligence chiefs worry about access control on large commercial constellations; lawmakers ask who owns the data when a crisis erupts. What looks like an engineering question quickly becomes a constitutional one.

Consider early warning satellites. These platforms track missile launches, enabling minutes of warning for cities and forces on the ground. For years, only a few nations possessed them. They were large, complex spacecraft in high orbits, designed for immunity rather than redundancy. But an adversary with kinetic anti-satellite weapons or powerful jammers could, in theory, blind a nation with a single strike. The emergence of proliferated infrared sensors—smaller, cheaper detectors hosted on commercial buses—offers an alternative. Instead of relying on three or four crown jewels in geostationary orbit, a state could field dozens of persistent watchers in low Earth orbit. Loss of one barely registers. Loss of ten is an inconvenience, not a crisis.

This shift forces a deeper question: what kind of security does a state prefer? Does it trust a fortress, or a swarm? Fortresses promise certainty. They can be wrapped in defensive payloads, guarded by encrypted links, shielded from radiation, and supported by dedicated ground control. Swarms promise continuity. They can survive attrition, hide among commercial traffic, and refresh hardware with each launch cycle. The choice reflects a nation's faith in control versus adaptability.

Hardened satellites, for all their strengths, age poorly. A spacecraft tested for a decade of service may watch its software ossify as ground networks evolve. Updating firmware across encrypted flight systems is slow and risky. In contrast, proliferated constellations refresh continually. Hardware flown last year becomes obsolete next year; vulnerabilities are patched in orbit or replaced wholesale. Innovation becomes routine. But routine is expensive. Launching hundreds of satellites demands stable access to rockets, ground licences, spectrum, and debris mitigation planning. Proliferation is not a free lunch; it is a logistical empire.

Security establishments also struggle with trust. A proliferated constellation often relies on commercial partners who manufacture buses, operate ground stations, and provide cloud storage. Intelligence services bristle at the prospect of sensitive data passing through private hands or multinational supply chains. Few ministers enjoy explaining that a critical reconnaissance feed is hosted on civilian infrastructure. Hardened government satellites, by contrast, are sovereign instruments. Their ground segment is locked behind guards and blast-resistant doors. Their vulnerabilities remain state secrets. But secrecy is costly too. When only a handful of technicians understand a system, talent bottlenecks emerge. When a nation refuses to use commercial infrastructure, it must build its own—and justify the bill to taxpayers.

Another division arises from ethics. Commercial proliferated networks blur the line between civilian and military assets. When governments rely on the same constellation that provides broadband to villages, hospitals, and farms, an adversary attacking the system risks harming civilians. This entanglement can deter aggression. It can also inflame escalation. A missile fired at a hardened military satellite is one thing; a strike that shutters schools and clinics is another. But ministries that base their defence on dual-use systems lose some control. They cannot order a private operator to sacrifice satellites without compensation or legal authority. In a hardened programme, command is centralised. In a proliferated commercial model, command is negotiated.

There is also geography to consider. Hardened satellites often occupy higher orbits—geostationary, highly elliptical, or cislunar trajectories—where they see vast swathes of Earth and communicate over long distances. Proliferated satellites crowd low Earth orbit, providing granularity and latency advantages but limited field of view. A nation may find that certain missions simply cannot be done cheaply. Deep-space tracking, nuclear detonation detection, and global broadcast still benefit from altitude and heavy payloads. Here, protection remains essential. But even heavy platforms can gain resilience by networking with smaller nodes—offloading data, relaying commands, and hiding in plain sight.

Some policymakers argue for hybrid constellations: a hardened core surrounded by a proliferated shell. The core preserves critical functions with high assurance. The shell absorbs attacks and preserves continuity. This architecture mirrors biological systems, where vital organs are shielded and redundancy exists at the cellular level. But hybrid models demand coordination between procurement cultures that rarely cooperate. The agency that launches a billion-pound satellite does not always enjoy sharing budgets with the one that launches ten thousand-pound spacecraft.

Cost shapes the battlefield as much as physics. A single hardened satellite may cost more than an entire proliferated constellation. That price reflects radiation shielding, secure processors, bespoke propulsion, and exhaustive testing. But cost buys control. A ministry owning its own spacecraft owns its destiny. A ministry relying on commercial rideshares and outsourced ground stations may lose leverage at the worst moment. History is littered with examples of governments discovering that commercial agreements contain inconvenient clauses when crises arrive.

Yet commercial operators bring agility that ministries struggle to match. They accept faster risk cycles, they design for mass production, they embrace off-the-shelf parts, and they iterate in months, not years. Militaries accustomed to procurement timelines measured in decades find this pace intoxicating and destabilising. It undermines legacy programmes and threatens entrenched suppliers. It challenges comfortable assumptions that defence technology should be bespoke. The spread of proliferated constellations is not only a technical revolution; it is an industrial revolt.

Adversaries face dilemmas too. A hardened asset demands precision to destroy; a proliferated network demands persistence. A missile strike can kill a single exquisite satellite. But jamming, spoofing, or cyber intrusion must be sustained across hundreds of targets to matter. And while proliferated systems appear fragile in isolation, their collective resilience frustrates attackers. Even if an adversary destroys dozens, replacements can be launched within weeks. In contrast, a destroyed hardened satellite can take years to replace. A state choosing protection stakes its credibility on a small number of launch pads and manufacturing lines. If those are disrupted, capability collapses.

Still, proliferation breeds complacency if misunderstood. Numbers alone do not guarantee resilience. A thousand cheap satellites that all depend on the same ground gateway are no safer than one. A constellation that routes all traffic through a single cloud provider can be crippled by a software update gone wrong. Diversity matters: orbital planes, link paths, data storage, manufacturers, encryption chains. Proliferation is effective only when paired with architectural imagination.

Protection carries its own blind spots. Hardened systems often assume that their enemies will attack kinetically, not digitally. They prepare for debris and missile defence, but underestimate software corruption, supply chain poisoning, or insider sabotage. A spacecraft may survive a blast but fail after a firmware exploit. The question is not only how a satellite withstands force, but how its operators withstand deception.

There is no universal answer. The right mix depends on geography, threat environment, industrial base, and political temperament. Small nations may embrace proliferation because it offers capability once unaffordable. Large nations may cling to hardened assets because they distrust dependence. Alliances complicate matters further: a constellation shared among partners distributes cost and risk, but also sovereignty. A member state with access to the network may leak data—deliberately or through incompetence. Trust is safer when hardware is centralised. Resilience is safer when hardware is dispersed.

In the end, the debate circles back to that quiet conference room. The minister wanted machines that would not die. The engineer believed in systems that would not care if they did. Each feared a different kind of vulnerability: physical destruction versus operational paralysis. Both recognised that the sky above is no longer a sanctuary. It is a theatre, contested at radio frequencies, probed by cyber intrusion, scanned by space situational awareness networks, and littered with the remnants of past arrogance.

Perhaps the most revealing question is not *which* strategy to choose, but *when* to switch. When does a nation decide that its hardened satellites are too slow, too few, too predictable? When does a proliferated constellation grow so large that it must begin hardening itself? At what point does the cost of numbers exceed the value of durability? There is no formula. Only judgement.

Somewhere in a laboratory, a new bus is being printed, cheap enough to throw away yet powerful enough to matter. Somewhere in a bunker, a hardened spacecraft is being assembled, designed to outlive its builders. The future may belong to both. Or to neither.

The real question is whether the world will choose abundance before it learns, painfully, that protection was never quite enough.

Smart ground, smarter space

The command centre was silent when the satellite went dark—not destroyed, not jammed, simply cut off from its ground link by a storm of interference. In earlier decades, that would have been the end of the story: a helpless machine drifting above Earth, waiting for contact. Instead, the spacecraft continued its task, logging targets, triaging data, compressing imagery and routing packets to peers that still had clear channels. Hours later, when its links cleared, it transmitted a distilled summary—critical alerts first, secondary telemetry later, trivia not at all. The interruption barely registered. Resilience came not from hardened armour or heroic operators, but from a quiet shift in philosophy: intelligence aboard the satellite, not just beneath it.

For most of spacefaring history, satellites have been obedient servants. They sensed, they listened, they relayed, but they rarely *thought*. Decisions were made on the ground, at the pace of human operators and centralised mission control. That model worked when constellations were small, frequencies were quiet, and adversaries sparse. Today, it strains under the weight of thousands of spacecraft, contested spectrum, cyber intrusion, and near-continuous manoeuvre. The choke point is no longer in orbit; it is in the downlink. When every byte must travel to Earth before meaning can be extracted, the system exposes a single vulnerable artery. Hence the pivot to smarter space.

Onboard autonomy rewrites the contract between spacecraft and operators. Rather than asking permission at every turn, an intelligent satellite can classify imagery, detect anomalies, schedule its own slews, and even execute evasive manoeuvres during proximity hazards. Edge AI—miniaturised machine learning models running on radiation-tolerant hardware—filters raw sensor feeds into usable intelligence. Instead of sending gigabytes of cloud-covered Earth to the ground, it sends a handful of annotated targets worth attention. This does not remove humans from the loop, but it moves decision-making closer to the point of sensing, cutting latency and shrinking the attack surface that an adversary can exploit.

Consider maritime surveillance: traditional systems downlink vast radar swaths, leaving analysts to hunt for vessels that have switched off their AIS transponders. An autonomous satellite can detect hull signatures, classify ship types, track courses, and alert coastal states without ever waiting for ground approval. The logic is not science fiction; commercial firms already use onboard processing to spot illegal fishing and oil dumping. Military operators, seeing the same advantages, increasingly insist that reconnaissance platforms carry their own analytic brains.

This autonomy matters twice over. First, when power and waveform are contested, as during jamming or geomagnetic storms, bandwidth is precious. A satellite that can decide what not to send wastes none of it. Second, when ground stations are compromised—whether by cyber attack, physical strike, or political coercion—a spacecraft that can continue partial missions buys time. Graceful degradation in orbit complements graceful degradation on Earth.

But smarter space is only half the equation. Smart ground matters just as much. Historically, ground segments have been brittle architectures: fixed dishes, fixed locations, fixed operators. They were efficient when threats were low; they are liabilities when adversaries can geolocate and target them. To reduce exposure, modern ground networks distribute antennae across continents, maritime platforms, and airborne relays. Virtualised mission control allows operators to switch stations seamlessly, splitting command authority across hardened centres and cloud-hosted backups. The ground becomes a fluid web, not a castle.

Resilient ground must also speak many languages. A satellite that only communicates through one proprietary protocol, to one vendor's antenna farm, is a hostage to fortune. Interoperability—across allies, agencies, and commercial networks—creates routing options. If one path goes dark, another opens. Defence ministries once resisted this for fear of dependency; now they court it for resilience. Shared infrastructure does not erase sovereignty; it strengthens survival.

There is philosophical tension in autonomy. Militaries prize control, yet autonomy demands trust. A spacecraft that reroutes its own data or chooses its own manoeuvres challenges the instinct for central command. Engineers propose safeguards—permission structures, abort commands, audit trails—but no system is perfect. What if the AI misclassifies a friendly radar site as hostile? What if a corrupted model hallucinates threats? Autonomy introduces new failure modes, which must be confronted honestly, not buried beneath hype.

Nevertheless, the alternative—total dependence on ground control—is increasingly indefensible. Ground links are noisy. Latency kills opportunities. A reconnaissance satellite that must ask permission to pivot risks missing fleeting activity: a missile on a transporter-erector, a submarine surfacing beneath cloud cover, a convoy scattering into civilian traffic. Autonomy buys initiative.

Smart ground plays another role: cyber defence. Spacecraft are computers that cannot be patched by hand. When a vulnerability emerges, operators must beam updates across millions of kilometres, hoping the code takes and the attacker does not interfere. Resilient ground architecture pre-emptively segments networks, isolates compromised nodes, and rejects malicious command patterns. It treats satellites as part of a broader distributed system, not fragile antiques.

As autonomy grows, satellites become teammates rather than dependants. A radar satellite tasking an optical neighbour to re-image a moving object; a weather satellite flagging a volcanic eruption; a communications node allocating bandwidth based on priority queues—all without human micromanagement. The more the network learns, the more it behaves like a single organism rather than a flock of dumb metal.

Onboard processing also lowers the value of intercepting downlinks. An adversary that captures raw imagery may glean intelligence; one that intercepts curated metadata may learn little. Compression and encryption at source shift the cost curve in favour of defenders. Even if a link is compromised, the damage is contained.

Autonomy has humanitarian implications too. In disaster zones, weather satellites with onboard flood-mapping algorithms can send evacuation maps directly to terminals in affected regions, bypassing bureaucratic bottlenecks. Earth-observation networks can share crop-stress alerts with farmers before harvests fail. In conflict zones, autonomous platforms can detect power outages and collapsed bridges, guiding relief convoys through safer corridors. These are not marginal gains; they save lives.

Still, intelligence without oversight is dangerous. Nations must resist the temptation to treat autonomous satellites as infallible oracles. Bias in training data can mislead. Adversaries can spoof sensors. Radiation-induced bit flips can corrupt models. The romance of autonomy must be tempered by rigorous testing, red-teaming, and ethical guardrails.

Smart ground introduces its own dilemmas. Virtualised mission control depends on cloud infrastructure that may be susceptible to legal subpoenas, supply-chain compromise, or insider leaks. Ministries that once owned every bolt of their ground stations now outsource storage and compute to commercial partners. This raises sovereignty questions: whose jurisdiction governs the data? Who holds the encryption keys? What happens if a provider is pressured by a hostile state?

Yet the alternative—building fully sovereign, fully redundant ground networks—quickly becomes unaffordable. Most nations cannot sustain dozens of globally distributed antenna farms. They turn to shared services, alliances, and commercial leases. Smart ground is therefore a compromise between ambition and reality: distributed enough to survive attack, integrated enough to coordinate, flexible enough to adapt.

When space becomes smarter, it stops being a remote asset and becomes part of the operational fabric. Armies on the ground, fleets at sea, and humanitarian teams in crisis zones do not wait for analysts in distant centres to interpret imagery; they receive actionable insight in near real time. Satellites cease to be cameras in the sky and become partners in decision-making.

The next frontier is cooperative autonomy: satellites negotiating with each other to allocate tasks, conserve power, and avoid collision. Such behaviour demands trust frameworks, cryptographic identity schemes, and consensus algorithms robust to cyber deception. It transforms constellations into federated systems, where no single node holds the fate of the mission.

There is a quiet dignity in this shift. The era of heroic ground controllers, typing commands into terminals and waiting for a distant beep of acknowledgement, is not gone, but it is evolving. Operators become supervisors of systems that think and learn. The ground becomes a conductor, not a puppeteer.

Some will recoil at the loss of direct control. Others will celebrate the liberation from bottlenecks. The truth lies between: autonomy and resilience are not luxuries, but necessities in a crowded and contested orbit. Spacecraft that cannot think will die. Ground networks that cannot adapt will fail.

The transformation is already under way. Satellites learn to prioritise. Ground stations learn to hide. Networks learn to heal. Intelligence migrates upwards, and fragility drains away. Somewhere above us, a machine is making a decision that once required a human hand.

Whether that decision is right or wrong will shape the battles—and the rescues—of the future.

Logistics in orbit

The most expensive wreckage in human history is not lying at the bottom of the ocean or rusting in a desert boneyard. It surrounds us, silent and invisible, circling Earth at thousands of kilometres per hour. Some of it is the detritus of carelessness; much of it is the residue of a deeper problem. Satellites die not because their sensors fail or their logic stops working, but because they run out of the single commodity we still treat as disposable:

propulsion. When the fuel is spent, a billion-dollar machine becomes a drifting liability. If that logic governed aviation, airports would be scrapyards. Instead, aircraft queue up at gates, refuel, fly again. Space, by contrast, has never known a service station. Until now.

The idea is deceptively simple: rather than launching replacements for every satellite that nears the end of life, meet the spacecraft where it is. Top up its propellant. Swap a component. Tug it to a higher orbit. In terrestrial terms, this is unremarkable—refuelling and servicing are mundane acts. In orbit, they are revolutionary. For decades, engineers assumed satellites were single-use artefacts: launch, operate, burn up. The economic model of space was built around obsolescence. But as constellations proliferate and budgets tighten, the prospect of throwing away perfectly functional platforms becomes untenable. Logistics in orbit is not a luxury; it is a rational response to scale.

The first wave of on-orbit servicing was timid: robotic arms nudging debris, experimental missions practising docking with cooperative targets. The next wave is bolder. Spacecraft designed explicitly as tugs carry extra propellant and grappling mechanisms, capable of pushing or pulling dead or dying satellites into more useful or safer positions. Some missions demonstrate "docking collars" or standardised interfaces, turning satellites into modular Lego rather than sealed coffins. The Canadian "arm" tradition, the European robotic servicing initiatives, and American life-extension vehicles hint at a future where a satellite is not a terminal product but a maintainable asset.

There is profound strategic logic here. Every ministry of defence knows that its most valuable geostationary platforms—the communications behemoths and missile-warning sentinels—run on countdown clocks. Propellant is spent not only when satellites change station, but when they counteract the persistent drag of space weather. Once the tank runs dry, gravity takes over, and the spacecraft must be moved to a graveyard orbit. With refuelling, that timeline stretches. A fleet that once lasted fifteen years could endure twenty, perhaps thirty. The fiscal impact is staggering: a single life-extension mission may save billions in deferred procurement. The military impact is just as sharp: continuity of service matters more than new paint.

But logistics in orbit is more than topping up tanks. Servicing can repair faulty appendages, install new processors, or replace ageing sensors. A satellite built in 2020 can fly in 2040 with modernised payloads, avoiding the cycle of obsolescence that currently drives rapid launch cadence. This blurs the line between spacecraft and infrastructure. The first satellites were machines; the next are platforms.

Yet servicing raises dilemmas. A tug that can dock with friendly satellites can dock with adversarial ones. A robot that can refuel a crippled satellite can push another out of position. Dual-use shadows are long, and every state understands that logistics can be a weapon. One nation's orbital mechanic is another's orbital threat. To mitigate suspicion, commercial operators emphasise transparent servicing experiments with cooperative targets. Defence agencies speak of "mission assurance" rather than "manipulation". The semantics matter: public trust in orbital servicing depends on framing it as repair, not interference.

Refuelling itself is not trivial. Spacecraft use different propellants—hydrazine, xenon, green fuels—stored under pressure in tanks never meant to be opened. Docking requires exquisite precision, often with targets that lack standard ports or alignment markings. The act of approaching an ageing satellite risks collision, fragmentation, and diplomatic fallout. Early missions therefore prefer cooperative targets, pre-fitted with grappling points. But the ambition is broader: a future where servicing vehicles can grip unprepared satellites, mitigating the dead mass accumulating in geostationary orbit.

There is a philosophical shift underway: from disposal to stewardship. Humanity has littered orbit for sixty years; logistics offers a cleaner alternative. Rather than launching replacements that join the orbital traffic jam, servicing keeps the sky usable. Environmental logic aligns with economic sense. Operators begin to ask not, "What is the next satellite?" but, "How do we extend the one we already have?"

Logistics also changes power projection. Nations with servicing fleets enjoy resilience others cannot match. An adversary that seeks to degrade a constellation must reckon with the capacity to repair and reconstitute. Just as aerial refuelling gave air forces global reach, orbital servicing gives space forces endurance. The destruction of a satellite becomes less strategic if it can be revived; the calculus of attack shifts.

At the commercial level, servicing disrupts business models. Satellite manufacturers have long relied on replacement cycles to drive revenue. If clients can refresh on-orbit, the game changes: service contracts replace hardware sales. Insurance markets, too, must adjust. A damaged satellite currently means a claim payout and a new procurement. With servicing, insurers may opt to fund repairs instead—cheaper, faster, less risky.

There are early signs of how this future might unfold. Life-extension vehicles have already attached themselves to ageing communications satellites, taking over station-keeping duties and squeezing out extra years of service. Experimental missions have demonstrated fluid transfer in microgravity, a proof of concept once considered near impossible. Earth-observation firms contemplate small tugs that reposition satellites into new orbits to chase lucrative imaging windows. Militaries explore servicing as a means of strategic persistence: a constellation that refuels is a constellation that refuses to die.

Orbital logistics also touches the realm of autonomy. Servicing missions cannot rely on second-by-second commands from ground control; latency makes that unworkable. Instead, tugs require algorithms to detect anomalies, maintain safe approach corridors, and abort when risk thresholds are crossed. This autonomy must be trustworthy; a mistake risks debris fields that would haunt orbit for decades. Consequently, servicing pushes the frontier of robotic judgement. Space becomes a lab for machine ethics, not just engineering.

There is, however, a darker question: who gets saved? Life-extension missions are expensive and scarce. Commercial logic favours profitable assets; geopolitical logic favours strategic ones. Operators will triage: some satellites will be rescued, others abandoned. In orbit, as on Earth, logistics is a rationing mechanism. Power lies not only in launching satellites, but in deciding which ones deserve another chance.

Then there is the supply chain. Servicing vehicles themselves need fuel depots: cryogenic stores, transfer modules, or captured propellant from decommissioned stages. Some propose orbital fuel stations stocked by reusable launchers. Others imagine harvesting resources from derelict satellites. Still others talk of ISRU—using lunar water for propellant—which borders on the speculative but no longer on the impossible. If fuel becomes a tradable commodity in orbit, expect markets, monopolies, and diplomacy to follow.

Orbital tugs also enable choreography. Instead of launching replacement satellites into bespoke orbits, operators could launch to a convenient transfer path, then hire a tug to deliver payloads to final positions. This lowers the energy requirements for spacecraft propulsion and lets operators prioritise mass for sensors and communications. Supply chains in space start to resemble those at sea: vessels, depots, towboats, and lanes.

Not everyone welcomes this complexity. Critics argue that servicing increases the number of active manoeuvres, raising collision risks. They warn of "ambulance congestion" in already crowded orbits. Others fear monopolisation: a single servicing provider dominating the geostationary belt. There are also legal uncertainties. Who is responsible if a servicing attempt goes wrong and scatters debris across valuable orbital slots? Which treaties apply? How do states verify that a tug is not a disguised weapon?

Yet doing nothing carries its own risks. Orbit becomes more congested every year. Debris begets debris; a few catastrophic collisions could render key altitudes unusable for generations. Servicing removes derelicts, extending useful life and reducing replacement launches. The most sustainable space environment is one where assets are cared for, not abandoned. Logistics is therefore a form of environmental security.

Life-extension also shapes national strategy. A country that invests in servicing sidesteps the tyranny of launch bottlenecks. When rockets are scarce, servicing keeps fleets alive. When geopolitical crises choke supply chains, logistic spacecraft provide breathing room. In that sense, orbital servicing is a sovereignty tool. It reduces dependence on launch windows and foreign vendors. It buys time.

There is symbolism in this shift. For decades, space was a theatre of expendability—single-use boosters, disposable satellites, one-off missions. Logistics transforms that mindset. It treats space not as a frontier to be conquered, but as infrastructure to be maintained. The metaphor changes: from conquest to cultivation.

The most compelling reason for logistics in orbit is not technical, economic, or strategic. It is moral. We have built an environment in which every piece of debris threatens new generations of spacecraft and astronauts. We have an obligation to clean up after ourselves. Servicing is the first step in taking responsibility for the celestial commons.

Still, uncertainty lingers. Will governments trust commercial servicers to handle national assets? Will insurance firms embrace repair over replacement? Will standardised docking ports become universal, or will proprietary interfaces fragment the market? Will tugs become silent custodians or contested instruments of power?

Somewhere above us, a satellite nearing end-of-life waits for a tug now months instead of years away. The engineers who built it assumed it would die in place. The operators who command it assume it will fly again. That presumption—of second chances—is the quiet revolution.

One day, perhaps, orbital logistics will be ordinary. Spacecraft will refuel as casually as aircraft, components will be swapped like server blades, and graveyard orbits will shrink instead of swell. Or perhaps the politics of suspicion will choke the promise, and servicing will remain a niche, resented capability.

Either way, the first stations are being built. The first tugs are flying. The first satellites have tasted borrowed life. Orbit is no longer a one-way trip. The question is no longer whether logistics in space is possible, but who will control it—and what they will choose to save.

Testing the untestable

No engineer can detonate a satellite in orbit to watch the debris bloom across the skies, yet every nation fears that moment. No operations centre can practise in real time the loss of half a constellation to a solar storm, yet it must be ready when the Sun misbehaves. Space punishes experimentation. The environment is hostile, unpredictable, and unforgiving of rehearsal. A launch failure is public, irreversible, and ruinously expensive. A botched manoeuvre can create fragments that haunt orbits for decades. And still, systems are expected to withstand sabotage, radiation surges, cyber intrusion, and collisions with invisible objects. The paradox at the heart of modern space operations is simple: we must be prepared for disasters we hope never to see, and cannot safely recreate.

To cope with this contradiction, the sector has begun to build worlds within worlds. High-fidelity simulators model orbital mechanics, environmental noise, and adversarial behaviour with astonishing precision. Digital twins—software replicas of satellites and ground networks—age, degrade, and fail as their real counterparts would. Operators can suspend time inside these synthetic realms, replaying attacks, tweaking variables, and exploring paths that would be suicidal in reality. In effect, space powers have built laboratories for catastrophe.

There is a candour to this approach that contrasts sharply with the optimism of the past. Early satellite programmes assumed failure was improbable if hardware was carefully qualified. Today, the mindset has shifted. Failure is inevitable; only preparedness is optional. A modern constellation is not complete until it has been attacked—virtually—by its creators. Red teams of hackers, aerospace engineers, and intelligence specialists probe ground stations, jam simulated uplinks, and feed corrupted telemetry into the twin. They hunt for the seams where complacency hides. When they succeed, everyone learns.

The stakes justify the intensity. When a critical satellite fails, consequences cascade. Power grids lose timing signals. Financial markets stagger. Troops in the field lose communications. Civilian aircraft lose navigation redundancy. In peacetime, this is disruptive. In conflict, it is crippling. Planners know that no amount of manufacturing excellence guarantees survival. Instead, they pursue graceful collapse: systems that continue to function, even in degraded states. But designing for resilience demands knowledge of how things break. That knowledge comes from testing the untestable.

Tabletop exercises are the most visible expression of this philosophy. Picture a control room where senior operators, scientists, and liaison officers gather around map projections and telemetry feeds. A hypothetical scenario unfolds: a debris cloud has entered a valuable orbital shell. Predictive models show the cloud thickening as fragments collide with dormant satellites. Warning times shrink from hours to minutes. Communications links falter under bandwidth triage. Decisions must be made: move which satellites first? Sacrifice which assets? Who receives service priority? And what if the debris field is a deliberate, covert attack rather than an accident? The room wrestles with the ethical weight of each choice. There is no perfect outcome, only less catastrophic ones. Every exercise etches lessons into doctrine.

This is not theatre. The 2007 destruction of a satellite by China and the 2009 collision between Iridium 33 and Cosmos 2251 scattered thousands of pieces of long-lived debris. Those events were not simulations; they were warnings. Since then, operators have developed risk matrices for every conjunction alert, ranking threats and plotting evasive manoeuvres. But as constellations grow into the tens of thousands, manual tracking becomes futile. Hence the rise of automated collision-avoidance algorithms, tested against swarms of synthetic hazards. Only by pushing these algorithms to their limits—overloading them, corrupting them, confusing them—can engineers find the blind spots.

The same principle applies to cyber defence. Satellites are computers in radiation baths, linked to ground stations vulnerable to intrusion. Some attacks seek to jam or spoof; others aim to inject malicious code. Real attacks are mercifully rare, but simulated ones occur daily. Digital twins make this possible. They allow adversarial testing without risking live assets. Engineers slip malware into the twin's virtual memory, reroute commands, mimic insider threats, and watch for unexpected behaviour. A surprising proportion of vulnerabilities arise not from exotic hacks but from mundane assumptions: a forgotten default password, a misconfigured firewall, a sloppy command protocol. The discipline of red-teaming exposes the banal fragilities of high technology.

Beyond cyber and debris, there are environmental nightmares that no human can influence. Solar storms can strip satellites of power, corrupt data, and overwhelm shielding. Flares have disabled satellites before and will again. Yet predicting their precise impact demands complex modelling. Agencies run space weather simulations tied to digital twins, injecting bursts of radiation, heating satellite surfaces, and forcing emergency power modes. They uncover corner cases: batteries that discharge too quickly, memory that corrupts silently, antennas that misalign because thermal expansion is worse than assumed. Armed with these insights, designers reconfigure components, alter power budgets, and adjust response scripts.

Which leads to a fundamental tension. Simulations lure us into believing we have tamed uncertainty. Digital twins are seductive. They offer completeness: a universe built of equations and logic where every event has a cause and every fault a lesson. But reality is not a closed system. Unknown unknowns exist. Software reflects assumptions; if those assumptions are incomplete, the twin may fail to predict the very catastrophe it was built to avert. Some critics argue that the industry risks overconfidence, believing its virtual worlds are faithful representations when they are simplifications. The remedy is humility: simulations must be constantly updated with real-world telemetry, anomalies, and post-mortems. Testing is not a ritual; it is a feedback loop.

The most forward-thinking agencies now blend simulation with live "shadow missions". An operational satellite silently mirrors commands sent to a twin. When the model predicts a fault, engineers compare twin behaviour against live data. When an anomaly occurs in orbit, the twin is forced to replicate it. This co-evolution strengthens both. Over time, the twin becomes a faithful historian of the spacecraft, and the spacecraft gains a guardian that anticipates trouble.

Testing the untestable also forces organisational maturity. In the analogue era, missions were built by small, insular teams. Today, constellations require collaborative operations across countries, companies, and supply chains. Tabletop exercises bring these actors together, stress-testing not only software but governance: who authorises manoeuvres? Who informs civil aviation when debris threatens? Who decides when to decommission a crippled satellite? The answers shape crisis response as much as engineering.

Another frontier is behavioural simulation. Imagine an adversary quietly shadowing a critical satellite with a suspicious spacecraft. Is it inspecting? Preparing to jam? Poised to ram? Operators rehearse these ambiguous scenarios, testing geopolitical nerves as much as orbital physics. Diplomats and military planners join the room, not to press buttons, but to weigh escalation risks. In these sessions, space becomes recognisable: not a sterile vacuum, but a domain where strategy, psychology, and technology collide.

Yet even the most elaborate simulations cannot eliminate risk. Testing trains instincts, but instincts must be exercised under pressure. After-action reports reveal a sobering truth: during stress, humans cling to familiar patterns, even when a situation demands improvisation. Some agencies therefore role-play "chaos injects", adding false alarms and conflicting telemetry to shake complacency. In one exercise, operators discovered that a critical system automatically rebooted during a simulated solar storm, breaking communications at the moment leadership needed clarity. No one had anticipated a fail-safe triggering at precisely the wrong time. The finding was uncomfortable, then invaluable.

The ambition grows. New research explores using artificial intelligence to generate adversarial events—synthetic attacks that seek out system weaknesses with creativity exceeding human imagination. In these environments, satellites and ground networks spar against digital predators that evolve as quickly as defences. It is a glimpse of a future where resilience is a dynamic contest.

Still, a deeper philosophical question lingers. Can we ever truly test the untestable? Or are we constructing elaborate illusions of control to ease our anxiety in a domain that remains fundamentally unpredictable? The answer may be both. Simulation does not erase uncertainty; it reduces ignorance. It teaches us where we are brittle, where we are complacent, and where our clever designs hide silent flaws. It reminds us that space is an arena without mercy, and that preparation is the only kindness we can offer ourselves.

Somewhere tonight, a team is rehearsing the loss of a satellite that is still healthy. They are arguing over how many minutes to spend calculating a new trajectory. They are debating how to explain an outage to the public. They are practising grief for a machine that has not yet died. It is a strange ritual, yet profoundly rational. In space, the difference between shock and composure is rehearsal.

One day, a real emergency will come—a debris storm, a hostile attack, a solar flare. The simulations will not make the moment easy. They will make it survivable. And if there is any measure of success in testing the untestable, it lies in that quiet promise: when the worst arrives, we will not be meeting it for the first time.

Chapter 12

Rules That Actually Work

The laws of space were written for a quieter sky. They were drafted when a handful of superpowers placed a few dozen machines in orbit and agreed, in broad strokes, not to poison the heavens with weapons of mass destruction. Those rules succeeded in what they set out to do. They stopped nuclearised space platforms and orbital doomsday devices. But they never imagined constellations of thousands, commercial fleets that cross borders as easily as photons, or private firms with capabilities once reserved for nation-states. The treaties endure, but their silence has grown deafening. Every year the sky grows more crowded, the stakes richer, and the risks sharper. Yet the formal rulebook barely budges.

There is a dangerous comfort in assuming that laws follow technology in due time. History suggests otherwise. When innovation outruns governance, the void is filled by improvisation and brinkmanship. In space, those improvisations play out in a transparent arena where every mistake becomes shrapnel. A single irresponsible manoeuvre can scatter fragments that remain lethal for centuries. A sloppy software update can blind a region's communications. A careless approach to a rival's satellite can be read as espionage—or sabotage. Silent incidents accumulate, each one a brush with disaster politely left unremarked.

The most telling sign of the imbalance is that responsible actors already behave according to rules that do not formally exist. Operators avoid close passes unless necessary. They notify neighbours before moving large satellites. They publish ephemerides, encrypt uplinks, and conduct de-orbit planning even when no treaty requires it. These behaviours were not negotiated in marble halls; they emerged from survival instincts. They prove that viable rules need not be encyclopaedic or utopian. They must simply make sense.

This chapter is about rules of that sort: lean, verifiable, incentive-compatible, and technologically neutral. Rules that reward good behaviour without demanding sainthood. Rules that make worse choices more expensive and better choices harder to ignore. They are not silver bullets. They are seatbelts—mundane until the day they save a life.

The first principle is brutal in its simplicity: a rule that cannot be verified is not a rule. Many well-meaning proposals for space law fail on that point. They want to ban particular payloads or restrict particular capabilities, forgetting that satellites are black boxes, often dual-use by nature. A sensor that aids weather forecasting can help missile targeting. A tug that repairs satellites can ram them. A cryptographic upgrade can be for security—or subversion. Attempts to legislate based on imagined intent collapse on contact with physics and politics. Behaviour, on the other hand, can be observed. A satellite that approaches another without notice reveals malign or negligent practice. One that publishes accurate positions and respects keep-out distances demonstrates the opposite. A norm that can be checked can be trusted. And a rule that can be trusted reshapes incentives.

Transparency is the next hinge, but only the kind that matters. Publishing every coordinate of every manoeuvre is neither realistic nor safe. What matters are the specific signals that reduce misunderstanding: proximity notifications, logs of major manoeuvres, and timely sharing of collision warnings. Public ephemerides let operators cross-check each other. They also create a forensic record if something goes wrong. These mundane data trails do for space what brake-lights and indicators do for roads: they let everyone understand what everyone else intends. The point is not to reveal secrets; it is to prevent accidents that masquerade as aggression.

Commercial operators have already shown what such norms look like in practice. When rival constellations risk passing within kilometres of each other, their control centres exchange data directly. They verify ephemerides, agree who will manoeuvre, and report to traffic watchdogs. It is quiet, civil, and astonishingly effective. These are embryonic compacts—proto-rules forged not by diplomats but by flight dynamics teams. Codifying them is not political fantasy; it is recognising reality.

Yet voluntary behaviour has limits. Some operators cut corners. Some hope to free-ride on the caution of others. A few may flirt with dangerous ambiguity for strategic advantage. That is why norms alone are not enough; incentives must align with safety. Governments have a powerful instrument for this: procurement. When ministries choose satellite services, they can award points for debris-free end-of-life, for transparent manoeuvre logs, for collision avoidance protocols, for resilient architectures. Suddenly, safer behaviour becomes profitable. A market signal can achieve what treaties struggle to enforce.

The idea applies even more strongly to emerging technologies. On-orbit servicing, refuelling, and debris removal offer enormous benefits, but they also introduce risks. A servicing robot capable of docking gently is also capable of interfering. A debris tug able to tow junk could tow something more valuable. Rather than banning such capabilities—which only pushes them into secrecy—rules can focus on conduct. Declare intentions before approaching another operator's satellite. Maintain telemetry logs of each action. Agree to independent inspection after a servicing mission. Publish data on momentum exchange and disposal of scrap. These are specific, measurable acts. No one needs to prove innocence; they merely need to demonstrate compliance.

If rules and incentives form the skeleton, commercial compacts provide the connective tissue. Industry codes already exist in fields like aviation, maritime shipping, and undersea cables. Companies agree on radio etiquette, emergency coordination, and interference protocols, because disruption costs money and reputation. Space is following the same trajectory. Major operators are discussing shared escalation channels—dedicated hotlines for when something looks wrong. Others propose common procedures for handling mutual collision alerts. Some are exploring reciprocal assistance during cyber incidents. These agreements lack the pomp of treaties, yet they solve real problems.

The most interesting proposals are regional pilots for civil orbital pacts. Instead of waiting for a global treaty—an impossible task in a fractured geopolitical climate—coalitions of willing states and firms can adopt a minimal set of commitments. They can agree to publish manoeuvre notices, to maintain end-of-life disposal standards, to notify others before close approaches, to keep verified logs of critical events, and to provide transparency during emergencies. Once the pilot works, others will join, not out of moral awakening but because failing to join marks an operator as reckless. Norms become contagious.

All of this rests on a philosophy that rejects perfectionism. Perfect rules are inert; workable rules are incremental. Instead of banning potentially dangerous technologies, shape their use. Instead of demanding universal transparency, require the specific disclosures that reduce miscalculation. Instead of building thousand-page treaties, define a dozen reliable behaviours and enforce them through incentives. Law becomes lighter, not weaker.

This approach also acknowledges a hard truth: space governance is not a morality play. States and firms act from interests. If safer conduct costs money, they will avoid it. If reckless manoeuvres risk blowback, they will refrain. A rule's brilliance is irrelevant if it is not incentive-compatible. That is why procurement scores, insurance premiums, and licensing conditions matter more than rhetorical declarations. They change calculus, not conscience.

Critics claim that voluntary or incentive-driven frameworks are too fragile. Why trust companies or states to behave prudently when strategic competition is sharpening? Because even rivals share one interest: keeping the orbital environment usable. The logic is unforgiving. Destructive behaviour pollutes shared lanes. Debris does not respect borders. A nation or company that poisons orbit endangers its own assets and future ambitions. This shared vulnerability is the seed of cooperation. Not kumbaya, but self-preservation.

A second criticism focuses on verification. How do we truly know a satellite is where it claims to be? How do we detect falsified logs? The answer lies in redundancy. Observatories, telescopes, and radar networks exist on every continent. Commercial tracking is booming. Peers cross-check each other. Independent bodies can audit logs, compare claims with observations, and spot anomalies. Deception is possible, but difficult—and costly if discovered.

The deeper philosophical shift, however, is recognising that rules in space are not about preventing conflict entirely. They are about preventing stupidity. They aim to stop incidents born from ambiguity, misinterpretation, and negligence. History shows that most crises are not acts of grand strategy; they are accidents that escalate. Space has no buffer for such mistakes. In orbit, error becomes physics: a fragment travelling seven kilometres per second, a collision that multiplies itself. Rules that actually work focus on those pivot points where prudence is cheap and catastrophe is irreversible.

The most profound consequence of workable rules may not be safety alone but legitimacy. When norms become habitual and incentives align, actors see responsible behaviour as the default. A satellite that approaches without notice draws suspicion. A firm that refuses disposal is seen as a pariah. A state that hides manoeuvres loses credibility. Informal enforcement—

market pressure, reputational cost, peer scrutiny—fills the gaps that treaties cannot reach.

A generation from now, people may be astonished that the global commons of orbit was once governed by hope and etiquette rather than structured commitments. But that future will not arrive through grand conferences or sweeping prohibitions. It will come from clear behavioural standards, transparent signals, commercial compacts, and regional pilots that prove safety can coexist with ambition.

The promise of this chapter lies in its premise: the rules that matter are the rules that can be lived. They are specific enough to guide, flexible enough to adapt, and credible enough to be enforced. If space is to remain a domain of innovation rather than attrition, its governance must be as modern as its technology. The path forward is narrow but navigable—and far wiser than waiting for the perfect treaty that never arrives.

Principles before pages

The easiest rule to write is the one that sounds noble and achieves nothing. Space governance is littered with such relics: declarations that celebrate peace, pledges that forbid imaginary weapons, treaties that bind only the well-intentioned. They read beautifully and work poorly. The uncomfortable lesson of the last half-century is that complexity does not create compliance. Verifiable, incentive-compatible, technology-agnostic norms do. In other words: principles that matter more than pages.

Consider the problem through a familiar metaphor. On Earth, traffic laws seldom dictate the shape of a vehicle's engine or the composition of its brakes. They regulate behaviour: speed limits, right of way, signals, prohibitions on drink-driving. A police officer does not tear apart every car to see whether it hides a dangerous modification; the officer observes how it moves. Compliance is observable. Transgressions are punishable. The public knows the rules and trusts that others do too. That clarity keeps roads usable. Imagine instead a legal world that banned certain brake systems, prohibited particular chassis designs, or required manufacturers to declare the moral purpose of each car. Chaos would follow, not safety. The principle applies just as brutally in orbit.

Space is full of dual-use ambiguity. A robotic arm can repair a satellite, or seize it. A propulsion system can dodge debris, or ram a rival. A high-resolution sensor can track weather, or track tanks. Attempting to legislate payloads is a fool's errand. Nations can mask capabilities under layers of proprietary housings and encrypted telemetry. Private firms jealously guard specifications. And anyway, intent cannot be read from hardware. A camera is a camera, no matter whose intelligence agency will later download the images. So rules that depend on unknowable internals inevitably collapse. They demand omniscience that no regulator possesses.

That is why the most promising frameworks shift from the "what" to the "how". Behavioural norms sidestep secrecy and deal instead with the visible consequences of choice. If a satellite approaches within a defined proximity of another, require notification. If a servicing vehicle intends to dock, demand publicly logged telemetry and consent from the owner. If a spacecraft performs a major manoeuvre, record the burn so that others can reconstruct its path. No one needs to declare their payload. No one needs to reveal their code. They simply need to behave in ways that can be observed and audited. The principle is not disarmament; it is predictability.

Verifiability is the first pillar. A rule without verification is opinion dressed in legalese. In orbit, verification is not exotic: it happens every day. The United States, Europe, Russia, China, India, Japan, and a flock of commercial companies track thousands of objects. Optical telescopes watch the glint of solar panels. Radar arrays chart trajectories to within metres. Increasingly, crowdsourced observations support independent confirmation. The sky itself is transparent. Operators might lie about intentions, but their satellites cannot hide their paths. This surveillance architecture already exists; governance can harness it.

Incentive-compatibility is the second pillar. Rules that punish the careful and reward the reckless will not last. Consider end-of-life disposal. De-orbiting a satellite, or moving it to a graveyard orbit, costs fuel—money, in other words. A firm that behaves responsibly incurs an expense its unscrupulous rivals may skip. Unless regulatory pressure or market incentives correct that imbalance, bad actors profit. Procurement offers one remedy. Governments purchase satellite bandwidth, imagery, and navigation services by the billion. If bids were scored, even modestly, on disposal records and collision-avoidance compliance, responsible operators would gain a competitive edge. Insurance is another. Premiums could be lower for companies that share telemetry, publish manoeuvre logs, and follow proximity etiquette. Financial gravity can drag behaviour towards safety faster than diplomatic sermons.

A third pillar is technological agnosticism. Rules that fixate on today's platforms age quickly. Space is not static; constellations scale, propulsion changes, autonomy grows, and new materials appear. A ban on a particular engine type or a particular instrument becomes obsolete the moment innovation sidesteps it. Worse, it encourages evasion: actors design around the letter of the rule while violating its spirit. Behavioural standards avoid this trap. "Share manoeuvre notices 24 hours prior." "Respect minimum separation distances." "Dispose of defunct satellites within X years." The rule works whether the vehicle is a CubeSat or a behemoth broadcasting terabits. The rocket equation does not care about legal definitions; it cares about physics. So should regulators.

These principles cut against a deep bureaucratic instinct: the urge to draft lengthy, high-resolution regulations. Pages feel like progress. Complexity masquerades as sophistication. Yet space teaches the opposite. Highly detailed rules invite loopholes and contestation. They also slow response, because every amendment requires tortuous negotiation. By the time consensus forms, the technology landscape has moved on. The better path is lean. Set clear thresholds, define observable behaviours, mandate minimum disclosures, and let actors innovate within those lines. Restraint by regulators creates flexibility for engineers.

Critics of this philosophy argue that thin rules lack deterrence. What stops a determined adversary from behaving responsibly until the moment it chooses not to? The same thing that stops aircraft from turning into weapons at cruising altitude: the expectation of consequences. If norms are narrow, verifiable, and widely adopted, violations stand out. A satellite that shadows another without notice becomes a suspect. A servicing mission conducted in silence attracts scrutiny. In a dense observation environment, secrecy is fragile, and exposure is costly. Reputation matters. Markets matter. Diplomacy matters. Escalation is risky. Even adversaries understand that igniting an orbital incident invites reciprocal action and creates long-term debris that harms their own fleets. Quiet deterrence is built into the economics and physics of space.

Others insist that without sweeping bans—on close approaches, on robotic arms, on dual-use sensors—bad actors will exploit loopholes. But sweeping bans collapse under basic reality. Space agencies need robotic arms for repairs. They need close approaches for servicing, salvage, and debris removal. They need high-resolution sensors for climate monitoring and disaster response. Prohibitions criminalise essential activities and punish innovators. In contrast, behavioural norms do not outlaw capability; they outlaw reckless practice. You may approach someone else's satellite, but only with consent and notification. You may operate powerful sensors, but must abide by interference rules. You may deploy an autonomous tug, but must log your actions. The principle is not disarmament; it is adult supervision.

Philosophically, principles-before-pages reflect a mature understanding of trust. Rules cannot rely on goodness. They must assume selfishness. If compliance becomes the rational choice—cheaper, safer, or more reputationally valuable—actors will comply regardless of virtue. Self-interest is not a design flaw; it is a design constraint. The most elegant treaty is useless if signatories quietly ignore it. The most modest norm is powerful if even rivals respect it. Good governance embraces human nature rather than fighting it.

The commercial world offers powerful evidence. In recent years, disparate companies operating vast constellations have quietly adopted shared etiquette. When collision alerts arise—and they arise daily—the operators exchange data to decide who should manoeuvre. When a satellite fails and begins to tumble, its owner warns neighbours. When two spacecraft must pass within dangerous proximity, control rooms coordinate. None of this is required by treaty. It emerged because it works. Informal behaviour norms proved more robust than formal law. Codifying them would not reinvent the wheel; it would simply attach brakes.

One of the most striking advantages of behavioural rules is their accessibility. Smaller nations and private firms can adopt them as easily as great powers. They do not demand intelligence agencies or exotic inspection tools. Publish your ephemerides. Notify others of manoeuvres. Maintain collision-avoidance logs. Honour disposal windows. These are modest, actionable steps. In a system where newcomers proliferate, accessibility matters. If governance excludes emerging actors, resentment festers and rule-breaking spreads. Tech-agnostic principles avoid that spiral.

There is also a democratic virtue here. When rules are simple, ordinary citizens and civil society organisations can verify compliance. Amateur astronomers track satellites. University programmes build telescopes. Journalists consult public ephemerides. If a state claims innocence after a suspicious conjunction, independent observers can check. This sunlight is not merely symbolic; it deters deception. When truth is decentralised, no single actor monopolises it.

None of this denies the need for law. Principles-before-pages is a legal strategy, not an abdication of responsibility. It demands that governments, firms, and regulators focus on the essential: preventing catastrophic miscalculation and environmental harm. There is philosophical discipline in deciding what *not* to regulate. Trying to forbid every conceivable malign act is impossible. Defining a few critical behaviours that keep space usable is achievable.

One of the most interesting tensions lies between secrecy and verification. Defence agencies instinctively guard orbital data. Commercial firms protect intellectual property. Transparency feels like vulnerability. Yet transparency is also insurance. When an operator publishes manoeuvre data, they gain credibility. If something goes wrong—a collision, an outage, a dead satellite—they can prove their innocence. Without that transparency, every incident invites suspicion. In a strategic climate already thick with mistrust, silence is toxic. The principle is painfully pragmatic: say enough to prevent misinterpretation.

Another tension sits between national pride and shared safety. Space remains a theatre of prestige. But prestige loses meaning if the theatre collapses. No state wants to be the first to compromise. Yet each knows that debris is a shared curse. Informal coordination often precedes formal agreement; regionally led pilots allow states to experiment with norms without sacrificing sovereignty. A handful of countries, joined by private firms and insurers, can adopt minimal behavioural standards. If the pilot works—if it reduces false alarms, speeds collision resolution, and earns market rewards—others will join out of pragmatism, not ideology.

Underlying all of this is a stark truth: space is becoming brittle. Constellations multiply. Orbits crowd. Kessler-style chain reactions move from fiction to risk assessment. The window for elegant treaties has closed; the window for practical norms remains open. The question is not whether humanity will write more pages. It is whether the principles behind them will actually work.

A rulebook that protects orbit will not be a monument of legal prose. It will be a modest scaffold of verifiable behaviours, backed by incentives that reward safety and punish negligence. It will not freeze technology; it will steer conduct. It will not trust intentions; it will measure outcomes. And it will change as the sky changes.

That future is not guaranteed. But it is possible. The path is visible. The challenge is to resist the temptation of theatrical regulation and embrace the dull, powerful discipline of principles before pages. The difference between a pristine orbit and a poisoned one may not be grand treaties at all, but a handful of norms that operators actually live by.

Transparency that matters

In 2019, a European satellite and a SpaceX Starlink spacecraft drifted towards an uncomfortable rendezvous over the Atlantic. The predicted probability of collision crept upward. One operator sent warnings. The other, overwhelmed by automated alerts, missed the message. Hours before impact, the European team fired its thrusters and veered away. Nothing was damaged, no debris cloud born. Yet the near miss shook the industry. Two competent actors, abundant sensors, and a sky full of data, and still the world nearly gained a preventable disaster. The lesson was brutal: transparency is not a moral accessory. It is infrastructure. Without it, even well-run systems can fail.

The incident also revealed something subtler. There was no wrongdoing, no malice—just a communication lapse. Nevertheless, for weeks, online forums swirled with speculation. Was it negligence? Was it secrecy? Was it commercial defensiveness? In a domain where every manoeuvre is visible in the night sky, a simple misunderstanding grew into a public narrative of risk. Transparency is not only about safety in orbit; it is about trust on Earth.

What, then, does real transparency look like? Not abstract declarations, nor vague promises from press offices. It is a concrete set of practices: logs of manoeuvres, notifications of close approaches, publicly accessible ephemerides, and agreed etiquette for proximity operations. Crucially, it must come with safeguards that respect national security and commercial confidentiality. The goal is not confession; the goal is predictability.

Start with logs. Every spacecraft already keeps them: fuel usage, thruster burns, station-keeping corrections. Operators know where their vehicles have been and where they intend to go. But logs locked in private archives help no one. When a satellite unexpectedly shifts course, neighbours grow nervous. Misinterpretation can spread faster than facts. Publishing basic manoeuvre records—time, location, magnitude—enables others to reconstruct trajectories. This matters in a crowded sky. It also matters when something goes wrong. Imagine a dead satellite begins to tumble, threatening a collision chain. If its logs are public, analysts can estimate fuel reserves, predict drag, and model probable paths. Without logs, they theorise in the dark.

Notifications are the second pillar. Space agencies déjà vu the problem from Earth: aircraft file flight plans, ships file sail plans. They do so not out of charity but necessity. If a tanker turns off its AIS transponder, navies and insurers raise eyebrows. If an aircraft stops talking to air traffic control, alarms ring. The same logic holds above the Kármán line. If a spacecraft intends a major manoeuvre—especially one that reduces separation with another object—it should notify. Notification is not full disclosure; it is a courtesy that prevents panic.

Public ephemerides form the third pillar. Ephemerides are simply tables of predicted positions. Most operators already share them with space-tracking authorities, some with universities, and a few release them openly. If published in standardised formats, with sufficient temporal resolution, the whole ecosystem benefits. Collision-avoidance software becomes more accurate. Amateur astronomers validate claims. Insurers price risk with precision. Crucially, open ephemerides reduce the chance that a manoeuvre is misread as an attack or rehearsal. In geopolitics, interpretation matters as much as intent.

A recurring objection is security. Why should a state reveal the orbit of a sensitive satellite? Why should a firm expose commercially valuable data? The answer is not that transparency is costless; it is that secrecy is expensive. When others cannot tell what a spacecraft is doing, they assume the worst. Threat analysts prepare response options. Politicians give speeches. Markets twitch. In a theatre where manoeuvres can be tracked with backyard telescopes, secrecy easily looks sinister. The smarter approach is not full disclosure, but structured disclosure: publish enough to demonstrate normal behaviour, keep the rest behind the curtain.

Safeguards make this possible. Ephemerides can be delayed, fuzzed, or published at reduced resolution. Logs can redact payload data while preserving manoeuvre vectors. Notifications can describe intentions without revealing purposes. A servicing mission might announce an upcoming close approach without specifying what panel it intends to fix. States already practice this on Earth; militaries file maritime notices long before they reveal exercises. The principle is the same: prevent surprise, not honesty.

The most transformative idea in this space is *standard proximity etiquette.* When one spacecraft approaches another, a set of polite rituals should apply. Request consent. Announce the window. Broadcast telemetry that confirms alignment. If the target satellite belongs to a rival state, transparency becomes a de-escalation tool. Without it, every close approach could look like a test of disablement. With it, a servicing mission looks like maintenance, not malice. Etiquette may appear soft, but it creates powerful expectations. Breaking etiquette becomes evidence of hostile intent.

Why is etiquette especially crucial now? Because refuelling, repair, debris removal, and salvage missions are becoming normal. The old rule—stay away from other satellites—no longer works in a world of orbital logistics. If tugboats are to tow dead craft to graveyards, they must approach. If debris is to be cleared, some vehicle must get close. Without etiquette, benign missions and hostile ones are indistinguishable. With it, the sky becomes legible.

Transparency also has a quieter benefit: it equalises. Small nations and new operators have historically complained that space was governed by whispers between superpowers. Official notices often travelled through diplomatic channels, not public repositories. Now, commercial trackers like LeoLabs, ExoAnalytic, and others publish conjunction alerts that anyone can read. Democratized awareness limits the ability of major powers to control the narrative. When a satellite breaks apart, open data exposes the facts. When a nation conducts a debris-generating test, no press release can hide the evidence. Transparency distributes power.

Yet transparency is not without tension. Defence officials worry that sharing telemetry invites tampering. Companies fear that publishing logs could reveal proprietary propulsion efficiency. Autocrats dislike being watched. This friction will not vanish. But it can be managed. Satellite operators can use hashed logs, proving authenticity without exposing detail. Governments can publish only the orbital element sets, not the mission data. Third-party custodians—perhaps universities or neutral space traffic management centres—can hold sensitive data behind access controls. The point is not that these solutions are effortless, but that they exist.

Transparency should also be reciprocal. If only one actor publishes logs, its rivals gain intelligence without contributing. Reciprocity creates fairness and encourages adoption. A region-led pilot—say, a consortium of spacefaring nations plus large commercial operators—could trial a transparency compact. They would agree to publish ephemerides in a shared format, notify close approaches, and maintain an archive of manoeuvre logs. If the pilot reduces false alarms and eases collision-avoidance work, others will join. Governance in space often grows from demonstration, not decree.

Philosophically, transparency speaks to the core challenge of the militarising sky: trust without friendship. Rival states will never love one another, but they can coexist. Transparent behaviour allows cooperation without sentiment. During the Cold War, hotlines and surveillance satellites reduced miscalculation. Today, transparency plays the same role. When every actor knows that every other actor can see, deception becomes harder and less useful. A world of quiet observation is a world of fewer surprises.

But transparency is not merely strategic. It is environmental. Space debris does not distinguish between flags. When two satellites collide, they threaten every constellation in the orbital lane. Transparency helps prevent the conditions that lead to chain reactions: missed warnings, misinterpreted manoeuvres, secrecy masquerading as indifference. In this sense, transparency is the closest thing space has to sanitation. Without it, contagion spreads.

A further virtue lies in the psychological realm. Humans fear the unknown. When opaque actors behave strangely, we imagine malice. When information is partial, we fill gaps with suspicion. Over time, those narratives ossify into doctrine. War colleges teach students to assume the worst. Legislatures fund countermeasures. The cycle hardens. Transparency interrupts this feedback loop. It introduces dull facts where rumours once flourished. Dull facts are a blessing.

Critically, transparency does not require everyone to participate from day one. Early adopters can set standards that others gradually match. Commercial firms often lead. After the 2019 near miss, several major operators improved their alert systems and began sharing more movement data. Insurance companies took note. Premiums shifted. Investors asked questions. In markets, prudence is contagious.

What happens if transparency fails? If logs vanish, if ephemerides are falsified, if proximity etiquette erodes? Then every approach becomes a provocation. Every manoeuvre is a signal. Every failure is a possible attack. The climate becomes volatile. In such a world, even routine events—solar storms, battery failures, thermal anomalies—take on strategic colour. A dead satellite could be sabotage. A broken antenna could be cyber interference. Escalation thrives on ambiguity.

There is an irony here. Many actors hoard data because they fear being misunderstood. In reality, the hoarding increases misunderstanding. The cure for misinterpretation is not silence but clarity. Publish enough to make malicious readings implausible. Stop short of betraying secrets. Transparency is not a confession booth; it is a window.

Perhaps the most powerful argument for transparency is its ordinariness. It is not revolutionary to keep logs, notify neighbours, or share orbital paths. These are tasks operators already perform internally. The innovation is only to do it publicly and predictably. Space governance does not need a utopian charter. It needs habits. Step-by-step, these habits will harden into norms, and norms into rules.

Yet nothing guarantees adoption. Some actors will cling to opacity until a preventable collision or misinterpreted manoeuvre forces reform. Others will insist that transparency is a Western invention, an intrusion, a strategic trap. Some will hide because secrecy has been their default for decades. The path forward will be uneven.

But there is momentum. Constellations grow. Launches multiply. The sky is no longer a gentleman's club of a few national agencies. It is a highway of thousands. Highways demand signals, signage, and rules of the road. Even the most defiant driver eventually learns to use headlights and indicators. The alternative is a crash.

Transparency that matters is not wide-eyed idealism. It is hard-edged pragmatism. Log your manoeuvres. Publish your ephemerides. Notify your neighbours. Follow proximity etiquette. Do it not because you are good, but because it protects you from being misunderstood. Do it not because others deserve trust, but because you deserve safety.

In a domain where one misread orbit can trigger geopolitical crisis, the smallest disclosure can be the difference between vigilance and panic. The question is no longer whether humanity will share the sky. It is whether we will make it legible.

Commercial compacts

A curious phenomenon emerged in the first age of NewSpace: entrepreneurs who would never trust a rival in business gladly shared the sky with them. Competitors launched side by side from Cape Canaveral. They bought insurance from the same underwriters, hired the same propulsion consultants, and queued for slots on the same rockets. In the vacuum of space, market logic was ruthless—but orbital survival was communal. The contradiction sharpened whenever a collision warning flashed across the screen: here were firms locked in competition on Earth, yet utterly dependent on each other's good behaviour above it. Out of that tension grew a simple realisation. If states could not write rules fast enough, companies would have to write their own.

The seeds of commercial compacts are not theoretical. They sprouted the day insurers raised premiums on satellites lacking deorbit plans, and launch providers quietly blacklisted clients whose debris mitigation looked performative. Space, once the exclusive frontier of national ambition, became a shared balance sheet. Operators understood that a single debris-generating event could trigger a cascade that threatened everyone's revenue. Collisions stop being geopolitical when bolts are flying at twelve kilometres per second. They become actuarial.

To grasp why commercial compacts matter, consider interference. Jamming a satellite, even briefly, is not always an act of war. Sometimes it is accidental: a poorly aimed uplink, an unlicensed ground terminal, a misconfigured modem. The result is the same—noise drowning out signal. In tightly packed frequency bands, one company's mistake can cripple another's service. Regulators try to police this, but enforcement is slow. After complaints and investigations, fines may come months later. In the meantime, users suffer. Firms know this, so informal agreements began to form. When interference is detected, operators call one another, compare logs, and isolate the source. Most incidents are resolved quietly, without diplomatic notes or press releases. This, in miniature, is a commercial compact: companies recognising that shared infrastructure requires shared responsibility.

Yet informal courtesy will not survive the scale of tomorrow. Thousands of satellites are being launched into low orbit, many for communication, some for navigation, some for imaging. They will beam across the same spectrum, rely on the same tracking services, and pass through the same congested altitudes. Courtesy is no longer enough. Codes must be written: common escalation ladders, data-sharing protocols, and transparent handling of interference claims. Imagine a standardised severity scale—minor, serious, critical—each with pre-agreed actions. Minor interference triggers notification and collaborative diagnosis. Serious interference triggers joint investigation, frequency coordination, and temporary mitigation steps. Critical interference—signal loss threatening life or strategic infrastructure—triggers emergency hotlines staffed 24/7. Nothing grandiose, just professionalism.

Debris demands a similar covenant. Many companies advertise deorbit plans, yet few submit to independent verification. Some vehicles require active propulsion to deorbit, but what happens if the thrusters fail? A compact could require firms to carry passive disposal mechanisms—drag sails, tethers, or controlled disintegration aids—that function when propulsion is lost. Firms already integrate backup batteries and redundant avionics; adding redundancy to end-of-life disposal is simply an extension of that logic. If a satellite dies in place, drifting and threatening others, the operator should share telemetry and provide custody of the object to an authorised debris-removal service. Refusal would breach the compact, and insurers could penalise it.

Crisis protocols may prove the most transformative. Consider a scenario where two satellites are predicted to collide in 36 hours. One operator initiates an avoidance manoeuvre; the other remains silent. Perhaps they are asleep. Perhaps they didn't receive the alert. Perhaps they are refusing to budge because moving would cost delta-v they cannot afford. Without a compact, the situation becomes a blame game. With one, the process is scripted. The firm that can manoeuvre most cheaply moves first. If both can manoeuvre, the one with higher fuel reserves adjusts. If neither can manoeuvre, third-party mediation—perhaps conducted by a space traffic management centre—allocates responsibility. Even partial coordination could prevent catastrophe.

These ideas sound straightforward, yet they collide with commercial instincts. Why should a company surrender autonomy to a code? Because autonomy without accountability is fragile. In orbit, no firm is self-sufficient. Satellites depend on ground networks, ground networks depend on spectrum rights, spectrum rights depend on international coordination. A compact creates reciprocity: you follow the rules, others follow them with you. Without reciprocity, every operator must treat neighbours as risks. A world of mutual suspicion is more expensive than a world of mutual predictability.

There is precedent. Maritime industries operate under codes that evolved from practice: collision regulations, standardised distress calls, shared search-and-rescue obligations. Shipping companies compete bitterly over cargo rates, yet cooperate instinctively when a ship is sinking. Similar norms exist in aviation: flight plans, transponders, and air traffic control are not optional. Airlines despise delays, but they endure them because the alternative is catastrophe. Space will follow the same arc, just faster. The stakes are too high, the orbits too narrow, the pace of launch too wild.

One might argue that commercial compacts are naïve in the face of state actors. What stops a government from hiding behind a private firm and breaking the rules? Nothing—except consequence. If a state uses a commercial facade to jam rivals or conduct hostile proximity operations, companies will document it, insurers will price the risk, and the facade will crumble. Markets are not perfect enforcers, but they are ruthless record-keepers. Reputation matters. Launch providers can refuse payloads. Ground station networks can terminate contracts. Satellite manufacturers can blacklist reckless clients. When norms align with self-interest, policing does not depend on benevolence.

A powerful driver of compacts lies in the fact that states increasingly rely on commercial constellations for critical functions—communications, navigation augmentation, Earth observation, and even military data. Governments need these networks to function. In the early months of the war in Ukraine, commercial operators maintained connectivity under cyber pressure, electromagnetic interference, and orbital congestion. Their resilience was not ordained by treaty; it was created through agile communication, transparency, and shared technical standards. Governments noticed. They realised that commercial behaviour can underpin national security. This shifts the incentives. States will pressure their vendors to join compacts, not out of altruism but out of necessity.

Consider crisis hotlines. During the Cold War, a direct line connected Washington and Moscow to prevent miscalculation. In space today, a similar hotline might connect major operators. If a constellation observes unexpected interference or a rogue rendezvous, it could immediately alert others and request clarification. Silence becomes suspicious. Communication becomes the default. Shared hotlines will not eliminate hostility, but they reduce the risk of permanent damage. In a domain where one error can create a thousand new projectiles, risk reduction has its own morality.

One difficult question animates the debate: who writes the code? There is no world parliament of private space firms. Some are American, some Chinese, some European, some from nations whose space ambition far exceeds their bureaucracy. The solution is incremental. A coalition of major constellations could draft a voluntary code: end-of-life disposal standards, interference reporting mechanisms, and emergency contact protocols. Even a modest agreement among five or six operators would cover thousands of satellites and set expectations for everyone else. Non-signatories would be noticed—and judged. Over time, insurers and launch providers could incorporate compact membership into their underwriting and contracting decisions. Safety becomes a competitive advantage.

None of this means that compacts replace regulation. They complement it. Laws move slowly. Treaties take years. Meanwhile, launches continue every week. Commercial operators have the agility regulators lack. They experiment. They refine. They iterate. When something works, it becomes precedent. When it becomes precedent, it becomes norm. When enough states endorse it, norm becomes practice. Most global regimes began this way: not with proclamations, but with habits.

There is a deeper philosophical point. Space, despite its grandeur, is an ecosystem built on invisible trust. Signals are invisible. Orbits are invisible. Debris is invisible until it collides. The environment only survives if actors behave predictably. Commercial compacts make the invisible visible. They do not ask operators to be saints; they ask them to be legible. Legibility is the precursor to cooperation.

Critics will say that compacts are fragile. What happens when a rogue actor ignores the code? What if a startup launches without a deorbit mechanism, or a state-backed operator refuses to share telemetry? Then the compact shows its teeth. Firms can publish evidence. Media will report it. Insurers will adjust premiums. Launch providers will hesitate. Satellites without responsible end-of-life plans might be denied access to ground networks or regulatory approvals. Selfish actions carry cost.

Another objection is that compacts privilege large firms. A start-up with limited capital cannot afford the compliance burden of redundancy, logging, and hotline staffing. Yet the opposite is true. Start-ups suffer most from accidents not of their own making. If a debris event forces operators to harden their spacecraft, the cost hits newcomers hardest. Prevention is cheaper than cleanup, especially for the small. A code that reduces the risk of catastrophe is an investment in survival.

Still, one danger remains: compacts can ossify. If codes become rigid, they can freeze innovation. The answer is not to abandon compacts, but to design them with revision built in. A review cycle—every two years, say—could update disposal thresholds, adjust telemetry requirements, and incorporate new technologies. As on-orbit servicing matures, the code could require operators to accept tow assistance rather than leave derelicts adrift. Rules can evolve without collapsing.

One day, a crisis will test all this. Perhaps a constellation will suffer a cascading failure of solar arrays. Perhaps a launch vehicle will scatter debris into a crowded lane. Perhaps a geopolitical confrontation will spill into orbit, deliberately or accidentally. In that moment, commercial compacts will show their worth. If operators have already shared telemetry, established escalation protocols, and agreed disposal norms, chaos becomes manageable. If not, panic spreads faster than fragments.

Commercial compacts are not the final architecture of space governance. They are the scaffolding from which something more enduring can be built. But scaffolding matters. Without it, the structure never rises.

So the question hanging over the next decade is simple: will firms shape their own safety, or wait for states to do it for them? The answer will not come from grand declarations at the United Nations. It will come from engineers drafting shared standards in conference rooms, insurers adjusting premiums, network operators agreeing to pick up the phone in the middle of the night.

In the end, a compact is not a document. It is a promise: if you protect my orbit, I will protect yours. A promise is a fragile thing—until the day it saves everyone who made it.

Buying resilience

The first myth of space governance is that laws shape behaviour. In truth, money does. Regulations can urge, warn, and shame, but procurement decides what gets built, launched, and sustained. When a ministry signs a contract for a constellation, it is writing policy in hardware. If that contract rewards resilience—redundancy, graceful degradation, safe disposal—engineers design for longevity. If it prioritises the lowest upfront price, they cut corners and pray. For decades, far too many governments chose the latter.

There is a grim irony to this. The public will fund a satellite at a cost of hundreds of millions, yet balk at investing a few million more to guarantee it will not become space junk. Launches are celebrated, failures buried in technical annexes. The incentives are backwards. Manufacturers know that resilience is expensive: shielding, fault-tolerant processors, radiation-hardened components, deorbit kits, propulsion redundancy, on-orbit inspection ports. Every one of these adds cost, mass, or complexity. If bids are judged on price alone, corners will be trimmed until the spacecraft is little more than a single point of failure drifting at 7.5 kilometres per second.

The turning point arrived quietly, when insurers began pricing risk with greater precision. Constellations built without end-of-life disposal plans saw premiums climb. Payloads with no redundancy paid more still.

Operators complained. Ministries noticed. Suddenly, the cheapest satellite was no longer the least expensive. It was merely the most vulnerable. At the same time, commercial mega-constellations demonstrated a truth governments had ignored: resilient architectures are achievable, scalable, and economically rational. The private sector was no longer waiting for permission. It was accelerating.

Buying resilience is not a slogan; it is a procurement philosophy. It begins by rewarding desirable behaviours. A request for proposals can require verifiable deorbit plans, audited propulsion models, and telemetry transparency. It can award extra points for satellites that degrade gracefully rather than fail catastrophically. It can demand operators publish collision-avoidance logs and share proximity data. These are not burdens. They are insurance against orbital tragedy.

Consider end-of-life disposal. A satellite that cannot remove itself from orbit is a threat to everyone, yet many procurement documents treat deorbit systems as optional extras. Governments should invert this. Make safe disposal mandatory. Make verifiable disposal rewarded. Score it so heavily that any bidder without a credible plan cannot win. Some agencies have begun doing this, tying launch licences to disposal expectations and requiring operators to demonstrate thruster reliability. Others remain hesitant, worried that tough rules will scare away bidders. The opposite is true. Firms that invest in resilience want a market that values it.

Resilience also means graceful degradation. A satellite should not drop offline the moment one subsystem fails. It should retreat to essential functions, shed non-critical tasks, and continue serving at reduced capacity. Spacecraft already carry redundant avionics and power distribution, yet too few adopt architectural redundancy at system level. One solar array fails; the second should carry life support. One antenna collapses; the narrowband channel should stay alive. Procurement can demand such design logic without prescribing the technology. Engineers are superb at improvisation when the incentives align.

There is a moral dimension as well. Governments owe their citizens stewardship of public space. Orbit is a shared domain. When a state launches a satellite that cannot dispose of itself responsibly, it is imposing risk on every other user. A procurement officer may never see a piece of debris, but they have power over it. By requiring bidders to submit debris-mitigation data and modelling, they bring transparency to an invisible problem.

Tender evaluations often include environmental impact, employment benefits, and regional development. Add orbital sustainability to the list.

Some will protest that resilience is expensive. That may be true in the short term. But failures are costlier. A single satellite collision can generate thousands of fragments, each capable of disabling another satellite. A chain reaction could cripple weather forecasting, communications, navigation, emergency services. The cost of one cascading failure dwarfs the incremental cost of resilience. And resilience saves money in less dramatic ways: longer satellite life, reduced launch frequency, lower insurance premiums, and fewer emergency manoeuvres.

Procurement can also reward innovation. A tender might specify outcomes, not technologies. Instead of mandating a particular deorbit system, it could require that any failed spacecraft will be removed from orbit within five years and verified by third-party tracking. This invites creativity. Some firms will propose drag sails. Others will use electric propulsion. Some may rely on future orbital tugs. The government need not choose. It need only demand results.

Resilient procurement does not stop in space. Ground networks are equally vulnerable. A resilient architecture spreads control across multiple ground stations, uses hardened cables, employs redundant gateways, and encrypts control uplinks. Governments could insist that providers demonstrate cyber resilience, signal authentication, and rapid failover. Constellations that can shift traffic from compromised stations to secure ones deserve preference.

There is a geopolitical layer. States often worry that imposing strict requirements will put domestic firms at a disadvantage. Yet every leading spacefaring nation depends increasingly on global suppliers. If major governments adopt resilience-based procurement, industry will adapt. International competition will play to higher standards. Spacecraft exported abroad will carry resilience by default. The norm will rise.

A different anxiety looms: what if resilience requirements clash with military secrecy? A satellite designed for covert operations may be reluctant to disclose telemetry or disposal methods. Yet secrecy does not require irresponsibility. A military spacecraft can be hardened, redundant, and capable of safe disposal without revealing capabilities. Classified annexes can protect sensitive details while still complying with sustainability criteria. Defence agencies should lead, not exempt themselves.

There is another powerful lever: financing. Development banks, sovereign wealth funds, and export credit agencies could condition support on resilience metrics. If a project lacks debris mitigation, they walk away. If a constellation shares telemetry and publishes proximity logs, financing becomes cheaper. Investors have no appetite for orbital pollution. They know that a debris cloud is not merely a scientific curiosity; it is a liability.

Procurement can even shape industrial behaviour in crisis. A contract might require operators to participate in emergency coordination: collision warnings, interference hotlines, and debris-removal efforts. Imagine a procurement clause that obliges operators to assist in towing disabled satellites if capable. This promotes a culture of shared responsibility.

In space, buying resilience is buying time. The more durable the architecture, the longer it serves before replacement. The more safely it disposes of itself, the less clutter accumulates. The more gracefully it degrades, the fewer sudden outages occur. Time is the ultimate currency. Every year gained before orbital congestion reaches crisis buys room for innovation and diplomacy.

Yet procurement officials do not always think this way. They operate under budget ceilings, political constraints, and audit pressures. They must justify costs to ministers, who prefer visible success to invisible prevention. A minister loves to cut ribbon on launch day, not to fund a deorbit system that will operate quietly a decade later. The challenge is to make prevention visible. Score it. Reward it. Show the public that responsible space design is patriotic, not bureaucratic.

There is a philosophical resonance here with environmental policy. The world learned—too slowly—that polluters must pay. Space is behind that curve, but the logic is identical. If you create a satellite, you must plan for its disposal. If you generate debris, you are liable. Procurement can accelerate that shift. By pricing irresponsibility into bids, it prevents free-riding and fosters stewardship.

One might fear that resilience-based procurement entrenches incumbents. It need not. Public tenders can create pathways for smaller firms to demonstrate innovative disposal methods or autonomous safety systems. Grants can reward start-ups that pioneer passive deorbit solutions. Governments can co-fund testbeds for orbital servicing and debris removal. The goal is not to burden industry—it is to reward ingenuity.

The trajectory is clear. Space agencies are already moving. NASA's procurement guidelines now score sustainability. The European Space Agency requires disposal within a fixed timeframe. Several national regulators have shortened permissible post-mission drift. These steps, modest though they appear, converge on a powerful idea: resilience is not charity. It is competence.

Still, a question lingers. Will governments have the courage to enforce their own standards when political pressure mounts to launch something quickly and cheaply? The temptation will always exist to grant waivers, to accept promises in place of proof. That is where procurement officers become guardians. Their decisions shape orbit for decades.

Buying resilience means buying a future in which space remains usable. It means rewarding those who design for safety and signalling to others that there is no market for negligence. It means recognising that governance is not only written in treaties, but wired into flight computers, embedded in propulsion, and printed in procurement scoring sheets.

The next time a government signs a launch contract, a simple question should echo: are we paying for capability, or are we paying for failure deferred? The answer will determine whether humanity inherits a sky of opportunity—or a scrapyard spinning above our heads.

A civil orbital pact

There is a curious silence in orbit. Thousands of satellites move at bullet speed, cross national boundaries every ninety minutes, and perform functions that shape economies and wars. Yet there are no traffic rules, no universally agreed signals, no standard etiquette for passing or approaching. Each operator behaves as they see fit, guided by custom, self-interest, and luck. On Earth, we would never tolerate such anarchy. Imagine a world in which cars, ships, or aircraft navigated without shared norms. We solved those problems a century ago. Space still waits.

The gap is not due to ignorance. Most operators understand the danger. No one wants a collision. No one wants debris. No one wants misunderstandings to escalate into conflict. The problem is that formal treaties are slow, diplomatic consensus is fragile, and space power has become an arena of suspicion. States hesitate to limit themselves when rivals might cheat. Firms hesitate to disclose telemetry for fear of revealing trade secrets. The result is paralysis. Every nation claims to support "responsible behaviour", but few are willing to be the first mover.

A civil orbital pact is a way out: a modest, voluntary, region-led agreement among states and firms to behave predictably and transparently. Instead of waiting for a grand treaty drafted by diplomats in New York or Geneva, a coalition could begin with a pilot. Europe might launch one. So might a consortium of Asia-Pacific states. Even a cluster of commercial operators could start. The pact would not require unanimity, only enough participation to build momentum. Once major players adopt it, norms become expectations; expectations become pressure.

What would such a pact contain? Not idealistic declarations. Practical commitments. Minimal rules that reduce risk without forcing anyone to reveal secrets or abandon sovereignty. The first is proximity etiquette. When one satellite plans to approach another within a defined radius, the operator should send a notification—automated, authenticated, logged. This is not disarmament. It is courtesy, like signalling before changing lanes. States can still conduct inspections, but the inspected satellite will not mistake a surprise overflight as the opening move of a hostile act. Aerospace firms already log their manoeuvres internally. Sharing a subset of that data is not costly.

The second commitment is standardised collision warnings. When sensors detect a conjunction risk—whether from debris or a malfunctioning satellite—the operator should issue alerts to all relevant parties. Today, many organisations already do this voluntarily, but practices vary. Some alerts are late, vague, or incomplete. A pact would improve quality by requiring structured formats and timestamps. This is as mundane as air traffic control. It does not constrain military operations or proprietary information. It simply prevents preventable accidents.

Third: public ephemerides with safeguards. Orbital positions need not be disclosed in perfect precision. A pact could require that basic tracking data be shared at a resolution sufficient for collision avoidance but coarse enough to protect sensitive missions. Think of radar blips rather than flight plans. Intelligence agencies will always maintain higher-fidelity tracking, but shared data would give small operators—and emerging space nations—the situational awareness they currently lack. Today, commercial sensors often track classified spacecraft more openly than governments admit. A pact would formalise what is already nearly unavoidable.

Fourth: end-of-life responsibility. A participating operator should commit to one of three options—controlled re-entry, graveyard orbit, or rendezvous with a servicing vehicle. This is not a ban on failure. Satellites malfunction. Propulsion systems misfire. A pact would merely require that operators document a disposal plan, update it when failures occur, and report whether the spacecraft successfully left its operational orbit. Even approximate compliance would shrink long-term debris risk.

States may object: what incentive exists to join a pact that binds only the responsible? The answer is insurance—political and economic. Participation would lower collision premiums, grant access to shared data, and open doors to partner launches. A commercial operator that follows pact norms can advertise itself as a safe neighbour. Governments looking to subsidise industry could prioritise pacts in their licensing and procurement. In time, the pact becomes not only a badge of honour, but a commercial advantage.

Critics will warn that voluntary arrangements are weak. That argument misunderstands how norms evolve. At sea, the first lifesaving rules of maritime conduct were customary. Only later did they become mandatory. In aviation, pilots followed standard radio etiquette before treaties formalised it. The absence of enforcement does not imply impotence. Reputational pressure, market power, and peer influence can move faster than diplomacy. When a major constellation operator signs on, its competitors will not want to appear reckless by comparison.

A civil orbital pact should also include crisis protocols. When an operator experiences a critical failure—a tumbling satellite, unexpected break-up, or loss of control—there must be a mechanism to alert others rapidly. Today, many incidents go unreported for hours or days, during which fragments spread unnoticed. A simple, automated broadcast channel would change this. Participating operators could share alerts through a neutral clearinghouse. No ownership of blame, no legal liability, just information. Even adversaries benefit. A state that receives early warning of debris can manoeuvre defensively without assuming hostile intent.

Another element could be deconfliction hotlines. The Cold War taught the value of communication channels when trust collapses. Space lacks them. Two operators—commercial or national—could agree to share contact details and protocols for escalation. If one believes the other is interfering, they call before accusing. A minute of conversation might avoid a war of press releases, sanctions, or sabre-rattling. The cost is trivial. The benefit is stability.

Regional pilots make sense because orbit is already regionalised by launch infrastructure, tracking networks, and industrial alliances. Europe coordinates through the European Space Agency and its member states.

The Asia-Pacific region hosts rapidly expanding constellations. Latin American and African space programmes are growing. Any regional pact could begin with a handful of willing states and firms. Once operational, it would prove its worth through practice rather than promises. Others would join.

Some will demand that the pact include anti-weaponisation clauses. That ambition is noble but naïve. No state with counterspace capability will sign away its right to defend itself. A minimal pact avoids this fight. It does not ban weapons; it reduces accidents. It does not prohibit manoeuvres; it ensures they are understood. It does not dictate disarmament; it encourages predictability. In diplomacy, the perfect cripples the possible.

There is a philosophical power in modest rules. They remind participants that space is not a battlefield by default. It is a domain of shared vulnerability. Every operator relies on predictability. Every satellite is fragile. Even the most powerful states could lose weather forecasts, global communications, and early-warning systems if space becomes chaotic. A civil orbital pact is not about idealism. It is about pragmatic self-preservation.

And yet, beneath the pragmatism lies a moral intuition. When a state or firm joins such a pact, it implicitly acknowledges that its satellites are neighbours, not sovereign islands. It accepts that its choices ripple outward. This is how civilisation expands outward—first to oceans, then to skies, now to orbit. Rules that begin with a small circle grow until they encompass many. Civilisation is a habit.

The deepest sceptics will ask a harsh question: why trust rivals? The answer is simpler than trust. mistrust costs more. A pact does not require affection. It requires predictability. Operators do not have to like one another, only to understand what they will do in routine and crisis. In international relations, predictability is sometimes the closest thing to peace.

If a civil orbital pact emerged tomorrow—signed by a dozen states and the largest commercial operators—it would not solve every challenge. But the next time a satellite fails, an alert would go out. The next time two spacecraft approach one another, notifications would flow. The next time debris threatens, operators would adjust. The skies would not fall silent. They would speak.

The question is not whether such a pact is possible. It is whether anyone will choose to act while space remains salvageable. Will governments wait for a catastrophe, or will a few visionary actors pilot a modest, voluntary code?

History rewards those who build before collapse. The orbital commons is still young. Its rules are unwritten. If we choose to write them now—lightly, reasonably, and with humility—future generations may never know how close we came to losing the sky.

About the Author

Emile Dorqan is a French aerospace historian and policy adviser who writes about how technology quietly reorganises power. After analysing programmes at the European Space Agency, he turned to the wider question: what happens to politics when our most important infrastructure orbits above law, borders, and public oversight? His work follows the full chain, from launch pads and ground stations to boardrooms and ministries, translating specialist language into civic understanding. Raised on tales of early balloonists crossing the Channel, he sees a through-line from fragile fabric to orbital mesh: every leap in altitude rewrites what states can do, and what they must restrain. He writes to equip readers with calm, usable frameworks for an era when satellites decide both convenience and catastrophe.

www.ingramcontent.com/pod-product-compliance
Lightning Source LLC
Chambersburg PA
CBHW021216250926
51852CB00006B/33